Bilingual

VISUAL

dictionary

Bilingual

VISUAL

dictionary

DK LONDON
Senior Editors Angeles Gavira, Angela Wilkes
Senior Art Editor Ina Stradins
Jacket Editor Claire Gell
Jacket Design Development Manager Sophia MTT
Preproduction Producer Andy Hilliard
Producer Alex Bell
Picture Researcher Anna Grapes
Project Manager Christine Stroyan
Art Director Karen Self
Publisher Liz Wheeler
Publishing Director Jonathan Metcalf

DK INDIA
Editor Arpita Dasgupta
Assistant Editor Priyanjali Narain
Art Editor Yashashvi Choudhary
DTP Designers Jaypal Chauhan Singh, Anita Yadav
Jacket Designer Tanya Mehrotra
Jackets Editorial Coordinator Priyanka Sharma
Preproduction Manager Balwant Singh
Production Manager Pankaj Sharma

Designed for DK by WaltonCreative.com
Art Editor Colin Walton, assisted by Tracy Musson
Designers Peter Radcliffe, Earl Neish, Ann Cannings
Picture Research Marissa Keating

Language content for DK by g-and-w PUBLISHING
Managed by Jane Wightwick, assisted by Ana Bremón
Translation and editing by Christine Arthur
Additional input by Dr. Arturo Pretel, Martin Prill,
Frédéric Monteil, Meinrad Prill, Mari Bremón,
Oscar Bremón, Anunchi Bremón, Leila Gaafar

This American Edition, 2019
First American Edition, 2009
Published in the United States by DK Publishing
1745 Broadway, 20th Floor, New York, NY 10019

Copyright © 2009, 2015, 2018 Dorling Kindersley Limited
DK, a Division of Penguin Random House LLC
23 24 25 26 11 10 9 8
017–308063–Feb/2018

A catalog record for this book
is available from the Library of Congress.
ISBN 978-1-4654-6919-9

DK books are available at special discounts when purchased in bulk
for sales promotions, premiums, fund-raising, or educational use.
For details, contact: DK Publishing Special Markets,
1745 Broadway, 20th Floor, New York, NY 10019
SpecialSales@dk.com

Printed and bound in China

For the curious
www.dk.com

MIX
Paper | Supporting
responsible forestry
FSC™ C018179

This book was made with Forest
Stewardship Council™ certified
paper - one small step in DK's
commitment to a sustainable future.
For more information go to
www.dk.com/our-green-pledge

目录
mùlù
contents

中文 zhōngwén • english

词典介绍

图片的应用经研究有助于对信息的理解和记忆。本着这个原则，这本有着丰富图片注释的英中双语词典包含了范围很广的词汇。

这本词典按照情景划分章节，从饮食到健身，从家居到工作，从太空到动物世界，包括了日常生活的所有细节。从这本词典中你也可以找到额外的常用词汇和词组以便口语练习和词汇量的扩大。

这本词典实用，生动，易用。对所有对语言有兴趣的人来说是一个重要的参考工具。

注意事项

本词典中的中文汉字同中华人民共和国官方汉字一样为简体汉字。

本词典为普通话注音，注音标记为拼音。拼音是中国人和中文学生最熟悉的一种音标。四声的变化也在拼音的结构中显示。

所有词语项都是以同样的顺序展示 –文字，拼音，英文。例如：

午餐	安全带
wǔcān	ānquándài
lunch	**seat belt**

动词在英文词尾以 (v) 作为标记。例如：

收获 shōuhuò | harvest (v)

所有词汇在书后也有总目录可以查阅。在总目录里你可以通过查询英文，或者查询拼音找到相应的页数。这样你可以很顺利地找到和拼音或英文相对应的中文文字翻译。

使用说明

不论你学习语言的目的是工作，兴趣，为旅行做准备还是仅仅在已学语言的基础上扩大词汇量，这本词典都是你语言学习的重要工具。你可以多方面地去运用它。

在学习一种新的语言的时候，注意同源词汇（即在不同语言中相似的词汇）和衍生词汇（即只在某种语言中有相似根源的词汇）。你可以发现语言和语言之间的联系。例如说，英文从中文中引用了一些关于食品的词汇，而同时也输出了一些关于科技和流行文化的词汇。

实用技巧

- 当你设身处地在家，工作场所或者学校的时候，试看看相对应自己所在环境的章节。这样一来你可以合上书，环视四周看看自己可以识别多少事物。

- 为自己做一些词汇卡片，一面英文一面中文和汉语拼音。时常携带这些卡片并且测试自己的记忆。记住每次测试之前要打乱卡片的顺序。

- 挑战自己尝试用某一页上的所有词汇写一个小故事，一封信或者一段对话。这样不但可以帮助你牢记这些词汇，而且可以帮助你记住它们的拼写。如果你想尝试写一篇长一点的文章，那么以至少含有2-3个词的句子为起点。

- 如果你有很强的视觉记忆，试着将书上的内容画出来或者在纸上诠释出来，然后合上书，在已有的图形下面填充词汇。

- 一但你变得更加自信，从中文目录中任意找一些词汇，检查自己是否在翻阅到相关页之前能知道其词意。

免费音频应用程序

此音频应用程序包括书中的全部单词和语句，中文和英文语音是由母语播音员录制的，吐字清晰，使得语音和重要词汇的学习更加准确和明了。

音频应用程序使用说明

- 在应用程序站（app store）搜索"DK Visual Dictionary"，免费下载此程序到手机或平板电脑设备中。
- 打开程序，然后扫描书后的国际标准书号（ISBN）去解锁，解锁后视觉辞典（Visual Dictionary）就会显示在图书馆中。
- 下载与书本相配套的语音资料
- 输入页码，然后上下翻动去查看此页上的词和句。
- 通过点击词或句去播放语音。
- 左右翻动去浏览前页和下页内容。
- 添加词和句到"特别喜爱的文档中"（Favourites）。

about the dictionary

The use of pictures is proven to aid understanding and the retention of information. Working on this principle, this highly-illustrated English–Chinese bilingual dictionary presents a large range of useful current vocabulary.

The dictionary is divided thematically and covers most aspects of the everyday world in detail, from the restaurant to the gym, the home to the workplace, outer space to the animal kingdom. You will also find additional words and phrases for conversational use and for extending your vocabulary.

This is an essential reference tool for anyone interested in languages—practical, stimulating, and easy-to-use.

A few things to note
The Chinese in the dictionary is presented in simplified Chinese characters, as used in the People's Republic of China.

The pronunciation included for the Chinese is given in the Mandarin dialect and is shown in Pinyin, the standard romanization familiar to most native speakers and learners of Chinese. Accents showing the Chinese tones are included on the Pinyin.

The entries are always presented in the same order—Chinese, Pinyin, English—for example:

午餐	安全带
wǔcān	ānquándài
lunch	**seat belt**

Verbs are indicated by a (v) after the English, for example:

收获 shōuhuò | **harvest (v)**

Each language also has its own index at the back of the book. Here you can look up a word in either English or Pinyin and be referred to the page number(s) where it appears. To reference the Chinese characters for a particular word, look it up in the Pinyin or English index and then go to the page indicated.

how to use this book

Whether you are learning a new language for business, pleasure, or in preparation for a holiday abroad, or are hoping to extend your vocabulary in an already familiar language, this dictionary is a valuable learning tool which you can use in a number of different ways.

When learning a new language, look out for cognates (words that are alike in different languages) and derivations (words that share a common root in a particular language). You can also see where the languages have influenced each other. For example, English has imported some terms for food from Chinese but, in turn, has exported some terms used in technology and popular culture.

Practical learning activities
• As you move about your home, workplace, or college, try looking at the pages which cover that setting. You could then close the book, look around you and see how many of the objects and features you can name.
• Make flashcards for yourself with English on one side and Chinese/Pinyin on the other side. Carry the cards with you and test yourself frequently, making sure you shuffle them between each test.
• Challenge yourself to write a story, letter, or dialogue using as many of the terms on a particular page as possible. This will help you retain the vocabulary and remember the spelling. If you want to build up to writing a longer text, start with sentences incorporating 2–3 words.
• If you have a very visual memory, try drawing or tracing items from the book onto a piece of paper, then close the book and fill in the words below the picture.
• Once you are more confident, pick out words in the foreign language index and see if you know what they mean before turning to the relevant page to check if you were right.

free audio app

The audio app contains all the words and phrases in the book, spoken by native speakers in both Mandarin Chinese and English, making it easier to learn important vocabulary and improve your pronunciation.

how to use the audio app

• Search for "DK Visual Dictionary" and download the free app on your smartphone or tablet from your chosen app store.
• Open the app and scan the barcode (or enter the ISBN) to unlock your Visual Dictionary in the Library.
• Download the audio files for your book.
• Enter a page number, then scroll up and down through the list to find a word or phrase.
• Tap a word to hear it.
• Swipe left or right to view the previous or next page.
• Add words to your Favorites.

人 rén
people

人体 réntǐ • body

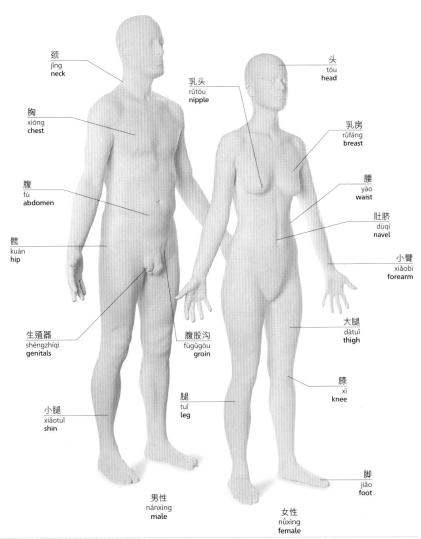

颈
jǐng
neck

乳头
rǔtóu
nipple

头
tóu
head

胸
xiōng
chest

乳房
rǔfáng
breast

腰
yāo
waist

腹
fù
abdomen

肚脐
dùqí
navel

髋
kuān
hip

小臂
xiǎobì
forearm

生殖器
shēngzhíqì
genitals

腹股沟
fùgǔgōu
groin

大腿
dàtuǐ
thigh

膝
xī
knee

小腿
xiǎotuǐ
shin

腿
tuǐ
leg

脚
jiǎo
foot

男性
nánxìng
male

女性
nǚxìng
female

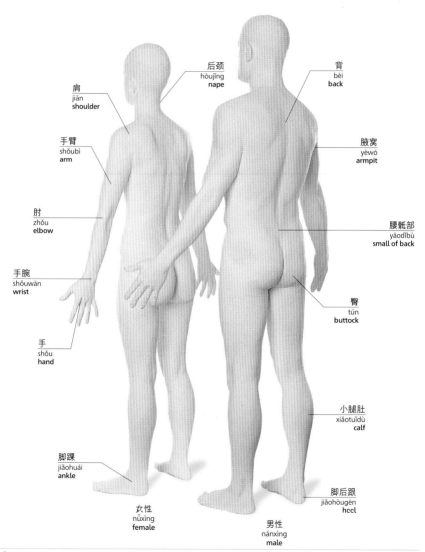

后颈
hòujǐng
nape

背
bèi
back

肩
jiān
shoulder

腋窝
yèwō
armpit

手臂
shǒubì
arm

肘
zhǒu
elbow

腰骶部
yāodǐbù
small of back

手腕
shǒuwàn
wrist

臀
tún
buttock

手
shǒu
hand

小腿肚
xiǎotuǐdù
calf

脚踝
jiǎohuái
ankle

脚后跟
jiǎohòugēn
heel

女性
nǚxìng
female

男性
nánxìng
male

面部 miànbù · **face**

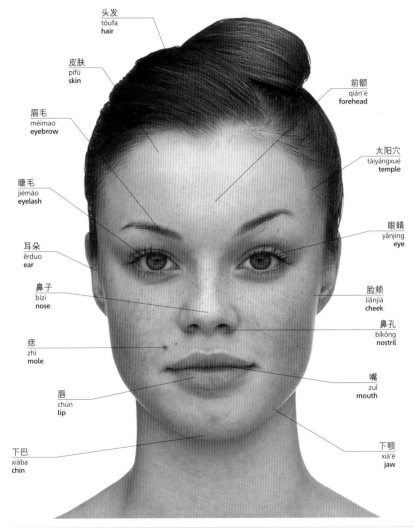

头发
tóufa
hair

皮肤
pífū
skin

前额
qián'é
forehead

眉毛
méimao
eyebrow

太阳穴
tàiyángxué
temple

睫毛
jiémáo
eyelash

眼睛
yǎnjing
eye

耳朵
ěrduo
ear

鼻子
bízi
nose

脸颊
liǎnjiá
cheek

鼻孔
bíkǒng
nostril

痣
zhì
mole

嘴
zuǐ
mouth

唇
chún
lip

下巴
xiàba
chin

下颚
xià'è
jaw

皱纹
zhòuwén
wrinkle

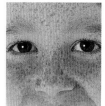

雀斑
quèbān
freckle

毛孔
máokǒng
pore

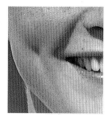

酒窝
jiǔwō
dimple

手 shǒu • hand

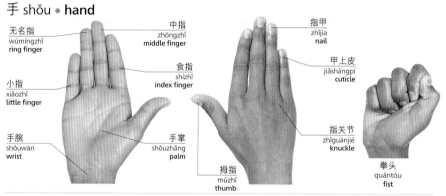

无名指
wúmíngzhǐ
ring finger

中指
zhōngzhǐ
middle finger

指甲
zhǐjiǎ
nail

食指
shízhǐ
index finger

甲上皮
jiǎshàngpí
cuticle

小指
xiǎozhǐ
little finger

指关节
zhǐguānjié
knuckle

手腕
shǒuwàn
wrist

手掌
shǒuzhǎng
palm

拇指
mǔzhǐ
thumb

拳头
quántóu
fist

脚 jiǎo • foot

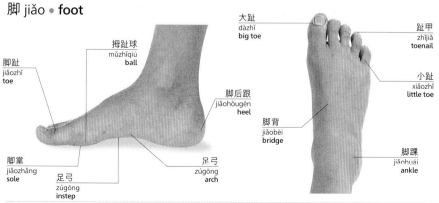

拇趾球
mǔzhǐqiú
ball

大趾
dàzhǐ
big toe

趾甲
zhǐjiǎ
toenail

脚趾
jiǎozhǐ
toe

小趾
xiǎozhǐ
little toe

脚后跟
jiǎohòugēn
heel

脚背
jiǎobèi
bridge

脚掌
jiǎozhǎng
sole

足弓
zúgōng
arch

足弓
zúgōng
instep

脚踝
jiǎohuái
ankle

肌肉 jīròu • muscles

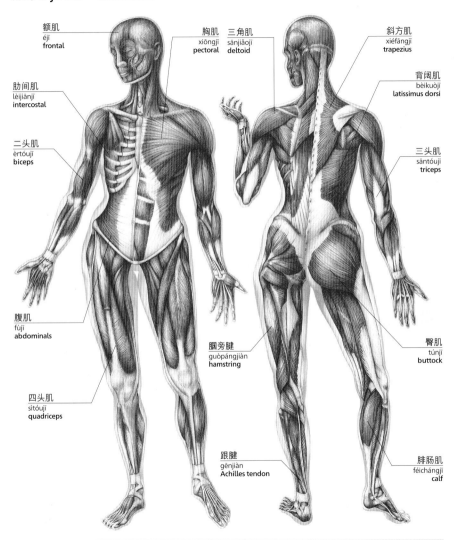

额肌
éjī
frontal

肋间肌
lèijiānjī
intercostal

二头肌
èrtóujī
biceps

腹肌
fùjī
abdominals

四头肌
sìtóujī
quadriceps

胸肌
xiōngjī
pectoral

三角肌
sānjiǎojī
deltoid

腘旁腱
guòpángjiàn
hamstring

跟腱
gēnjiàn
Achilles tendon

斜方肌
xiéfāngjī
trapezius

背阔肌
bèikuòjī
latissimus dorsi

三头肌
sāntóujī
triceps

臀肌
túnjī
buttock

腓肠肌
féichángjī
calf

骨骼 gǔgé • skeleton

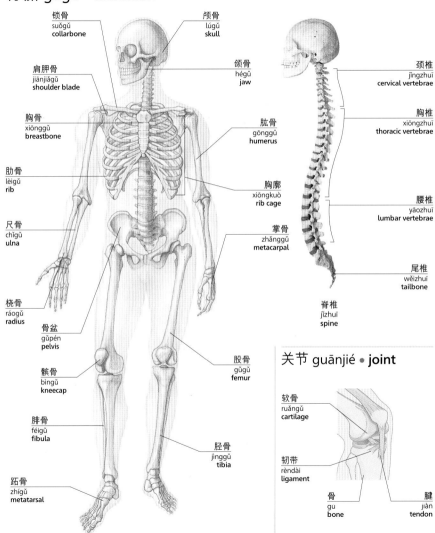

锁骨
suǒgǔ
collarbone

颅骨
lúgǔ
skull

肩胛骨
jiānjiǎgǔ
shoulder blade

颌骨
hégǔ
jaw

胸骨
xiōnggǔ
breastbone

肱骨
gōnggǔ
humerus

肋骨
lèigǔ
rib

胸廓
xiōngkuò
rib cage

尺骨
chǐgǔ
ulna

掌骨
zhǎnggǔ
metacarpal

桡骨
ráogǔ
radius

骨盆
gǔpén
pelvis

髌骨
bìngǔ
kneecap

股骨
gǔgǔ
femur

腓骨
féigǔ
fibula

胫骨
jìnggǔ
tibia

跖骨
zhígǔ
metatarsal

颈椎
jǐngzhuī
cervical vertebrae

胸椎
xiōngzhuī
thoracic vertebrae

腰椎
yāozhuī
lumbar vertebrae

尾椎
wěizhuī
tailbone

脊椎
jǐzhuī
spine

关节 guānjié • joint

软骨
ruǎngǔ
cartilage

韧带
rèndài
ligament

骨
gu
bone

腱
jiàn
tendon

内脏 nèizàng • internal organs

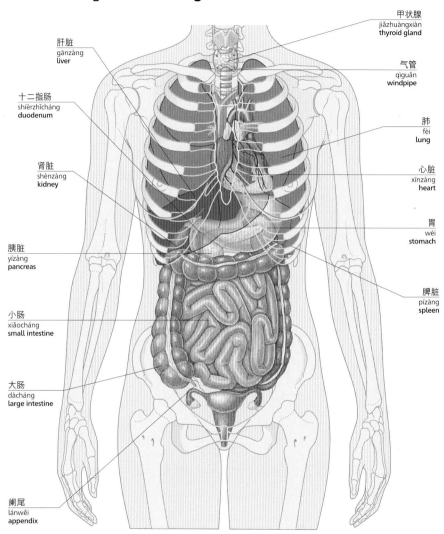

甲状腺
jiǎzhuàngxiàn
thyroid gland

肝脏
gānzàng
liver

气管
qìguǎn
windpipe

十二指肠
shíèrzhǐcháng
duodenum

肺
fèi
lung

肾脏
shènzàng
kidney

心脏
xīnzàng
heart

胃
wèi
stomach

胰脏
yízàng
pancreas

脾脏
pízàng
spleen

小肠
xiǎocháng
small intestine

大肠
dàcháng
large intestine

阑尾
lánwěi
appendix

头部 tóubù • head

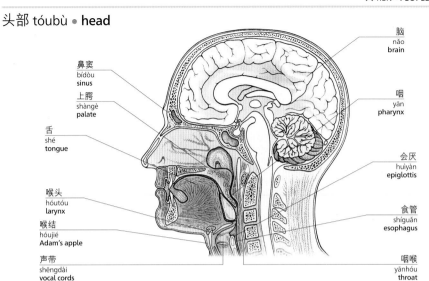

鼻窦
bídòu
sinus

上腭
shàngè
palate

舌
shé
tongue

喉头
hóutóu
larynx

喉结
hóujié
Adam's apple

声带
shēngdài
vocal cords

脑
nǎo
brain

咽
yān
pharynx

会厌
huìyàn
epiglottis

食管
shíguǎn
esophagus

咽喉
yānhóu
throat

人体系统 réntǐxìtǒng • body systems

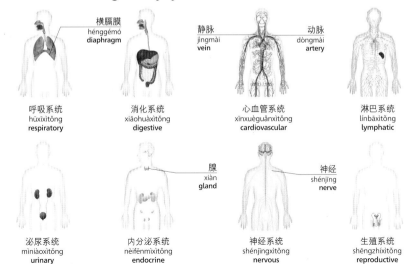

横膈膜
hénggémó
diaphragm

呼吸系统
hūxīxìtǒng
respiratory

消化系统
xiāohuàxìtǒng
digestive

静脉
jìngmài
vein

动脉
dòngmài
artery

心血管系统
xīnxuèguǎnxìtǒng
cardiovascular

淋巴系统
línbāxìtǒng
lymphatic

腺
xiàn
gland

泌尿系统
mìniàoxìtǒng
urinary

内分泌系统
nèifēnmìxìtǒng
endocrine

神经
shénjīng
nerve

神经系统
shénjīngxìtǒng
nervous

生殖系统
shēngzhíxìtǒng
reproductive

生殖器官 shēngzhíqìguān · **reproductive organs**

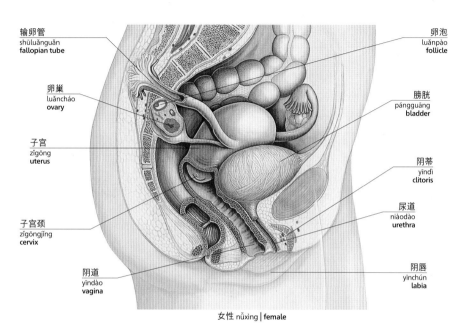

输卵管
shūluǎnguǎn
fallopian tube

卵泡
luǎnpào
follicle

卵巢
luǎncháo
ovary

膀胱
pángguāng
bladder

子宫
zǐgōng
uterus

阴蒂
yīndì
clitoris

尿道
niàodào
urethra

子宫颈
zǐgōngjǐng
cervix

阴道
yīndào
vagina

阴唇
yīnchún
labia

女性 nǚxìng | female

生殖 shēngzhí · **reproduction**

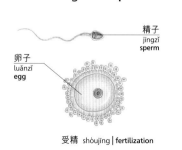

精子
jīngzǐ
sperm

卵子
luǎnzǐ
egg

受精 shòujīng | fertilization

词汇 cíhuì · **vocabulary**

荷尔蒙 hé'ěrméng **hormone**	阳痿 yángwěi **impotent**	有生殖能力的 yǒushēngzhínénglìde **fertile**
排卵 páiluǎn **ovulation**	怀孕 huáiyùn **conceive**	月经 yuèjīng **menstruation**
不育 bùyù **infertile**	性交 xìngjiāo **intercourse**	性病 xìngbìng **sexually transmitted disease**

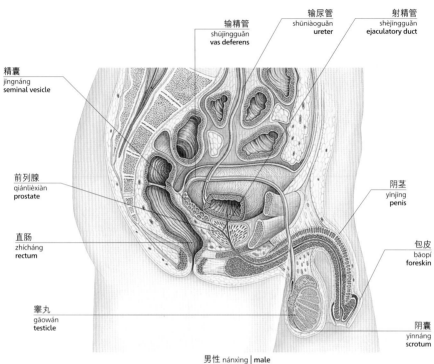

精囊
jīngnáng
seminal vesicle

输精管
shūjīngguǎn
vas deferens

输尿管
shūniàoguǎn
ureter

射精管
shèjīngguǎn
ejaculatory duct

前列腺
qiánlièxiàn
prostate

阴茎
yīnjīng
penis

直肠
zhícháng
rectum

包皮
bāopí
foreskin

睾丸
gāowán
testicle

阴囊
yīnnáng
scrotum

男性 nánxìng | male

避孕 bìyùn • contraception

子宫托
zǐgōngtuō
cervical cap

阴道隔膜
yīndàogémó
diaphragm

避孕套
bìyùntào
condom

宫内避孕器
gōngnèibìyùnqì
IUD

避孕药
bìyùnyào
pill

家庭 jiātíng • family

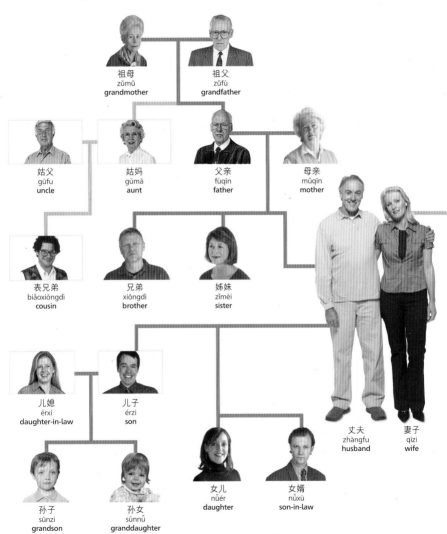

祖母
zǔmǔ
grandmother

祖父
zǔfù
grandfather

姑父
gūfu
uncle

姑妈
gūmā
aunt

父亲
fùqīn
father

母亲
mǔqīn
mother

表兄弟
biǎoxiōngdì
cousin

兄弟
xiōngdì
brother

姊妹
zǐmèi
sister

儿媳
érxí
daughter-in-law

儿子
érzi
son

丈夫
zhàngfu
husband

妻子
qīzi
wife

孙子
sūnzi
grandson

孙女
sūnnǚ
granddaughter

女儿
nǚér
daughter

女婿
nǚxù
son-in-law

词汇 cíhuì • vocabulary

亲戚 qīnqi relatives	父母 fùmǔ parents	孙子女 / 外孙子女 sūnzǐnǚ/wàisūnzǐnǚ **grandchildren**	继母 jìmǔ stepmother	继子 jìzǐ stepson	配偶 pèiǒu partner
世代 shìdài generation	孩子 háizi children	祖父母 / 外祖父母 zǔfùmǔ / wàizǔfùmǔ **grandparents**	继父 jìfù stepfather	继女 jìnǚ stepdaughter	双胞胎 shuāngbāotāi twins

成长阶段 chéngzhǎngjiēduàn • stages

岳母
yuèmǔ
mother-in-law

岳父
yuèfù
father-in-law

婴儿
yīng'ér
baby

儿童
értóng
child

妻妹(姐)夫
qīmèi(jiě)fū
brother-in-law

妻妹(姐)
qīmèi(jiě)
sister-in-law

男孩
nánhái
boy

女孩
nǚhái
girl

外甥女
wàishēngnǚ
niece

外甥
wàishēng
nephew

太太
tàitai
Mrs.

青少年
qīngshàonián
teenager

成年人
chéngniánrén
adult

称谓 chēngwèi • titles

先生
xiānsheng
Mr.

小姐
xiǎojiě
Miss/Ms.

男人
nánrén
man

女人
nǚrén
woman

人际关系 rénjìguānxì • relationships

助理
zhùlǐ
assistant

经理
jīnglǐ
manager

生意伙伴
shēngyìhuǒbàn
**business
partner**

雇主
gùzhǔ
employer

雇员
gùyuán
employee

同事
tóngshì
colleague

办公室 bàngōngshì | **office**

邻居
línjū
neighbor

朋友
péngyou
friend

熟人
shúrén
acquaintance

笔友
bǐyǒu
pen pal

男朋友
nánpéngyou
boyfriend

女朋友
nǚpéngyou
girlfriend

未婚夫
wèihūnfū
fiancé

未婚妻
wèihūnqī
fiancée

情侣 qínglǚ | **couple**

未婚夫妻 wèihūnfūqī | **engaged couple**

情感 qínggǎn • emotions

微笑
wēixiào
smile

快乐
kuàilè
happy

悲伤
bēishāng
sad

兴奋
xīngfèn
excited

无聊
wúliáo
bored

皱眉
zhòuméi
frown

惊讶
jīngyà
surprised

惊恐
jīngkǒng
scared

愤怒
fènnù
angry

困惑
kùnhuò
confused

忧虑
yōulǜ
worried

紧张
jǐnzhāng
nervous

自豪
zìháo
proud

自信
zìxìn
confident

尴尬
gāngà
embarrassed

羞涩
xiūsè
shy

词汇 cíhuì • vocabulary

烦恼 fánnǎo upset	笑 xiào laugh (v)	叹息 tànxī sigh (v)	叫喊 jiàohǎn shout (v)
震惊 zhènjīng shocked	哭 kū cry (v)	晕倒 yūndǎo faint (v)	打哈欠 dǎhāqian yawn (v)

人生大事 rénshēngdàshì · life events

出生
chūshēng
be born (v)

入学
rùxué
start school (v)

交友
jiāoyǒu
make friends (v)

毕业
bìyè
graduate (v)

就业
jiùyè
get a job (v)

恋爱
liàn'ài
fall in love (v)

结婚
jiéhūn
get married (v)

生子
shēngzǐ
have a baby (v)

婚礼 hūnlǐ | wedding

词汇 cíhuì · vocabulary

洗礼 xǐlǐ christening	立遗嘱 lìyízhǔ make a will (v)
纪念日 jì'niànrì anniversary	出生证明 chūshēng zhèngmíng birth certificate
移民 yímín emigrate (v)	婚宴 hūnyàn wedding reception
退休 tuìxiū retire (v)	蜜月 mìyuè honeymoon
死亡 sǐwáng die (v)	犹太男孩成人(13岁)仪式 yóutài nánhái chéngrén (shísānsuì)yíshì bar mitzvah

离婚
líhūn
divorce

葬礼
zànglǐ
funeral

节庆 jiéqìng • celebrations

节日 jiérì •
festivals

生日聚会
shēngrìjùhuì
birthday party

贺卡
hèkǎ
card

礼物
lǐwù
present

生日
shēngrì
birthday

圣诞节
shèngdànjié
Christmas

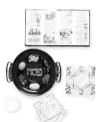

逾越节
yúyuèjié
Passover

新年
xīnnián
New Year

狂欢节 / 嘉年华会
kuánghuānjié / jiā'niánhuáhuì
carnival

游行
yóuxíng
procession

斋月
zhāiyuè
Ramadan

缎带
duàndài
ribbon

感恩节
gǎn'ēnjié
Thanksgiving

复活节
fùhuójié
Easter

万圣节
wànshèngjié
Halloween

排灯节
páidēngjié
Diwali

外表 wàibiǎo
appearance

童装 tóngzhuāng • children's clothing

婴儿 yīng'ér • baby

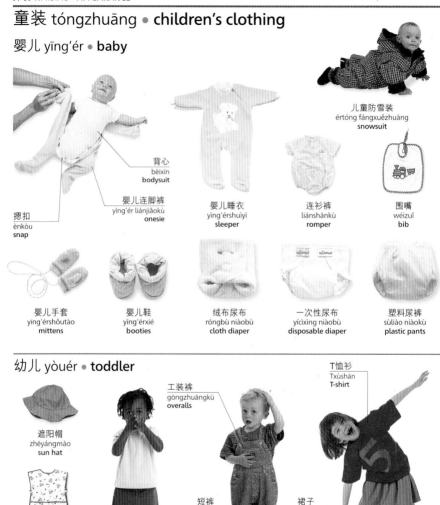

儿童防雪装
értóng fángxuězhuāng
snowsuit

背心
bèixīn
bodysuit

婴儿连脚裤
yīng'ér liánjiǎokù
onesie

摁扣
ènkòu
snap

婴儿睡衣
yīng'érshuìyī
sleeper

连衫裤
liánshānkù
romper

围嘴
wéizuǐ
bib

婴儿手套
yīng'érshǒutào
mittens

婴儿鞋
yīng'érxié
booties

绒布尿布
róngbù niàobù
cloth diaper

一次性尿布
yícìxìng niàobù
disposable diaper

塑料尿裤
sùliào niàokù
plastic pants

幼儿 yòuér • toddler

T恤衫
Txùshān
T-shirt

工装裤
gōngzhuāngkù
overalls

遮阳帽
zhēyángmào
sun hat

短裤
duǎnkù
shorts

裙子
qúnzi
skirt

围兜
wéidōu
apron

中文 zhōngwén • **english**

儿童 értóng • child

连衣裙
liányīqún
dress

风帽
fēngmào
hood

牛仔裤
niúzǎikù
jeans

背包
bēibāo
backpack

棒形纽扣
bàngxíng
niŭkòu
toggle

围巾
wéijīn
scarf

滑雪衫
huáxuěshān
parka

凉鞋
liángxié
sandals

长筒橡胶靴
chángtŏng
xiàngjiāoxuē
rain boots

夏天
xiàtiān
summer

雨衣
yŭyī
raincoat

秋天
qiūtiān
fall

粗呢外套
cūní wàitào
duffel coat

冬天
dōngtiān
winter

室内便袍
shìnèi biànpáo
robe

标志
biāozhì
logo

运动鞋
yùndòngxié
athletic shoes

儿童睡衣
értóng shuìyī
nightgown

拖鞋
tuōxié
slippers

睡衣
shuìyī
nightwear

足球球衣
zúqiú qiúyī
soccer uniform

运动服
yùndòngfú
jogging suit

紧身弹力裤
jǐnshēntánlìkù
leggings

词汇 cíhuì • vocabulary

天然纤维
tiānrán xiānwéi
natural fiber

合成的
héchéngde
synthetic

这可以机洗吗?
zhèkěyǐ jīxǐ ma?
Is it machine washable?

这适合两岁的孩子穿吗?
zhè shìhé liǎngsuìde háizi
chuān ma?
Will this fit a two-year-old?

男装 nánzhuāng · men's clothing

衣领
yīlǐng
collar

领带
lǐngdài
tie

腰带
yāodài
belt

翻领
fānlǐng
lapel

扣眼儿
kòuyǎn'ér
buttonhole

袖口
xiùkǒu
cuff

口袋
kǒudài
pocket

上装
shàngzhuāng
jacket

裤子
kùzi
pants

纽扣
niǔkòu
button

西装
xīzhuāng
business suit

雨衣
yǔyī
raincoat

衬里
chènlǐ
lining

皮鞋
píxié
leather shoes

词汇 cíhuì · vocabulary

羊毛衫 yángmáoshān cardigan	晨衣 chényī robe	外套 wàitào coat
运动服 yùndòngfú tracksuit	内衣裤 nèiyīkù underwear	长 cháng long
		短 duǎn short

有没有大/小一点儿的尺寸?
yǒuméiyǒu dà/xiǎo yìdiǎnr de chǐcùn?
Do you have this in a larger/smaller size?

我可以试穿一下吗?
wǒ kěyǐ shìchuān yíxià ma?
May I try this on?

v型领
Vxínglǐng
V-neck

圆领
yuánlǐng
crew neck

休闲上衣
xiūxián shàngyī
blazer

粗呢夹克
cūníjiákè
sport coat

马甲
mǎjiǎ
vest

T恤衫
Txùshān
T-shirt

滑雪衫
huáxuěshān
parka

运动衫
yùndòngshān
sweatshirt

衬衫
chènshān
shirt

牛仔裤
niúzǎikù
jeans

套头毛衣
tàotóumáoyī
sweater

睡衣
shuìyī
pajamas

背心
bèixīn
undershirt

休闲服
xiūxiánfú
casual wear

短裤
duǎnkù
shorts

三角内裤
sānjiǎonèikù
briefs

短衬裤
duǎnchènkù
boxer shorts

袜子
wàzi
socks

女装 nǚzhuāng • women's clothing

上装
shàngzhuāng
jacket

缝合线
fénghéxiàn
seam

袖子
xiùzi
sleeve

及脚踝长
jíjiǎohuái cháng
ankle length

无肩带
wújiāndài
strapless

无袖
wúxiù
sleeveless

晚礼服
wǎnlǐfú
evening dress

连衣裙
liányīqún
dress

裙子
qúnzi
skirt

女士衬衫
nǚshì chènshān
blouse

裙边
qúnbiān
hem

及膝长
jíxī cháng
knee length

裤子
kùzi
pants

连裤袜
liánkùwà
tights

鞋
xié
shoes

正装
zhèngzhuāng
formal

便装
biànzhuāng
casual

女用内衣 nǚyòng nèiyī · **lingerie**

肩带
jiāndài
strap

便袍
biànpáo
robe

衬裙
chènqún
slip

紧身内衣
jǐnshēn nèiyī
camisole

吊袜带
diàowàdài
garter straps

女式短上衣
nǚshì duǎnshàngyī
bustier

长筒袜
chángtǒngwà
stocking

连裤袜
liánkùwà
panty hose

胸罩
xiōngzhào
bra

女用内裤
nǚyòng nèikù
panties

女睡衣
nǚshuìyī
nightgown

婚礼 hūnlǐ · **wedding**

花边
huābiān
lace

头纱
tóushā
veil

花束
huāshù
bouquet

拖裾
tuōjū
train

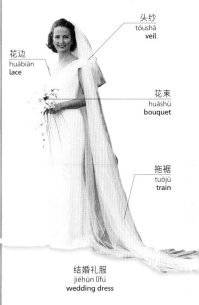

结婚礼服
jiéhūn lǐfú
wedding dress

词汇 cíhuì · **vocabulary**

束腹 shùfù corset	剪裁考究 jiǎncái kǎojiu tailored
松紧袜带 sōngjǐn wàdài garter	露背装 lùbèizhuāng halter neck
垫肩 diànjiān shoulder pad	内有金属丝的(胸罩) nèiyǒu jīnshǔsīde (xiōngzhào) underwire
腰带 yāodài waistband	运动胸罩 yùndòng xiōngzhào sports bra

配饰 pèishì • accessories

帽子
màozi
cap

礼帽
lǐmào
hat

围巾
wéijīn
scarf

腰带扣
yāodàikòu
buckle

腰带
yāodài
belt

柄
bǐng
handle

尖
jiān
tip

手帕
shǒupà
handkerchief

领结
lǐngjié
bow tie

领带别针
lǐngdàibiézhēn
tiepin

手套
shǒutào
gloves

伞
sǎn
umbrella

首饰 shǒushì • jewelry

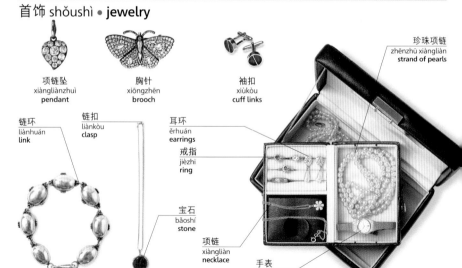

项链坠
xiàngliànzhuì
pendant

胸针
xiōngzhēn
brooch

袖扣
xiùkòu
cuff links

珍珠项链
zhēnzhū xiàngliàn
strand of pearls

链环
liànhuán
link

链扣
liànkòu
clasp

耳环
ěrhuán
earrings

戒指
jièzhi
ring

宝石
bǎoshí
stone

项链
xiàngliàn
necklace

手表
shǒubiǎo
watch

手镯
shǒuzhuó
bracelet

链子
liànzi
chain

首饰盒 shǒushìhé | jewelry box

包 bāo • bags

钱夹
qiánjiā
wallet

钱包
qiánbāo
change purse

扣环
kòuhuán
clasp

挎包
kuàbāo
shoulder bag

背带
bēidài
shoulder strap

提手
tíshǒu
handles

旅行袋
lǚxíngdài
duffel bag

公文包
gōngwénbāo
briefcase

手提包
shǒutíbāo
handbag

背包
bēibāo
backpack

鞋 xié • shoes

鞋带
xiédài
lace

鞋舌
xiéshé
tongue

鞋眼
xiéyǎn
eyelet

鞋底
xiédǐ
sole

鞋跟
xiégēn
heel

系带鞋
xìdàixié
lace-up

步行靴
bùxíngxuē
hiking boot

运动鞋
yùndòngxié
sneaker

靴子
xuēzi
boot

平底人字拖鞋
píngdǐ rénzi tuōxié
flip-flop

镂花皮鞋
lòuhuā píxié
dress shoe

高跟鞋
gāogēnxié
high-heeled shoe

坡跟鞋
pōgēnxié
wedge

凉鞋
liángxié
sandal

无带便鞋
wúdài biànxié
slip-on

平底单鞋
píngdǐ dānxié
pump

头发 tóufà · hair

发梳
fàshū
comb

梳头
shūtóu
comb (v)

发刷
fàshuā
brush

刷头发 shuātóufà | brush (v)

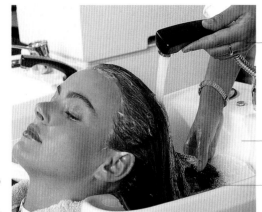

美发师
měifàshī
hairdresser

洗头盆
xǐtóupén
sink

顾客
gùkè
client

洗 xǐ | wash (v)

冲洗
chōngxǐ
rinse (v)

罩衫
zhàoshān
robe

剪
jiǎn
cut (v)

吹干
chuīgān
blow-dry (v)

定型
dìngxíng
set (v)

美发用品 měifà yòngpǐn · accessories

吹风机
chuīfēngjī
blow-dryer

洗发水
xǐfàshuǐ
shampoo

护发素
hùfàsù
conditioner

发胶
fàjiāo
gel

定型水
dìngxíngshuǐ
hairspray

卷发钳
juǎnfàqián
curling iron

剪刀
jiǎndāo
scissors

发箍
fàgū
headband

直发器
zhífàqì
hair straightener

发卡
fàqiǎ
bobby pins

发型 fàxíng · styles

马尾辫
mǎwěibiàn
ponytail

麻花辫
máhuābiàn
braid

法式盘头
fǎshì pántóu
French twist

发髻
fàjì
bun

小辫
xiǎobiàn
pigtails

女式短发
nǚshì duǎnfà
bob

短发
duǎnfà
crop

卷发
juǎnfà
curly

烫发
tàngfà
perm

直发
zhífà
straight

发根
fàgēn
roots

挑染
tiāorǎn
highlights

秃顶
tūdǐng
bald

假发
jiǎfà
wig

词汇 cíhuì · vocabulary

修剪
xiūjiǎn
trim (v)

拉直
lāzhí
straighten (v)

理发师
lǐfàshī
barber

头皮屑
tóupíxiè
dandruff

发梢分叉
fàshāo fēnchà
split ends

面包
miàn bāo
beard

油性(发质)
yóuxìng (fàzhì)
greasy

干性(发质)
gānxìng (fàzhì)
dry

中性(发质)
zhōngxìng (fàzhì)
normal

头皮
tóupí
scalp

发带
fàdài
hairband

小胡子
xiǎo hú zi
mustache

发色 fàsè · colors

金色
jīnsè
blonde

深褐色
shēnhèsè
brunette

红褐色
hónghèsè
auburn

红棕色
hóngzōngsè
red

黑色
hēisè
black

灰色
huīsè
gray

白色
báisè
white

染色的
rǎnsède
dyed

美容 měiróng · beauty

染发剂
rǎnfàjì
hair dye

眼影
yǎnyǐng
eye shadow

睫毛膏
jiémáogāo
mascara

眼线液
yǎnxiànyè
eyeliner

腮红
sāihóng
blush

粉底
fěndǐ
foundation

口红
kǒuhóng
lipstick

化妆 huàzhuāng · makeup

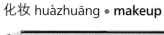

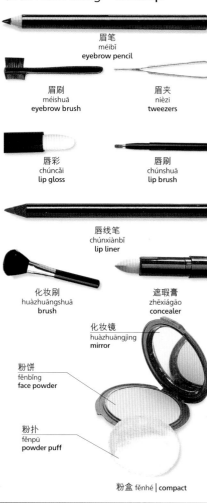

眉笔
méibǐ
eyebrow pencil

眉刷
méishuā
eyebrow brush

眉夹
nièzi
tweezers

唇彩
chúncǎi
lip gloss

唇刷
chúnshuā
lip brush

唇线笔
chúnxiànbǐ
lip liner

化妆刷
huàzhuāngshuā
brush

遮瑕膏
zhēxiágāo
concealer

化妆镜
huàzhuāngjìng
mirror

粉饼
fěnbǐng
face powder

粉扑
fěnpū
powder puff

粉盒 fěnhé | compact

美容护理 měirónghùlǐ • beauty treatments

面膜
miànmó
face mask

紫外线浴床
zǐwàixiàn yùchuáng
sunbed

面部护理
miànbùhùlǐ
facial

去死皮
qù sǐpí
exfoliate (v)

热蜡脱毛
rèlàtuōmáo
wax

趾甲护理
zhǐjiǎ hùlǐ
pedicure

化妆用品 huàzhuāng yòngpǐn • toiletries

洁面水
jiémiànshuǐ
cleanser

爽肤水
shuǎngfūshuǐ
toner

保湿霜
bǎoshīshuāng
moisturizer

黑肤霜
hēifūshuāng
self-tanning lotion

香水
xiāngshuǐ
perfume

淡香水
dànxiāngshuǐ
eau de toilette

指甲护理 zhǐjia hùlǐ • manicure

洗甲水
xǐjiǎshuǐ
nail polish remover

指甲锉
zhǐjiacuò
nail file

指甲油
zhǐjiayóu
nail polish

指甲剪
zhǐjiajian
nail scissors

指甲刀
zhǐjiadāo
nail clippers

词汇 cíhuì • vocabulary

肤色
fūsè
complexion

油性(皮肤)
yóuxìng(pífū)
oily

棕褐色皮肤
zōnghèsè pífū
tan

皮肤白皙
pífū báixī
fair

敏感性的
mǐngǎnxìngde
sensitive

纹身
wénshēn
tattoo

肤色较深
fūsè jiàoshēn
dark

低致敏的
dīzhìmǐnde
hypoallergenic

抗皱
kàngzhòu
antiwrinkle

干性(皮肤)
gānxìng(pífū)
dry

色调
sèdiào
shade

棉球
miánqiú
cotton balls

健康 jiànkāng
health

疾病 jíbìng · illness

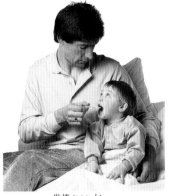

发烧 fāshāo | fever

头痛
tóutòng
headache

流鼻血
liúbíxiě
nosebleed

咳嗽
késou
cough

喷嚏
pēntì
sneeze

感冒
gǎnmào
cold

流感
liúgǎn
flu

气雾剂
qìwùjì
inhaler

哮喘
xiàochuǎn
asthma

痉挛
jìngluán
cramps

恶心
ěxin
nausea

水痘
shuǐdòu
chicken pox

皮疹
pízhěn
rash

词汇 cíhuì · vocabulary

中风 zhòngfēng stroke	糖尿病 tángniàobìng diabetes	湿疹 shīzhěn eczema	寒战 hánzhàn chill	呕吐 ǒutù vomit (v)	腹泻 fùxiè diarrhea
血压 xuèyā blood pressure	过敏 guòmǐn allergy	传染 chuánrǎn infection	胃痛 wèitòng stomachache	癫痫 diānxián epilepsy	麻疹 mázhěn measles
心肌梗塞 xīnjī gěngsè heart attack	枯草热 kūcǎorè hay fever	病毒 bìngdú virus	昏厥 hūnjué faint (v)	偏头痛 piāntóutòng migraine	腮腺炎 sāixiànyán mumps

医生 yīshēng · doctor
诊断 zhěnduàn · consultation

护士
hùshi
nurse

医生
yīshēng
doctor

X光片看片器
Xguāngpiàn kànpiànqi
X-ray viewer

处方
chǔfāng
prescription

患者
huànzhě
patient

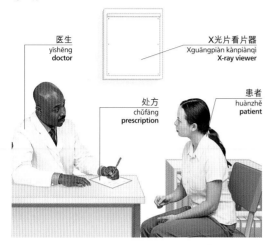

体重计
tǐzhòngjì
scale

充气袖带
chōngqì xiùdài
cuff

电子血压仪
diànzǐ xuèyā yí
**electric blood
pressure monitor**

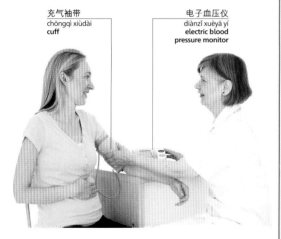

词汇 cíhuì · vocabulary

预约
yùyuē
appointment

接种
jiēzhòng
vaccination

诊疗室
zhěnliáoshì
doctor's office

体温计
tǐwēnjì
thermometer

候诊室
hòuzhěnshì
waiting room

体检
tǐjiǎn
**medical
examination**

我需要看医生。
wǒ xūyào kànyīshēng.
I need to see a doctor.

这儿疼。
zhè'er téng.
It hurts here.

创伤 chuāngshāng · injury

医用吊带
yīyòng
diàodài
sling

颈托
jǐngtuō
neck brace

扭伤 niǔshāng | sprain

骨折
gǔzhé
fracture

头颈部损伤
tóujǐngbù sǔnshāng
whiplash

割伤
gēshāng
cut

擦伤
cāshāng
graze

淤伤
yūshāng
bruise

刺伤
cìshāng
splinter

晒伤
shàishāng
sunburn

烧伤
shāoshāng
burn

咬伤
yǎoshāng
bite

蜇伤
zhēshāng
sting

词汇 cíhuì · vocabulary

事故 shìgù **accident**	大出血 dàchūxuè **hemorrhage**	中毒 zhòngdú **poisoning**	他/她没事吧? tā/tā méishì ba? **Will he/she be all right?**
紧急情况 jǐnjí qíngkuàng **emergency**	水泡 shuǐpào **blister**	电击 diànjī **electric shock**	哪里疼? nǎli téng? **Where does it hurt?**
伤口 shāngkǒu **wound**	脑震荡 nǎozhèndàng **concussion**	头部损伤 tóubù sǔnshāng **head injury**	请叫救护车。 qǐngjiào jiùhùchē. **Please call an ambulance.**

急救 jíjiù · first aid

药膏
yàogāo
ointment

创可贴
chuàngkětiē
adhesive
bandage

安全别针
ānquán biézhēn
safety pin

绷带
bēngdài
bandage

止痛药
zhǐtòngyào
painkillers

消毒湿巾
xiāodú shījīn
antiseptic wipe

镊子
nièzi
tweezers

剪刀
jiǎndāo
scissors

消毒剂
xiāodújì
antiseptic

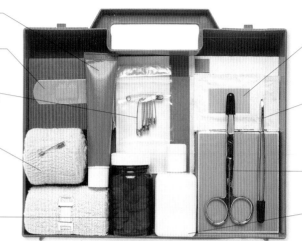

急救箱 jíjiùxiāng | first-aid kit

纱布
shābù
gauze

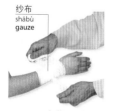

包扎
bāozā
dressing

医用夹板 yīyòngjiābǎn | splint

橡皮膏
xiàngpígāo
adhesive tape

复苏术
fùsūshù
resuscitation

词汇 cíhuì · vocabulary

休克 xiūkè shock	脉搏 màibó pulse	窒息 zhìxī choke (v)	您能帮帮我吗？ nín néng bāngbāng wǒ ma? Can you help?
不省人事 bùxǐng rénshì unconscious	呼吸 hūxī breathing	无菌 wújūn sterile	你会急救吗？ nǐ huì jíjiù ma? Do you know first aid?

医院 yīyuàn · hospital

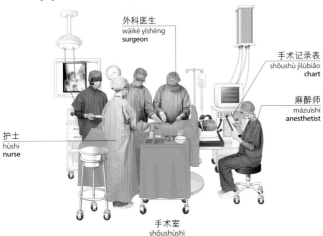

外科医生
wàikē yīshēng
surgeon

手术记录表
shǒushù jìlùbiǎo
chart

麻醉师
mázuìshī
anesthetist

护士
hùshi
nurse

手术室
shǒushùshì
operating room

验血
yànxuè
blood test

注射
zhùshè
injection

X光
Xguāng
X-ray

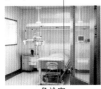

移动病床
yídòng bìngchuáng
gurney

呼叫按钮
hūjiào ànniǔ
call button

急诊室
jízhěnshì
emergency room

病房
bìngfáng
ward

轮椅
lúnyǐ
wheelchair

CT扫描
CT sǎomiáo
scan

词汇 cíhuì · vocabulary

手术 shǒushù operation	出院 chūyuàn discharged	探视时间 tànshì shíjiān visiting hours	儿童病房 értóng bìngfáng children's ward	加护病房 jiāhù bìngfáng intensive care unit
收治的 shōuzhìde admitted	诊所 zhěnsuǒ clinic	产科病房 chǎnkē bìngfáng maternity ward	单人病房 dānrén bìngfáng private room	门诊病人 ménzhěn bìngrén outpatient

科室 kēshì · departments

耳鼻喉科
ěrbíhóukē
ENT

心脏病科
xīnzàngbìngkē
cardiology

整形外科
zhěngxíngwàikē
orthopedics

妇科
fùkē
gynecology

理疗科
lǐliáokē
physiotherapy

皮肤科
pífūkē
dermatology

儿科
érkē
pediatrics

放射科
fàngshèkē
radiology

外科
wàikē
surgery

产科
chǎnkē
maternity

精神科
jīngshénkē
psychiatry

眼科
yǎnkē
ophthalmology

词汇 cíhuì · vocabulary

神经科 shénjīngkē **neurology**	泌尿科 mìniàokē **urology**	内分泌科 nèifēnmìkē **endocrinology**	病理科 bìnglǐkē **pathology**	结果 jiéguǒ **result**
肿瘤科 zhǒngliúkē **oncology**	矫形外科 jiǎoxíngwàikē **plastic surgery**	转诊 zhuǎnzhěn **referral**	检查 jiǎnchá **test**	专科医生 zhuānkē yīshēng **specialist**

牙医 yáyī · dentist

牙齿 yáchǐ · tooth

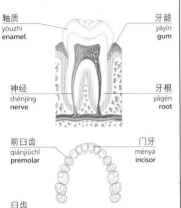

釉质
yòuzhì
enamel

牙龈
yáyín
gum

神经
shénjīng
nerve

牙根
yágēn
root

前臼齿
qiánjiùchǐ
premolar

门牙
ményá
incisor

臼齿
jiùchǐ
molar

犬齿
quǎnchǐ
canine

检查 jiǎnchá · checkup

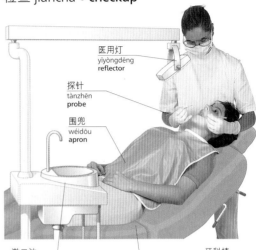

医用灯
yīyòngdēng
reflector

探针
tànzhēn
probe

围兜
wéidōu
apron

漱口池
shùkǒuchí
sink

牙科椅
yákēyǐ
dentist's chair

词汇 cíhuì · vocabulary

牙痛
yátòng
toothache

牙钻
yázuàn
drill

牙菌斑
yájūnbān
plaque

牙线
yáxiàn
dental floss

龋齿
qǔchǐ
decay

拔牙
báyá
extraction

填充物
tiánchōngwù
filling

齿冠
chǐguān
crown

用牙线洁齿
yòng yáxiàn jiéchǐ
floss (v)

刷牙
shuāyá
brush (v)

畸齿矫正器
jīchǐ jiǎozhèngqì
braces

X光
X guāng
dental X-ray

牙片
yápiàn
X-ray film

假牙
jiǎyá
dentures

配镜师 pèijìngshī · **optometrist**

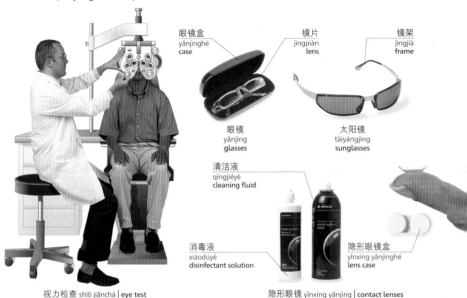

眼镜盒
yǎnjìnghé
case

镜片
jìngpiàn
lens

镜架
jìngjià
frame

眼镜
yǎnjìng
glasses

太阳镜
tàiyángjìng
sunglasses

清洁液
qīngjiéyè
cleaning fluid

消毒液
xiāodúyè
disinfectant solution

隐形眼镜盒
yǐnxíng yǎnjìnghé
lens case

视力检查 shìlì jiǎnchá | eye test

隐形眼镜 yǐnxíng yǎnjìng | contact lenses

眼睛 yǎnjìng · **eye**

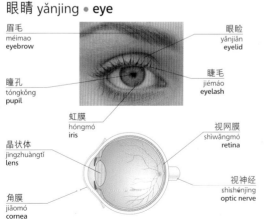

眉毛
méimao
eyebrow

眼睑
yǎnjiǎn
eyelid

瞳孔
tóngkǒng
pupil

睫毛
jiémáo
eyelash

虹膜
hóngmó
iris

晶状体
jīngzhuàngtǐ
lens

视网膜
shìwǎngmó
retina

视神经
shìshénjīng
optic nerve

角膜
jiǎomó
cornea

词汇 cíhuì · **vocabulary**

视力 shìlì vision	散光 sǎnguāng astigmatism
屈光度 qūguāngdù diopter	远视 yuǎnshì farsighted
眼泪 yǎnlèi tear	近视 jìnshì nearsighted
白内障 báinèizhàng cataract	双光的 shuāngguāngde bifocal

怀孕 huáiyùn · pregnancy

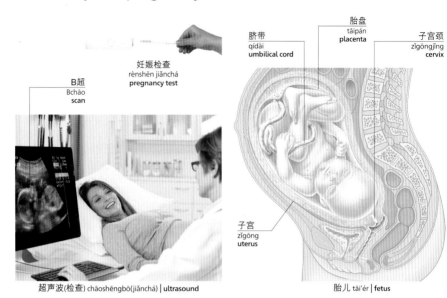

B超
Bchāo
scan

妊娠检查
rènshēn jiǎnchá
pregnancy test

脐带
qídài
umbilical cord

胎盘
tāipán
placenta

子宫颈
zǐgōngjǐng
cervix

子宫
zǐgōng
uterus

超声波(检查) chāoshēngbō(jiǎnchá) | ultrasound

胎儿 tāi'ér | fetus

词汇 cíhuì · vocabulary

排卵 páiluǎn ovulation	出生前 chūshēngqián prenatal	宫缩 gōngsuō contraction	扩张术 kuòzhāngshù dilation	分娩 fēnmiǎn delivery	臀位分娩 túnwèifēnmiǎn breech birth
怀孕 huáiyùn conception	胚胎 pēitāi embryo	破羊水 pòyángshuǐ break water (v)	硬膜外麻醉 yìngmó wài mázuì epidural	出生 chūshēng birth	早产的 zǎochǎnde premature
怀孕的 huáiyùnde pregnant	子宫 zǐgōng womb	羊水 yángshuǐ amniotic fluid	外阴切开术 wàiyīn qiēkāishù episiotomy	流产 liúchǎn miscarriage	妇科医生 fùkē yīshēng gynecologist
待产的 dàichǎnde expecting	怀孕三个月 huáiyùnsāngèyuè trimester	羊水穿刺诊断 yángshuǐ chuāncì zhěnduàn amniocentesis	剖腹产 pōufùchǎn cesarean section	缝合 fénghé stitches	产科医生 chǎnkē yīshēng obstetrician

分娩 fēnmiǎn · **childbirth**

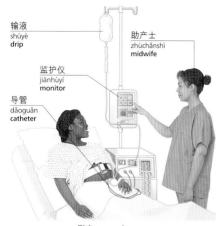

输液
shūyè
drip

助产士
zhùchǎnshì
midwife

监护仪
jiānhùyí
monitor

导管
dǎoguǎn
catheter

引产 yǐnchǎn | **induce labor (v)**

育婴箱 yùyīngxiāng | **incubator**

出生时体重 chūshēngshí tǐzhòng | **birth weight**

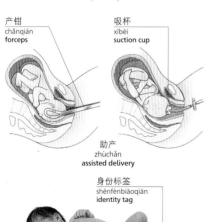

产钳
chǎnqián
forceps

吸杯
xībēi
suction cup

助产
zhùchǎn
assisted delivery

身份标签
shēnfènbiāoqiān
identity tag

新生儿 xīnshēng'ér | **newborn baby**

哺乳 bǔrǔ · **nursing**

吸乳器
xīrǔqì
breast pump

哺乳胸罩
bǔrǔ xiōngzhào
nursing bra

喂母乳
wèi mǔrǔ
breastfeed (v)

乳垫
rǔdiàn
nursing pads

替代疗法 tìdài liáofǎ • alternative therapy

瑜伽姿势
yújiāzìshì
yoga pose

垫子
diànzi
mat

瑜伽 yújiā | yoga

按摩
ànmó
massage

指压按摩
zhǐyā ànmó
shiatsu

脊柱按摩法
jǐzhù ànmófǎ
chiropractic

整骨疗法
zhěnggǔ liáofǎ
osteopathy

足底反射疗法
zúdǐ fǎnshè liáofǎ
reflexology

冥想
míngxiǎng
meditation

顾问
gùwèn
counselor

集体治疗
jítǐ zhìliáo
group therapy

灵气疗法
língqì liáofǎ
reiki

针灸
zhēnjiǔ
acupuncture

印度草药疗法
yìndù cǎoyào liáofǎ
ayurveda

催眠疗法
cuīmián liáofǎ
hypnotherapy

精油
jīngyóu
essential oils

本草疗法
běncǎo liáofǎ
herbalism

芳香疗法
fāngxiāng liáofǎ
aromatherapy

顺势疗法
shùnshì liáofǎ
homeopathy

指压疗法
zhǐyā liáofǎ
acupressure

治疗师
zhìliáoshī
therapist

精神疗法
jīngshén liáofǎ
psychotherapy

词汇 cíhuì · vocabulary

营养品 yíngyǎngpǐn **supplement**	自然疗法 zìrán liáofǎ **naturopathy**	放松 fàngsōng **relaxation**	药草 yàocǎo **herb**
水疗 shuǐliáo **hydrotherapy**	风水 fēngshuǐ **feng shui**	压力 yālì **stress**	水晶疗法 shuǐjīng liáofǎ **crystal healing**

家居 jiājū
home

房屋 fángwū · house

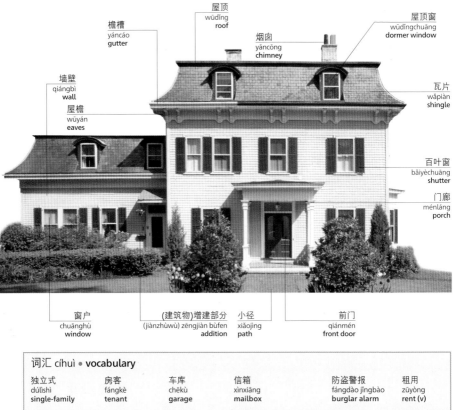

屋顶
wūdǐng
roof

檐槽
yáncáo
gutter

烟囱
yāncōng
chimney

屋顶窗
wūdǐngchuāng
dormer window

墙壁
qiángbì
wall

屋檐
wūyán
eaves

瓦片
wǎpiàn
shingle

百叶窗
bǎiyèchuāng
shutter

门廊
ménláng
porch

窗户
chuānghù
window

(建筑物)增建部分
(jiànzhùwù) zēngjiàn bùfen
addition

小径
xiǎojìng
path

前门
qiánmén
front door

词汇 cíhuì · vocabulary

独立式 dúlìshì single-family	房客 fángkè tenant	车库 chēkù garage	信箱 xìnxiāng mailbox	防盗警报 fángdào jǐngbào burglar alarm	租用 zūyòng rent (v)
半独立式 bàndúlìshì duplex	平房 píngfáng bungalow	阁楼 gélóu attic	门廊灯 ménlángdēng porch light	庭院 tíngyuàn courtyard	房租 fángzū rent
连栋房屋 liándòngfángwū townhouse	地下室 dìxiàshì basement	房间 fángjiān room	房东 fángdōng landlord	楼层 lóucéng floor	连排式 liánpáishì row house

入口 rùkǒu · entrance

公寓 gōngyù · apartment

扶手
fúshǒu
hand rail

楼梯平台
lóutī píngtái
landing

楼梯栏杆
lóutī lángān
banister

楼梯
lóutī
staircase

门厅
méntīng
foyer

阳台
yángtái
balcony

公寓楼
gōngyùlóu
apartment building

对讲器
duìjiǎngqì
intercom

门铃
ménlíng
doorbell

门垫
méndiàn
doormat

门环
ménhuán
door knocker

门链
ménliàn
door chain

钥匙
yàoshi
key

锁
suǒ
lock

门闩
ménshuān
bolt

电梯
diàntī
elevator

室内系统 shìnèi xìtǒng · **internal systems**

扇叶
shànyè
blade

风扇
fēngshàn
fan

暖器片
nuǎnqìpiàn
radiator

电暖器
diànnuǎnqì
space heater

对流式电暖器
duìliúshì diànnuǎnqì
convector heater

电 diàn · **electricity**

接地
jiēdì
ground

插片
chāpiàn
pin

零线
língxiàn
neutral

火线
huǒxiàn
live

节能灯泡
jiénéng dēngpào
energy-saving bulb

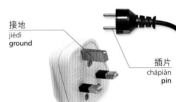

插头 chātóu | plug

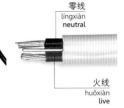

电线 diànxiàn | wires

词汇 cíhuì · **vocabulary**

电压 diànyā **voltage**	保险丝 bǎoxiǎnsī **fuse**	插座 chāzuò **outlet**	直流电 zhíliúdiàn **direct current**	停电 tíngdiàn **power outage**
安培 ānpéi **amp**	保险盒 bǎoxiǎnhé **fuse box**	开关 kāiguān **switch**	变压器 biànyāqì **transformer**	供电系统 gōngdiàn xìtǒng **household current**
电力 diànlì **power**	发电机 fādiànjī **generator**	交流电 jiāoliúdiàn **alternating current**	电表 diànbiǎo **electric meter**	

管道装置 guǎndào zhuāngzhì · **plumbing**

洗涤槽 xǐdícáo · **sink**

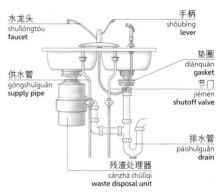

水龙头
shuǐlóngtóu
faucet

手柄
shǒubǐng
lever

垫圈
diànquān
gasket

供水管
gōngshuǐguǎn
supply pipe

节门
jiémén
shutoff valve

排水管
páishuǐguǎn
drain

残渣处理器
cánzhā chǔlǐqì
waste disposal unit

抽水马桶 chōushuǐ mǎtǒng · **toilet**

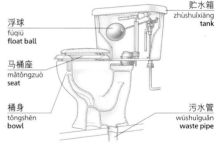

浮球
fúqiú
float ball

贮水箱
zhùshuǐxiāng
tank

马桶座
mǎtǒngzuò
seat

桶身
tǒngshēn
bowl

污水管
wūshuǐguǎn
waste pipe

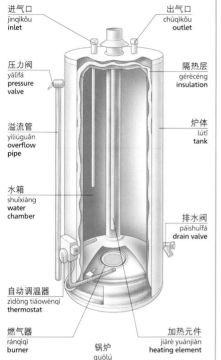

进气口
jìnqìkǒu
inlet

出气口
chūqìkǒu
outlet

压力阀
yālìfá
pressure
valve

隔热层
gérècéng
insulation

溢流管
yìliúguǎn
overflow
pipe

炉体
lútǐ
tank

水箱
shuǐxiāng
water
chamber

排水阀
páishuǐfá
drain valve

自动调温器
zìdòng tiáowēnqì
thermostat

燃气器
ránqìqì
burner

锅炉
guōlú
water heater

加热元件
jiārè yuánjiàn
heating element

垃圾处理 lājīchǔlǐ · **waste disposal**

瓶子
píngzi
bottle

垃圾回收箱
lājī huíshōuxiāng
recycling bin

盖子
gàizi
lid

踏板
tàbǎn
pedal

垃圾桶
lājītǒng
trash can

分类箱
fēnlèixiāng
sorting unit

有机废物
yǒujī fèiwù
organic waste

起居室 qǐjūshì · **living room**

壁灯
bìdēng
wall light

壁炉
bìlú
fireplace

天花板
tiānhuābǎn
ceiling

花瓶
huāpíng
vase

靠垫
kàodiàn
pillow

灯
dēng
lamp

茶几
chájī
coffee table

沙发
shāfā
sofa

地板
dìbǎn
floor

画框
huàkuàng
frame

画
huà
painting

窗帘
chuānglián
curtain

窗幔
chuāngmàn
sheer curtain

百叶窗
bǎiyèchuāng
Venetian blind

卷帘
juǎnlián
roller shade

装饰脚线
zhuāngshì jiǎoxiàn
molding

扶手椅
fúshǒuyǐ
armchair

书架
shūjià
bookshelf

沙发床
shāfāchuáng
sofa bed

地毯
dìtǎn
rug

书房 shūfáng | study

餐厅 cāntīng • dining room

胡椒粉
hújiāofěn
pepper

盐
yán
salt

餐桌
cānzhuō
table

陶瓷餐具
táocí cānjù
crockery

餐具
cānjù
cutlery

椅子
yǐzi
chair

椅背
yǐbèi
back

座位
zuòwèi
seat

椅子腿
yǐzituǐ
leg

词汇 cíhuì • vocabulary

摆桌子 bǎizhuōzi set the table (v)	饿 è hungry	午餐 wǔcān lunch	饱 bǎo full	主人 zhǔrén host	请再给我加一些，好吗？ qǐng zàigěi wǒ jiā yìxiē, hǎoma? Can I have some more, please?
上菜 shàngcài serve (v)	桌布 zhuōbù tablecloth	晚餐 wǎncān dinner	一份 yífèn portion	女主人 nǚzhǔrén hostess	我吃饱了，谢谢。 wǒ chībǎole, xièxie. I've had enough, thank you.
吃 chī eat (v)	早餐 zǎocān breakfast	餐具垫 cānjùdiàn placemat	饭菜 fàncài meal	客人 kèrén guest	很好吃。 hěn hǎochī. That was delicious.

餐具 cānjù • crockery and cutlery

马克杯
mǎkèbēi
mug

咖啡杯
kāfēibēi
coffee cup

茶杯
chábēi
teacup

茶匙
cháchí
teaspoon

盘子
pánzi
plate

碗
wǎn
bowl

咖啡壶
kāfēihú
French press

茶壶
cháhú
teapot

带柄水壶
dàibǐngshuǐhú
pitcher

蛋杯
dànbēi
eggcup

酒杯
jiǔbēi
wine glass

平底玻璃杯
píngdǐbōlibēi
tumbler

玻璃器皿
bōlí qìmǐn
glassware

餐巾套环
cānjīn tàohuán
napkin ring

甜点盘
tiándiǎnpán
side plate

正餐用盘
zhèngcān
yòngpán
dinner plate

汤盘
tāngpán
soup bowl

汤匙
tāngchí
soup spoon

餐叉
cānchā
fork

餐具摆放
cānjù bǎifàng
place setting

餐匙
cānchí
spoon

餐刀
cāndāo
knife

餐巾
cānjīn
napkin

厨房 chúfáng · kitchen

搁架
gējià
shelves

防溅挡板
fángjiàn dǎngbǎn
backsplash

水龙头
shuǐlóngtóu
faucet

洗涤槽
xǐdícáo
sink

抽屉
chōutì
drawer

抽油烟机
chōuyóuyānjī
ventilation hood

陶瓷炉台
táocí lútái
ceramic
stovetop

操作台
cāozuòtái
countertop

烤箱
kǎoxiāng
oven

橱柜
chúguì
cabinet

厨房电器 chúfáng diànqì · appliances

搅拌容器
jiǎobànróngqì
mixing bowl

盖子
gàizi
lid

刀片
dāopiàn
blade

微波炉
wēibōlú
microwave oven

电水壶
diànshuǐhú
electric kettle

烤面包机
kǎomiànbāojī
toaster

食品加工器
shípǐn jiāgōngqì
food processor

搅拌器
jiǎobànqì
blender

洗碗机
xǐwǎnjī
dishwasher

制冰室
zhìbīngshì
ice maker

冷冻室
lěngdòngshì
freezer

冰箱
bīngxiāng
refrigerator

搁板
gēbǎn
shelf

蔬菜保鲜格
shūcài bǎoxiāngé
crisper

双门冰箱 shuāngmén bīngxiāng
side-by-side refrigerator

词汇 cíhuì · vocabulary

餐具沥水架 cānjù lìshuǐjià **draining board**	冷冻 lěngdòng **freeze (v)**
火炉 huǒlú **burner**	解冻 jiědòng **defrost (v)**
炉盘 lúpán **stovetop**	蒸 zhēng **steam (v)**
垃圾桶 lājītǒng **garbage can**	炒 chǎo **sauté (v)**

烹饪 pēngrèn · cooking

削皮
xiāopí
peel (v)

切片
qiēpiàn
slice (v)

擦碎
cāsuì
grate (v)

注水
zhùshuǐ
pour (v)

搅拌
jiǎobàn
mix (v)

搅打
jiǎodǎ
whisk (v)

煮沸
zhǔfèi
boil (v)

煎
jiān
fry (v)

擀
gǎn
roll (v)

搅动
jiǎodòng
stir (v)

文火煻/煨/炖
wénhuǒshāo, wēi, dùn
simmer (v)

沸水煮
fèishuǐzhǔ
poach (v)

烘制
hōngzhì
bake (v)

烤制
kǎozhì
roast (v)

烧烤
shāokǎo
broil (v)

厨具 chújù • kitchenware

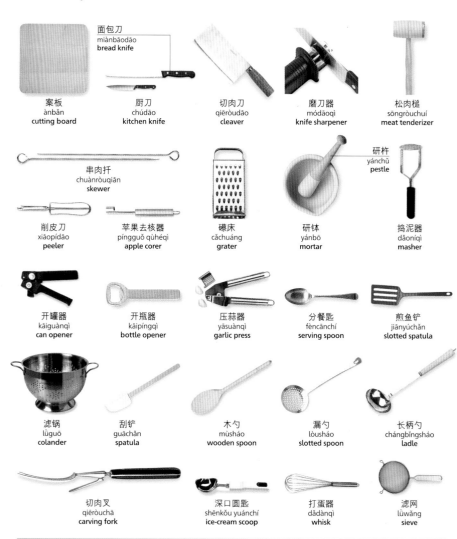

面包刀
miànbāodāo
bread knife

案板
ànbǎn
cutting board

厨刀
chúdāo
kitchen knife

切肉刀
qiēròudāo
cleaver

磨刀器
módāoqì
knife sharpener

松肉槌
sōngròuchuí
meat tenderizer

串肉扦
chuànròuqiān
skewer

研杵
yánchǔ
pestle

削皮刀
xiāopídāo
peeler

苹果去核器
píngguǒ qùhéqì
apple corer

礤床
cǎchuáng
grater

研钵
yánbō
mortar

捣泥器
dǎoníqì
masher

开罐器
kāiguànqì
can opener

开瓶器
kāipíngqì
bottle opener

压蒜器
yāsuànqì
garlic press

分餐匙
fēncānchí
serving spoon

煎鱼铲
jiānyúchǎn
slotted spatula

滤锅
lùguō
colander

刮铲
guāchǎn
spatula

木勺
mùsháo
wooden spoon

漏勺
lòusháo
slotted spoon

长柄勺
chángbǐngsháo
ladle

切肉叉
qiēròuchā
carving fork

深口圆匙
shēnkǒu yuánchí
ice-cream scoop

打蛋器
dǎdànqì
whisk

滤网
lǜwǎng
sieve

锅盖
guōgài
lid

不粘锅
bùzhānguō
nonstick

煎锅
jiānguō
frying pan

长柄深平底锅
chángbǐng shēn píngdǐguō
saucepan

烤架盘
kǎojiàpán
grill pan

炒锅
chǎoguō
wok

陶制炖锅
táozhìdùnguō
earthenware dish

玻璃
bōlí
glass

耐热
nàirè
ovenproof

搅拌碗
jiǎobànwǎn
mixing bowl

舒芙蕾模子
shūfúlěi múzi
soufflé dish

烘烤菜肴盘
hōngkǎo càiyáopán
gratin dish

干酪蛋糕模
gānlào dàngāomú
ramekin

砂锅
shāguō
casserole dish

蛋糕制作 dàngāo zhìzuò • baking cakes

秤
chèng
scale

量壶
liánghú
measuring cup

蛋糕烤模
dàngāo kǎomú
cake pan

馅饼烤模
xiànbǐng kǎomú
pie pan

奶油蛋糕烤模
nǎiyóudàngāo kǎomú
quiche pan

面粉刷 miànfěnshuā
pastry brush

擀面杖 gǎnmiànzhàng | rolling pin

蛋糕裱花袋 dàngāo
biǎohuādài | piping bag

松饼烤盘
sōngbǐng kǎopán
muffin pan

烤盘
kǎopán
cookie sheet

冷却架
lěngquèjià
cooling rack

烤箱手套
kǎoxiāng shǒutào
oven mitt

围裙
wéiqún
apron

卧室 wòshì · **bedroom**

衣橱
yīchú
wardrobe

床头灯
chuángtóudēng
bedside lamp

床头板
chuángtóubǎn
headboard

床头柜
chuángtóuguì
nightstand

五斗橱
wǔdǒuchú
chest of drawers

抽屉	床	床垫	床罩	枕头
chōutì	chuáng	chuángdiàn	chuángzhào	zhěntou
drawer	**bed**	**mattress**	**bedspread**	**pillow**

暖水袋
nuǎnshuǐdài
hot-water bottle

时钟收音机
shízhōng shōuyīnjī
clock radio

闹钟
nàozhōng
alarm clock

纸巾盒
zhǐjīnhé
box of tissues

衣架
yījià
coat hanger

床上用品 chuángshàng yòngpǐn · bed linen

枕套
zhěntào
pillowcase

镜子
jìngzi
mirror

床单
chuángdān
sheet

床帷
chuángwéi
dust ruffle

梳妆台
shūzhuāngtái
dressing table

羽绒被
yǔróngbèi
comforter

棉被
miánbèi
quilt

毯子
tǎnzi
blanket

地板
dìbǎn
floor

词汇 cíhuì · vocabulary

单人床 dānrénchuáng **twin bed**	床脚板 chuángjiǎobǎn **footboard**	失眠 shīmián **insomnia**	醒来 xǐnglái **wake up (v)**	设定闹钟 shèdìng nàozhōng **set the alarm (v)**
双人床 shuāngrénchuáng **full bed**	弹簧床面 tánhuáng chuángmiàn **bedspring**	上床睡觉 shàngchuáng shuìjiào **go to bed (v)**	起床 qǐchuáng **get up (v)**	打鼾 dǎhān **snore (v)**
电热毯 diànrètǎn **electric blanket**	地毯 dìtǎn **carpet**	入睡 rùshuì **go to sleep (v)**	整理床铺 zhěnglǐ chuángpù **make the bed (v)**	内嵌式衣橱 nèiqiànshì yīchú **closet**

浴室 yùshì · bathroom

毛巾架
máojīnjià
towel rack

淋浴隔门
línyù gémén
shower door

冷水龙头
lěngshuǐ lóngtóu
cold faucet

热水龙头
rèshuǐ lóngtóu
hot faucet

淋浴喷头
línyù pēntóu
shower head

洗手池
xǐshǒuchí
sink

塞子
sāizi
plug

淋浴
línyù
shower

地漏
dìlòu
drain

马桶座
mǎtǒngzuò
toilet seat

抽水马桶
chōushuǐ mǎtǒng
toilet

马桶刷
mǎtǒngshuā
toilet brush

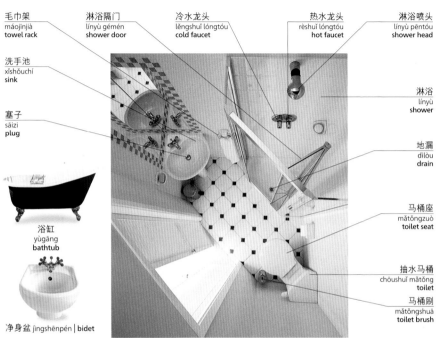

浴缸
yùgāng
bathtub

净身盆 jìngshēnpén | bidet

词汇 cíhuì · vocabulary

家用药箱
jiāyòng yàoxiāng
medicine cabinet

浴室防滑垫
yùshì fánghuádiàn
bath mat

卫生纸
wèishēngzhǐ
toilet paper

淋浴隔帘
línyù gélián
shower curtain

洗淋浴
xǐlínyù
take a shower (v)

洗澡
xǐzǎo
take a bath (v)

口腔卫生 kǒuqiāng wèishēng · dental hygiene

牙刷
yáshuā
toothbrush

牙线
yáxiàn
dental floss

牙膏
yágāo
toothpaste

漱口液
shùkǒuyè
mouthwash

海绵
hǎimián
sponge

浮石
fúshí
pumice stone

背刷
bèishuā
back brush

除臭剂
chúchòujì
deodorant

肥皂盒
féizàohé
soap dish

肥皂
féizào
soap

沐浴乳
mùyùrǔ
shower gel

面霜
miànshuāng
face cream

泡泡浴液
pàopào yùyè
bubble bath

擦手巾
cāshǒujīn
hand towel

浴巾
yùjīn
bath towel

毛巾
máojīn
towels

润肤露
rùnfūlù
body lotion

爽身粉
shuǎngshēnfěn
talcum powder

浴袍
yùpáo
bathrobe

剃须 tìxū • shaving

电动剃须刀
diàndòng tìxūdāo
electric razor

剃须泡沫
tìxūpàomò
shaving foam

一次性剃须刀
yícìxìng tìxūdāo
disposable razor

剃刀刀片
tìdāo dāopiàn
razor blade

须后水
xūhòushuǐ
aftershave

育婴室 yùyīngshì · **nursery**

婴儿护理 yīng'ér hùlǐ · **baby care**

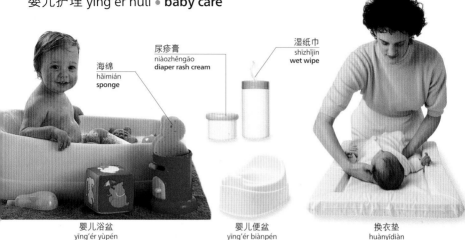

尿疹膏
niàozhěngāo
diaper rash cream

湿纸巾
shīzhǐjīn
wet wipe

海绵
hǎimián
sponge

婴儿浴盆
yīng'ér yùpén
baby bath

婴儿便盆
yīng'ér biànpén
potty

换衣垫
huànyīdiàn
changing mat

睡眠 shuìmián · **sleeping**

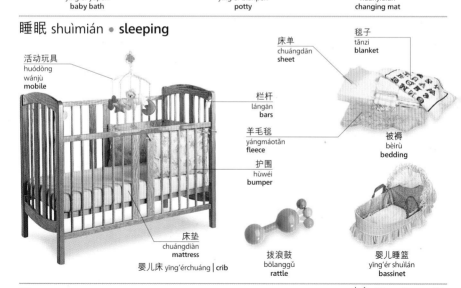

床单
chuángdān
sheet

毯子
tǎnzi
blanket

活动玩具
huódòng
wánjù
mobile

栏杆
lángàn
bars

羊毛毯
yángmáotǎn
fleece

护围
hùwéi
bumper

被褥
bèirù
bedding

床垫
chuángdiàn
mattress

婴儿床 yīng'érchuáng | **crib**

拨浪鼓
bōlànggǔ
rattle

婴儿睡篮
yīng'ér shuìlán
bassinet

游戏 yóuxì • playing

娃娃
wáwa
doll

长毛绒玩具
chángmáoróng wánjù
stuffed toy

娃娃屋
wáwawū
dollhouse

玩具屋
wánjùwū
playhouse

泰迪熊
tàidíxióng
teddy bear

玩具
wánjù
toy

球
qiú
ball

玩具篮
wánjùlán
toy basket

游戏围栏
yóuxì wéilán
playpen

安全 ānquán • safety

儿童安全锁
értóng ānquánsuǒ
child lock

婴儿监视器
yīng'ér jiānshìqì
baby monitor

楼梯门栏
lóutī ménlán
stair gate

饮食 yǐnshí • eating

高脚椅
gāojiǎoyǐ
high chair

奶嘴
nǎizuǐ
nipple

婴儿杯
yīng'érbēi
drinking cup

奶瓶
nǎipíng
bottle

外出 wàichū • going out

折叠式婴儿车
zhédiéshì yīng'érchē
stroller

卧式婴儿车
wòshìyīng'érchē
baby carriage

遮阳篷
zhēyángpéng
hood

尿布
niàobù
diaper

手提式婴儿床
shǒutíshì yīng'érchuáng
carrier

婴儿衣物袋
yīng'ér yīwùdài
diaper bag

婴儿吊带
yīng'ér diàodài
baby sling

家务间 jiāwùjiān · **utility room**

洗涤 xǐdí · **laundry**

干净衣物
gānjìng yīwù
clean clothes

脏衣物
zāngyīwù
dirty laundry

洗衣篮
xǐyīlán
laundry basket

洗衣机
xǐyījī
washing machine

洗衣干衣机
xǐyī gānyījī
washer-dryer

滚筒式烘干机
gǔntǒngshì hōnggānjī
tumble dryer

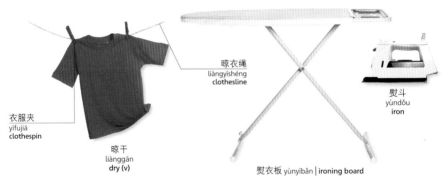

晾衣绳
liàngyīshéng
clothesline

衣服夹
yīfujiā
clothespin

晾干
liànggān
dry (v)

熨斗
yùndǒu
iron

熨衣板 yùnyībǎn | ironing board

词汇 cíhuì · **vocabulary**

装入 zhuāngrù load (v)	甩干 shuǎigān spin (v)	熨烫 yùntàng iron (v)
漂洗 piǎoxǐ rinse (v)	甩干机 shuǎigānjī spin dryer	织物柔顺剂 zhīwù róushùnjì fabric softener

洗衣机怎么用?
xǐyījī zěnmeyòng?
How do I operate the washing machine?

如何设定洗染色/白色衣物?
rúhé shèdìng xǐ rǎnsè/báisè yīwù?
What is the setting for colors/whites?

清洁用具 qīngjiéyòngjù • cleaning equipment

吸管
xīguǎn
suction hose

短柄扫帚
duǎnbǐng sàozhou
brush

簸箕
bòji
dustpan

漂白剂
piǎobáijì
bleach

水桶
shuǐtǒng
bucket

去污粉
qùwūfén
powder

洗涤液
xǐdíyè
liquid

抹布
mābù
dust cloth

吸尘器
xīchénqì
vacuum cleaner

拖把
tuōbǎ
mop

清洁剂
qīngjiéjì
detergent

上光剂
shàngguāngjì
polish

扫除 sǎochú • activities

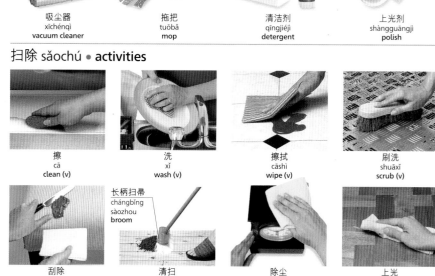

擦
cā
clean (v)

洗
xǐ
wash (v)

擦拭
cāshì
wipe (v)

刷洗
shuāxǐ
scrub (v)

刮除
guāchú
scrape (v)

长柄扫帚
chángbǐng
sàozhou
broom

清扫
qīngsǎo
sweep (v)

除尘
chúchén
dust (v)

上光
shàngguāng
polish (v)

工作间 gōngzuòjiān • workshop

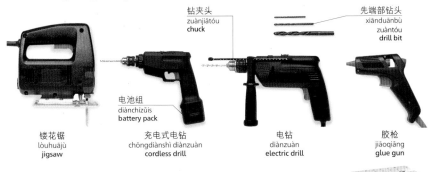

钻夹头
zuànjiātóu
chuck

先端部钻头
xiānduānbù
zuàntóu
drill bit

电池组
diànchízǔis
battery pack

镂花锯
lòuhuājù
jigsaw

充电式电钻
chōngdiànshì diànzuàn
cordless drill

电钻
diànzuàn
electric drill

胶枪
jiāoqiāng
glue gun

夹钳
jiāqián
clamp

刃
rèn
blade

台钳
táiqián
vise

打磨机
dǎmójī
sander

圆锯
yuánjù
circular saw

工作台
gōngzuòtái
workbench

木材胶
mùcáijiāo
wood glue

工具架
gōngjùjià
tool rack

槽刨
cáobào
router

手摇曲柄钻
shǒuyáo
qūbǐngzuàn
bit brace

刨花
bàohuā
wood shavings

电源箱延长线
diànyuánxiāng
yánchángxiàn
extension cord

技术 jìshù • techniques

切割
qiēgē
cut (v)

锯
jù
saw (v)

钻孔
zuànkǒng
drill (v)

钉
dīng
hammer (v)

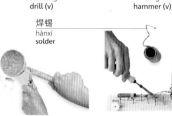

焊锡
hànxī
solder

刨 páo | plane (v)

车削 chēxiāo | turn (v)

雕刻 diāokè | carve (v)

焊接 hànjiē | solder (v)

材料 cáiliào • materials

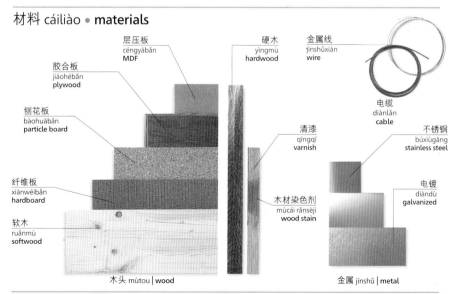

层压板
céngyābǎn
MDF

胶合板
jiāohébǎn
plywood

刨花板
bàohuābǎn
particle board

纤维板
xiānwéibǎn
hardboard

软木
ruǎnmù
softwood

硬木
yìngmù
hardwood

金属线
jīnshǔxiàn
wire

电缆
diànlǎn
cable

清漆
qīngqī
varnish

不锈钢
búxiùgāng
stainless steel

木材染色剂
mùcái rǎnsèjì
wood stain

电镀
diàndù
galvanized

木头 mùtou | wood

金属 jīnshǔ | metal

工具箱 gōngjùxiāng • toolbox

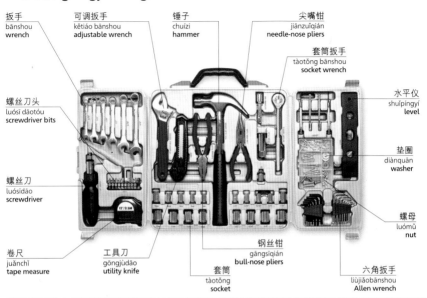

扳手
bānshou
wrench

可调扳手
kětiáo bānshou
adjustable wrench

锤子
chuízi
hammer

尖嘴钳
jiānzuǐqián
needle-nose pliers

套筒扳手
tàotǒng bānshou
socket wrench

螺丝刀头
luósī dāotóu
screwdriver bits

水平仪
shuǐpíngyí
level

垫圈
diànquān
washer

螺丝刀
luósīdāo
screwdriver

螺母
luómǔ
nut

卷尺
juǎnchǐ
tape measure

工具刀
gōngjùdāo
utility knife

钢丝钳
gāngsīqián
bull-nose pliers

套筒
tàotǒng
socket

六角扳手
liùjiǎobānshou
Allen wrench

钻头 zuàntóu • drill bits

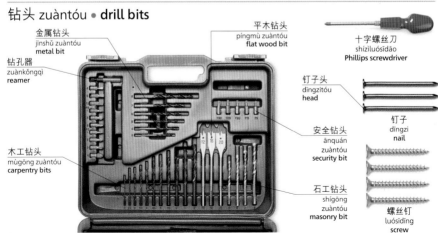

金属钻头
jīnshǔ zuàntóu
metal bit

平木钻头
píngmù zuàntóu
flat wood bit

十字螺丝刀
shízìluósīdāo
Phillips screwdriver

钻孔器
zuànkǒngqì
reamer

钉子头
dīngzitóu
head

钉子
dīngzi
nail

木工钻头
mùgōng zuàntóu
carpentry bits

安全钻头
ānquán
zuàntóu
security bit

石工钻头
shígōng
zuàntóu
masonry bit

螺丝钉
luósīdīng
screw

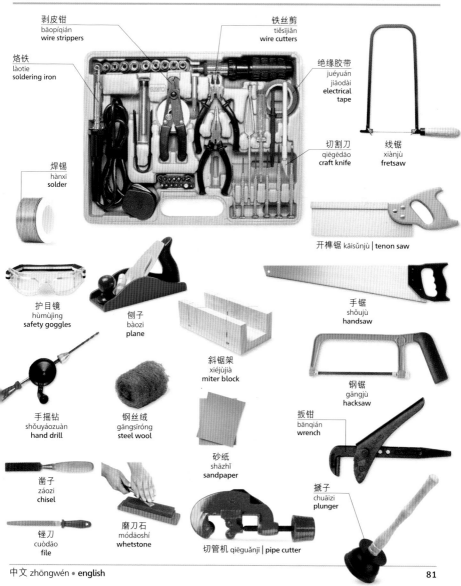

剥皮钳
bāopíqián
wire strippers

铁丝剪
tiěsījiǎn
wire cutters

烙铁
làotiě
soldering iron

绝缘胶带
juéyuán
jiāodài
electrical
tape

切割刀
qiēgēdāo
craft knife

线锯
xiànjù
fretsaw

焊锡
hànxī
solder

开榫锯 kāisǔnjù | tenon saw

护目镜
hùmùjìng
safety goggles

刨子
bàozi
plane

斜锯架
xiéjùjià
miter block

手锯
shǒujù
handsaw

钢锯
gāngjù
hacksaw

手摇钻
shǒuyáozuàn
hand drill

钢丝绒
gāngsīróng
steel wool

砂纸
shāzhǐ
sandpaper

扳钳
bānqián
wrench

凿子
záozi
chisel

磨刀石
módāoshí
whetstone

撬子
chuāizi
plunger

锉刀
cuòdāo
file

切管机 qiēguǎnjī | pipe cutter

装修 zhuāngxiū • decorating

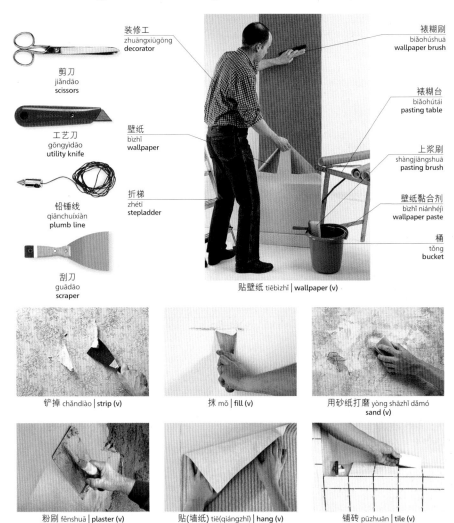

剪刀
jiǎndāo
scissors

工艺刀
gōngyìdāo
utility knife

铅锤线
qiānchuíxiàn
plumb line

刮刀
guādāo
scraper

装修工
zhuāngxiūgōng
decorator

壁纸
bìzhǐ
wallpaper

折梯
zhétī
stepladder

裱糊刷
biǎohúshuā
wallpaper brush

裱糊台
biǎohútái
pasting table

上浆刷
shàngjiāngshuā
pasting brush

壁纸黏合剂
bìzhǐ niánhéjì
wallpaper paste

桶
tǒng
bucket

贴壁纸 tiēbìzhǐ | **wallpaper (v)**

铲掉 chǎndiào | **strip (v)**

抹 mǒ | **fill (v)**

用砂纸打磨 yòng shāzhǐ dǎmó
sand (v)

粉刷 fěnshuā | **plaster (v)**

贴(墙纸) tiē(qiángzhǐ) | **hang (v)**

铺砖 pūzhuān | **tile (v)**

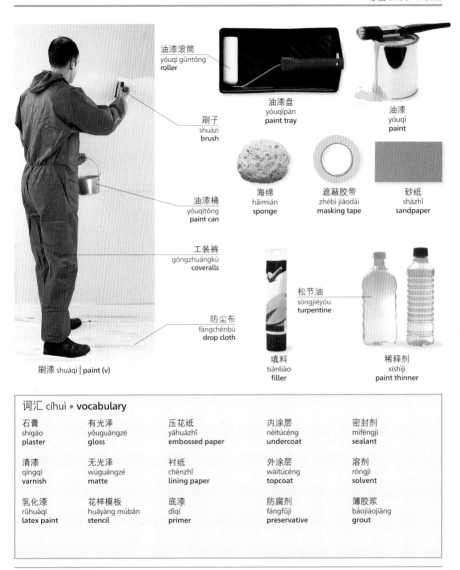

油漆滚筒
yóuqī gǔntǒng
roller

油漆盘
yóuqīpán
paint tray

油漆
yóuqī
paint

刷子
shuāzi
brush

海绵
hǎimián
sponge

遮蔽胶带
zhēbì jiāodài
masking tape

砂纸
shāzhǐ
sandpaper

油漆桶
yóuqītǒng
paint can

工装裤
gōngzhuāngkù
coveralls

松节油
sōngjiéyóu
turpentine

防尘布
fángchénbù
drop cloth

填料
tiánliào
filler

稀释剂
xīshìjì
paint thinner

刷漆 shuāqī | paint (v)

词汇 cíhuì • vocabulary

石膏 shígāo plaster	有光泽 yǒuguāngzé gloss	压花纸 yāhuāzhǐ embossed paper	内涂层 nèitúcéng undercoat	密封剂 mìfēngjì sealant
清漆 qīngqī varnish	无光泽 wúguāngzé matte	衬纸 chènzhǐ lining paper	外涂层 wàitúcéng topcoat	溶剂 róngjì solvent
乳化漆 rǔhuàqī latex paint	花样模板 huāyàng múbǎn stencil	底漆 dǐqī primer	防腐剂 fángfǔjì preservative	薄胶浆 báojiāojiāng grout

花园 huāyuán • garden

花园风格 huāyuánfēnggé • garden styles

内院 nèiyuàn | patio garden

屋顶花园
wūdǐng huāyuán
roof garden

吊篮
diàolán
hanging basket

岩石园
yánshíyuán
rock garden

法式花园 fǎshì huāyuán | formal garden

庭院 tíngyuàn | courtyard

花格屏 huāgéping | trellis

乡间花园
xiāngjiān huāyuán
cottage garden

香草花园
xiāngcǎo huāyuán
herb garden

水景花园
shuǐjǐng huāyuán
water garden

藤架
téngjià
arbor

石面路
shímiànlù
paving

小径
xiǎojìng
path

肥料堆
féiliàoduī
compost pile

门
mén
gate

花坛
huātán
flowerbed

土壤 tǔrǎng •
soil

表层土
biǎocéngtǔ
topsoil

沙土
shātǔ
sand

石灰石
shíhuīshí
chalk

棚屋
péngwū
shed

温室
wēnshì
greenhouse

篱笆
líba
fence

绿草带
lǚcǎodài
herbaceous border

草坪
cǎopíng
lawn

池塘
chítáng
pond

树篱
shùlí
hedge

拱门
gǒngmén
arch

菜圃
càipǔ
vegetable garden

淤泥
yūní
silt

黏土
niántǔ
clay

露台甲板
lùtáijiǎbǎn
deck

喷泉 pēnquán | fountain

花园植物 huāyuánzhíwù · **garden plants**

植物种类 zhíwùzhǒnglèi · **types of plants**

一年生(植物)
yìniánshēng (zhíwù)
annual

二年生(植物)
èrniánshēng (zhíwù)
biennial

多年生(植物)
duōniánshēng (zhíwù)
perennial

球茎植物
qiújīng zhíwù
bulb

蕨类植物
juélèi zhíwù
fern

灯心草
dēngxīncǎo
cattail

竹子
zhúzi
bamboo

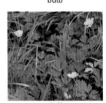

杂草
zácǎo
weeds

药草
yàocǎo
herb

水生植物
shuǐshēng zhíwù
water plant

树
shù
tree

棕榈
zōnglǘ
palm

针叶树
zhēnyèshù
conifer

常绿(植物)
chánglǜ (zhíwù)
evergreen

落叶(植物)
luòyè (zhíwù)
deciduous

剪型植物
jiǎnxíngzhíwù
topiary

高山植物
gāoshān zhíwù
alpine

肉质植物
ròuzhì zhíwù
succulent

仙人掌
xiānrénzhǎng
cactus

盆栽植物
pénzāi zhíwù
potted plant

阴地植物
yīndì zhíwù
shade plant

攀缘植物
pānyuán
zhíwù
climber

开花灌木
kāihuā guànmù
flowering shrub

地被植物
dìbèi zhíwù
ground cover

匍匐植物
púfú zhíwù
creeper

观赏(植物)
guānshǎng
(zhíwù)
ornamental

草
cǎo
grass

园艺工具 yuányì gōngjù · garden tools

搂草耙
lōucǎopá
lawn rake

堆肥
duīféi
compost

种子
zhǒngzi
seeds

骨粉
gǔfěn
bone meal

铲
chǎn
shovel

叉
chā
fork

长柄修篱剪
chángbǐng xiūlíjiǎn
long-handled shears

耙子
pázi
rake

锄头
chútou
hoe

碎石
suìshí
gravel

草袋
cǎodài
grass bag

马达
mǎdá
motor

把手
bǎshou
handle

浅底篮
qiǎndǐlán
gardening basket

防护盘
fánghùpán
shield

支架
zhījià
stand

剪草器
jiǎncǎoqì
trimmer

剪草机
jiǎncǎojī
lawnmower

独轮手推车
dúlún shǒutuīchē
wheelbarrow

手叉
shǒuchā
hand fork

移植铲
yízhíchǎn
trowel

刃
rèn
blade

修篱剪
xiūlíjiǎn
shears

手锯
shǒujù
handsaw

修枝剪
xiūzhījiǎn
pruners

育苗盘
yùmiáopán
seed tray

杀虫剂
shāchóngjì
pesticide

园艺手套
yuányì shǒutào
gardening gloves

合股线
hégǔxiàn
twine

园艺标签
yuányìbiāoqiān
labels

捆绑细丝
kǔnbǎng xìsī
twist ties

固枝环
gùzhīhuán
ring ties

支撑杆
zhīchēnggǎn
canes

筛子
shāizǐ
sieve

花盆
huāpén
plant pot

橡胶靴
xiàngjiāoxuē
rubber boots

浇灌 jiāoguàn · watering

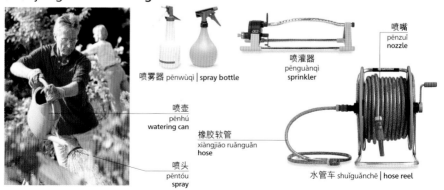

喷雾器 pēnwùqì | spray bottle

喷灌器
pēnguànqì
sprinkler

喷嘴
pēnzuǐ
nozzle

喷壶
pēnhú
watering can

橡胶软管
xiàngjiāo ruǎnguǎn
hose

喷头
pēntóu
spray

水管车 shuǐguǎnchē | hose reel

园艺 yuányì ∙ **gardening**

草地
cǎodì
lawn

树篱
shùlí
hedge

花坛
huātán
flowerbed

割草机
gēcǎojī
lawnmower

树木支桩
shùmù zhīzhuāng
stake

割草 gēcǎo | mow (v)

铺草皮
pūcǎopí
sod (v)

扎孔透气
zhākǒngtòuqì
spike (v)

耙
pá
rake (v)

修枝
xiūzhī
trim (v)

挖
wā
dig (v)

播种
bōzhǒng
sow (v)

土表施肥
tǔbiǎo shīféi
top-dress (v)

浇水
jiāoshuǐ
water (v)

支撑杆
zhīchēnggān
cane

整枝
zhěngzhī
train (v)

摘除枯花
zhāichú kūhuā
deadhead (v)

喷水
pēnshuǐ
spray (v)

插条
chātiáo
cutting

嫁接
jiàjiē
graft (v)

繁殖
fánzhí
propagate (v)

修剪
xiūjiǎn
prune (v)

用杆支撑
yònggān zhīchēng
stake (v)

移植
yízhí
transplant (v)

清除杂草
qīngchú zácǎo
weed (v)

加护盖物
jiā hùgàiwù
mulch (v)

收获
shōuhuò
harvest (v)

词汇 cíhuì • vocabulary

栽培 zāipéi cultivate (v)	园艺设计 yuányì shèjì landscape (v)	施肥 shīféi fertilize (v)	筛 shāi sift (v)	有机(栽培)的 yǒujī(zāipéi)de organic	秧苗 yāngmiáo seedling	底土 dǐtǔ subsoil
护理 hùlǐ tend (v)	把…种于盆内 bǎ…zhòng yú pénnèi pot (v)	采摘 cǎizhāi pick (v)	松土 sōngtǔ aerate (v)	排水 páishuǐ drainage	肥料 féiliào fertilizer	除草剂 chúcǎojì weedkiller

服务 fúwù
services

急救 jíjiù • emergency services

救护车 jiùhùchē • ambulance

救护车 jiùhùchē | ambulance

担架
dānjià
stretcher

急救人员 jíjiù rényuán | paramedic

警察 jǐngchá • police

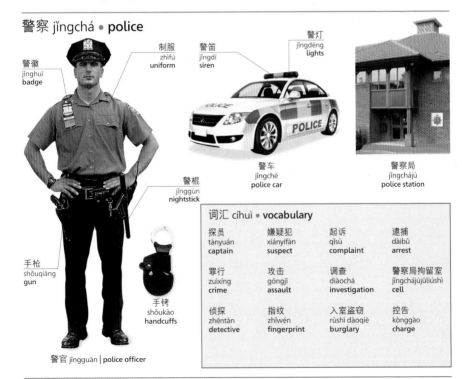

警徽
jǐnghuī
badge

制服
zhìfú
uniform

警笛
jǐngdí
siren

警灯
jǐngdēng
lights

警棍
jǐnggùn
nightstick

手枪
shǒuqiāng
gun

手铐
shǒukào
handcuffs

警官 jǐngguān | police officer

警车
jǐngchē
police car

警察局
jǐngchájú
police station

词汇 cíhuì • vocabulary

探员 tànyuán captain	嫌疑犯 xiányífàn suspect	起诉 qǐsù complaint	逮捕 dàibǔ arrest
罪行 zuìxíng crime	攻击 gōngjī assault	调查 diàochá investigation	警察局拘留室 jǐngchájújūliúshì cell
侦探 zhēntàn detective	指纹 zhǐwén fingerprint	入室盗窃 rùshì dàoqiè burglary	控告 kònggào charge

消防队 xiāofángduì · fire department

头盔
tóukuī
helmet

烟
yān
smoke

水龙带
shuǐlóngdài
hose

吊篮
diàolán
basket

水柱
shuǐzhù
water jet

消防队员
xiāofángduìyuán
firefighters

悬臂
xuánbì
boom

消防梯
xiāofángtī
ladder

驾驶室
jiàshǐshì
cab

火情 huǒqíng | fire

消防站
xiāofángzhàn
fire station

消防通道
xiāofángtōngdào
fire escape

消防车
xiāofángchē
fire engine

烟雾报警器
yānwù bàojǐngqì
smoke alarm

火灾警报器
huǒzāi jǐngbàoqì
fire alarm

消防斧
xiāofángfǔ
ax

灭火器
mièhuǒqì
fire extinguisher

消防栓
xiāofángshuān
hydrant

我需要警察/消防队/救护车。
wǒ xūyào jǐngchá/xiāofángduì/
jiùhùchē.
I need the police/fire department/
ambulance.

在...有火情。
zài...yǒu huǒqíng.
There's a fire at ...

发生了事故。
fāshēngle shìgù.
There's been an accident.

报警!
bàojǐng!
Call the police!

银行 yínháng • bank

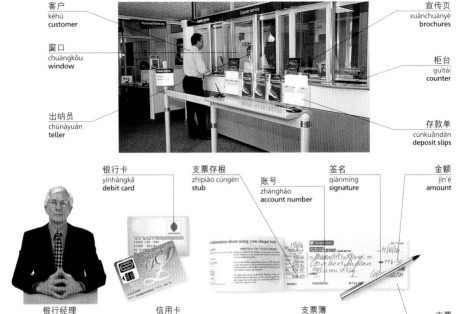

客户
kèhù
customer

窗口
chuāngkǒu
window

出纳员
chūnàyuán
teller

宣传页
xuānchuányè
brochures

柜台
guìtái
counter

存款单
cúnkuǎndān
deposit slips

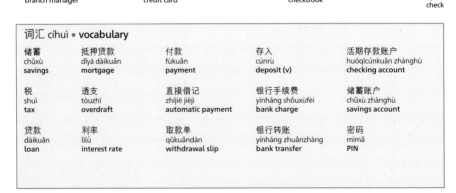

银行卡
yínhángkǎ
debit card

银行经理
yínháng jīnglǐ
branch manager

信用卡
xìnyòngkǎ
credit card

支票存根
zhīpiào cúngēn
stub

账号
zhànghào
account number

支票簿
zhīpiàobù
checkbook

签名
qiānmíng
signature

金额
jīn'é
amount

支票
zhīpiào
check

词汇 cíhuì • vocabulary

储蓄 chǔxù savings	抵押贷款 dǐyā dàikuǎn mortgage	付款 fùkuǎn payment	存入 cúnrù deposit (v)	活期存款账户 huóqīcúnkuǎn zhànghù checking account
税 shuì tax	透支 tòuzhī overdraft	直接借记 zhíjiē jièjì automatic payment	银行手续费 yínháng shǒuxùfèi bank charge	储蓄账户 chǔxù zhànghù savings account
贷款 dàikuǎn loan	利率 lìlǜ interest rate	取款单 qǔkuǎndān withdrawal slip	银行转账 yínháng zhuǎnzhàng bank transfer	密码 mìmǎ PIN

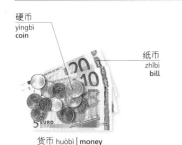

硬币
yìngbì
coin

纸币
zhǐbì
bill

货币 huòbì | money

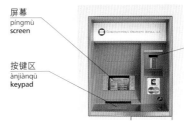

屏幕
píngmù
screen

插卡口
chākǎkǒu
card reader

按键区
ànjiànqū
keypad

提款机 tíkuǎnjī | ATM

外币 wàibì • foreign currency

外币兑换处
wàibì duìhuànchù
currency exchange

旅行支票
lǚxíng zhīpiào
traveler's check

汇率
huìlǜ
exchange rate

金融 jīnróng • finance

股票价格
gǔpiào jiàgé
share price

投资顾问
tóuzī gùwèn
financial advisor

股票经纪人
gǔpiào jīngjìrén
stockbroker

证券交易所 zhèngquàn jiāoyìsuǒ
stock exchange

词汇 cíhuì • vocabulary

兑现
duìxiàn
cash (v)

股份
gǔfèn
shares

货币面额
huòbì miàn'é
denomination

股息
gǔxī
dividends

佣金
yòngjīn
commission

会计师
kuàijìshī
accountant

投资
tóuzī
investment

有价证券组合
yǒujià zhèngquàn zǔhé
portfolio

证券
zhèngquàn
stocks

股权
gǔquán
equity

我能兑换吗？
wǒ néng duìhuàn ma?
Can I change this please?

今天的汇率是多少？
jīntiān de huìlǜ shì duōshǎo?
What's today's exchange rate?

通讯 tōngxùn • communications

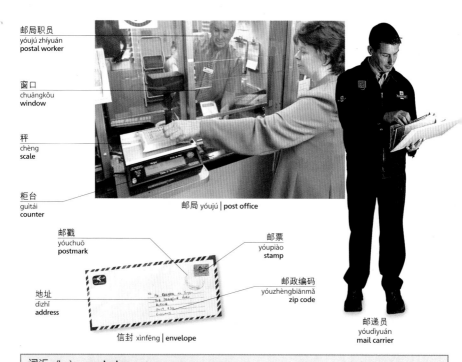

邮局职员
yóujú zhíyuán
postal worker

窗口
chuāngkǒu
window

秤
chèng
scale

柜台
guìtái
counter

邮局 yóujú | post office

邮戳
yóuchuō
postmark

邮票
yóupiào
stamp

地址
dìzhǐ
address

邮政编码
yóuzhèngbiānmǎ
zip code

信封 xìnfēng | envelope

邮递员
yóudìyuán
mail carrier

词汇 cíhuì • vocabulary

信 xìn letter	寄信人地址 jìxìnrén dìzhǐ return address	递送 dìsòng delivery	易损坏 yìsǔnhuài fragile	勿折 wùzhé do not bend (v)
航空邮件 hángkōng yóujiàn by airmail	签名 qiānmíng signature	汇票 huìpiào money order	邮袋 yóudài mailbag	此面向上 cǐmiàn xiàngshàng this way up
挂号邮件 guàhào yóujiàn registered mail	(从邮筒中)取信 (cóng yóutǒng zhōng) qǔxìn pickup	邮资 yóuzī postage	电报 diànbào telegram	

邮筒
yóutǒng
mailbox

信箱
xìnxiāng
letter slot

包裹
bāoguǒ
package

速递
sùdì
courier

电话 diànhuà • telephone

话机
huàjī
handset

机座
jīzuò
base station

无绳电话
wúshéng diànhuà
cordless phone

答录机
dálùjī
answering machine

电话亭
diànhuàtíng
phone booth

听筒
tīngtǒng
receiver

智能手机
zhìnéng shǒujī
smartphone

移动电话
yídòng diànhuà
cell phone

按键区
ànjiànqū
keypad

退币口
tuìbìkǒu
coin return

付费电话
fùfèi diànhuà
payphone

词汇 cíhuì • vocabulary

电话号码查询台 diànhuàhàomǎcháxúntái **directory assistance**	接听电话 jiētīng diànhuà **answer (v)**	接线员 jiēxiànyuán **operator**	你能告诉我…的号码吗? nǐ néng gàosù wǒ…de hàomǎ ma? **Can you give me the number for …?**
对方付费电话 duìfāng fùfèi diànhuà **collect call**	短信 duǎnxìn **text (SMS)**	占线 zhànxiàn **busy**	…的拨叫号码是多少? …de bōjiào hàomǎ shì duōshǎo? **What is the area code for …?**
拨号 bōhào **dial (v)**	语音讯息 yǔyīn xùnxī **voice message**	断线 duànxiàn **disconnected**	请短信通知我 qǐng duǎnxìn tōngzhī wǒ **Text me!**
APP/应用程序 APP/yìngyòng chéngxù **app**	密码 mìmǎ **passcode**		

旅馆 lǚguǎn · hotel
大厅 dàtīng · lobby

客人
kèrén
guest

房间钥匙
fángjiān yàoshi
room key

留言
liúyán
messages

分类架
fēnlèijià
pigeonhole

接待员
jiēdàiyuán
receptionist

登记簿
dēngjìbù
register

柜台
guìtái
counter

接待总台 jiēdài zǒngtái | reception

行李
xíngli
luggage

行李车
xínglǐchē
cart

搬运工 bānyùngōng | porter

电梯 diàntī | elevator

房间号码
fángjiān hàomǎ
room number

房间 fángjiān · rooms

单人间
dānrénjiān
single room

双人间
shuāngrénjiān
double room

双床间
shuāngchuángjiān
twin room

专用浴室
zhuānyòngyùshì
private bathroom

服务 fúwù • services

客房清洁服务
kèfáng qīngjié fúwù
maid service

洗衣服务
xǐyī fúwù
laundry service

早餐盘
zǎocānpán
breakfast tray

房间送餐服务 fángjiān sòngcān fúwù | room service

小冰箱
xiǎobīngxiāng
minibar

餐厅
cāntīng
restaurant

健身房
jiànshēnfáng
gym

游泳池
yóuyǒngchí
swimming pool

词汇 cíhuì • vocabulary

提供住宿和早餐
tígōng zhùsù hé zǎocān
bed and breakfast

供应三餐
gōngyìng sāncān
all meals included

半食宿
bànshísù
some meals included

有空房间吗?
yǒu kōng fángjiān ma?
Do you have any vacancies?

我预定了房间。
wǒ yùdìngle fángjiān.
I have a reservation.

我想要一个单人间,
wǒ xiǎngyào yīgè dānrénjiān,
I'd like a single room.

我要一个房间,住三天。
wǒ yào yīgèfángjiān, zhù sāntiān.
I'd like a room for three nights.

住一晚多少钱?
zhù yīwǎn duōshǎoqián?
What is the charge per night?

我什么时候得腾房?
wǒ shénme shíhou děi téng fáng?
When do I have to check out?

购物 gòuwù
shopping

购物 GÒUWÙ · **SHOPPING**

购物中心 gòuwùzhōngxīn • **shopping center**

大厅
dàtīng
atrium

招牌
zhāopái
sign

电梯
diàntī
elevator

三层
sāncéng
third floor

二层
èrcéng
second floor

自动扶梯
zìdòng fútī
escalator

一层
yīcéng
ground floor

顾客
gùkè
customer

词汇 cíhuì • **vocabulary**

儿童用品部
értóng yòngpǐnbù
children's department

箱包部
xiāngbāobù
luggage department

鞋靴部
xiéxuēbù
shoe department

购物指南
gòuwù zhǐnán
store directory

售货员
shòuhuòyuán
salesclerk

客户服务
kèhù fúwù
customer services

更衣室
gēngyīshì
fitting rooms

婴儿间
yīng'érjiān
baby changing room

卫生间
wèishēngjiān
restroom

这个多少钱?
zhège duōshǎo qián?
How much is this?

我可以换一件吗?
wǒ kěyǐ huàn yījiàn ma?
May I exchange this?

104　　中文 zhōngwén • **english**

百货商店 bǎihuò shāngdiàn • department store

男装
nánzhuāng
menswear

女装
nǚzhuāng
womenswear

女用内衣
nǚyòng nèiyī
lingerie

香水
xiāngshuǐ
perfumes

美容用品
měiróng yòngpǐn
cosmetics

家用纺织品
jiāyòng fǎngzhīpǐn
linens

家具
jiājù
home furnishings

缝纫用品
féngrèn yòngpǐn
notions

厨房用品
chúfáng yòngpǐn
kitchenware

瓷器
cíqì
china

电子产品
diànzǐ chǎnpǐn
electronics

灯具
dēngjù
lighting

体育用品
tǐyù yòngpǐn
sportswear

玩具
wánjù
toys

文具
wénjù
stationery

食品
shípǐn
groceries

超级市场 chāojí shìchǎng • supermarket

过道
guòdào
aisle

货架
huòjià
shelf

传送带
chuánsòngdài
conveyor belt

收银员
shōuyínyuán
checker

促销海报
cùxiāo hǎibào
specials

收款台 shōukuǎntái | checkout

顾客
gùkè
customer

收款机
shōukuǎnjī
cash register

购物袋
gòuwùdài
shopping bag

食品杂货
shípǐn záhuò
groceries

提手
tíshǒu
handle

780863 185779

条形码
tiáoxíngmǎ
bar code

购物车 gòuwùchē | grocery cart

购物篮 gòuwùlán | basket

条形码扫描器 tiáoxíngmǎ
sǎomiáoqì | scanner

烘烤食品
hōngkǎo shípǐn
bakery

乳制品
rǔzhìpǐn
dairy

早餐麦片
zǎocān màipiàn
breakfast cereals

罐装食品
guànzhuāng shípǐn
canned food

甜食
tiánshí
candy

蔬菜
shūcài
vegetables

水果
shuǐguǒ
fruit

肉禽
ròuqín
meat and poultry

鱼
yú
fish

熟食
shúshí
deli

冷冻食品
lěngdòng shípǐn
frozen food

方便食品
fāngbiàn shípǐn
prepared food

饮料
yǐnliào
drinks

家庭日用品
jiātíng rìyòngpǐn
household products

化妆品
huàzhuāngpǐn
toiletries

婴儿用品
yīng'ér yòngpǐn
baby products

家用电器
jiāyòng diànqì
electrical goods

宠物饲料
chǒngwù sìliào
pet food

杂志 zázhì | magazines

药店 yàodiàn · drugstore

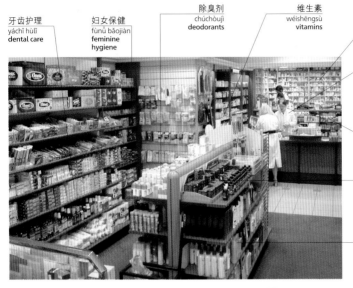

牙齿护理
yáchǐ hùlǐ
dental care

妇女保健
fùnǚ bǎojiàn
feminine hygiene

除臭剂
chúchòujì
deodorants

维生素
wéishēngsù
vitamins

药剂室
yàojìshì
pharmacy

药剂师
yàojìshī
pharmacist

止咳药
zhǐkéyào
cough medicine

草药
cǎoyào
herbal remedies

皮肤护理
pífū hùlǐ
skin care

晒后护肤液
shàihòu hùfūyè
aftersun lotion

防晒霜
fángshàishuāng
sunscreen

防晒液
fángshàiyè
sunblock

驱虫剂
qūchóngjì
insect repellent

湿纸巾
shīzhǐjīn
wet wipe

纸巾
zhǐjīn
tissue

卫生巾
wèishēngjīn
sanitary napkin

卫生棉条
wèishēng miántiáo
tampon

卫生护垫
wèishēng hùdiàn
panty liner

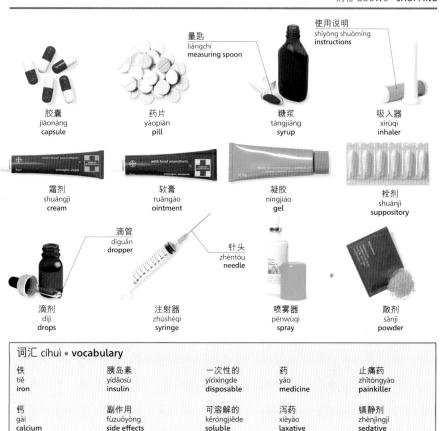

胶囊
jiāonáng
capsule

药片
yàopiàn
pill

量匙
liàngchí
measuring spoon

糖浆
tángjiāng
syrup

使用说明
shǐyòng shuōmíng
instructions

吸入器
xīrùqì
inhaler

霜剂
shuāngjì
cream

软膏
ruǎngāo
ointment

凝胶
níngjiāo
gel

栓剂
shuānjì
suppository

滴管
dīguǎn
dropper

针头
zhēntóu
needle

滴剂
dījì
drops

注射器
zhùshèqì
syringe

喷雾器
pēnwùqì
spray

散剂
sànjì
powder

词汇 cíhuì • vocabulary

铁 tiě iron	胰岛素 yídǎosù insulin	一次性的 yícìxìngde disposable	药 yào medicine	止痛药 zhǐtòngyào painkiller
钙 gài calcium	副作用 fùzuòyòng side effects	可溶解的 kěróngjiěde soluble	泻药 xièyào laxative	镇静剂 zhènjìngjì sedative
镁 měi magnesium	有效期限 yǒuxiào qīxiàn expiration date	剂量 jìliàng dosage	腹泻 fùxiè diarrhea	安眠药 ānmiányào sleeping pill
多种维生素制剂 duōzhǒng wéishēngsù zhìjì multivitamins	晕车药 yùnchēyào travel-sickness pills	药物治疗 yàowù zhìliáo medication	润喉片 rùnhóupiàn throat lozenge	消炎药 xiāoyányào anti-inflammatory

花店 huādiàn • florist

花
huā
flowers

百合
bǎihé
lily

洋槐
yánghuái
acacia

康乃馨
kāngnǎixin
carnation

盆栽植物
pénzāi zhíwù
potted plant

剑兰
jiànlán
gladiolus

鸢尾
yuānwěi
iris

雏菊
chújú
daisy

菊花
júhuā
chrysanthemum

满天星
mǎntiānxing
gypsophila

紫罗兰
zǐluólán
stocks

非洲菊
fēizhōujú
gerbera

叶簇
yècù
foliage

玫瑰
méiguī
rose

小苍兰
xiǎocānglán
freesia

中文 zhōngwén • english

花瓶
huāpíng
vase

兰花
lánhuā
orchid

牡丹
mǔdān
peony

花束
huāshù
bunch

茎
jīng
stem

黄水仙
huángshuǐxiān
daffodil

花苞
huābāo
bud

包装纸
bāozhuāngzhǐ
wrapping

郁金香 yùjīnxiāng | tulip

插花 chāhuā · **arrangements**

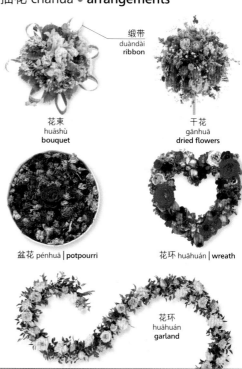

缎带
duàndài
ribbon

花束
huāshù
bouquet

干花
gānhuā
dried flowers

盆花 pénhuā | potpourri

花环 huāhuán | wreath

花环
huāhuán
garland

我能附上留言吗?
wǒ néng fùshàng liúyán ma?
Can I attach a message?

能帮我包一下吗?
néng bāng wǒ bāo yíxià ma?
Can I have them wrapped?

能不能将它们送到...?
néngbùnéng jiāng tāmen
sòngdào...?
Can you send them to ...?

这些花能开多久?
zhèxiē huā néng kāi duōjiǔ?
How long will these last?

这些花香吗?
zhèxiē huā xiāng ma?
Are they fragrant?

我想买一束...
wǒ xiǎng mǎi yíshù...
Can I have a bunch of ... please.

报刊亭 bàokāntíng · newsstand

香烟
xiāngyān
cigarettes

烟盒
yānhé
pack of cigarettes

邮票
yóupiào
stamps

连环画
liánhuánhuà
comic book

杂志
zázhì
magazine

报纸
bàozhǐ
newspaper

明信片
míngxìnpiàn
postcard

吸烟 xīyān · smoking

烟草
yāncǎo
tobacco

打火机
dǎhuǒjī
lighter

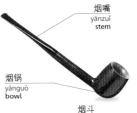

烟嘴
yānzuǐ
stem

烟锅
yānguō
bowl

烟斗
yāndǒu
pipe

雪茄
xuějiā
cigar

糖果店 tángguǒdiàn · candy store

巧克力盒
qiǎokèlíhé
box of chocolates

零食
língshí
snack bar

薯片
shǔpiàn
potato chips

甜食店 tiánshídiàn | candy store

词汇 cíhuì · vocabulary

牛奶巧克力 niúnǎiqiǎokèlì **milk chocolate**	焦糖 jiāotáng **caramel**
黑巧克力 hēiqiǎokèlì **dark chocolate**	松露巧克力 sōnglùqiǎokèlì **truffle**
白巧克力 báiqiǎokèlì **white chocolate**	饼干 bǐnggān **cookie**
杂拌糖果 zábàntángguǒ **pick and mix**	

糖果 tángguǒ · confectionery

巧克力
qiǎokèlì
chocolate

块状巧克力板
kuàizhuàng qiǎokèlibǎn
chocolate bar

糖果
tángguǒ
hard candy

棒棒糖
bàngbàngtáng
lollipop

太妃糖 tàifēitáng | **toffee**

奶油杏仁糖
nǎiyóuxìngréntáng | **nougat**

棉花软糖
miánhuāruǎntáng
marshmallow

薄荷糖
bòhetáng
mint

口香糖
kǒuxiāngtáng
chewing gum

软心豆粒糖
ruǎnxīndòulìtáng
jellybean

果味橡皮糖
guǒwèixiàngpítáng
gumdrop

甘草糖
gāncǎotáng
licorice

其他店铺 qítā diànpù ● other stores

面包店
miànbāodiàn
bakery

糕点店
gāodiǎndiàn
pastry shop

肉铺
ròupù
butcher shop

水产店
shuǐchǎndiàn
fish counter

蔬菜水果店
shūcàishuǐguǒdiàn
produce stand

食品杂货店
shípǐnzáhuòdiàn
grocery store

鞋店
xiédiàn
shoe store

五金店
wǔjīndiàn
hardware store

古董店
gǔdǒngdiàn
antique store

礼品店
lǐpǐndiàn
gift shop

旅行社
lǚxíngshè
travel agency

首饰店
shǒushìdiàn
jewelry store

书店
shūdiàn
bookstore

音像店
yīnxiàngdiàn
record store

酒类专卖店
jiǔlèizhuānmàidiàn
liquor store

宠物商店
chǒngwùshāngdiàn
pet store

家具店
jiājùdiàn
furniture store

时装店
shízhuāngdiàn
boutique

词汇 cíhuì • vocabulary

房地产商
fángdìchǎnshāng
real estate office

园艺用品店
yuányì yòngpǐndiàn
garden center

干洗店
gānxǐdiàn
dry cleaner

投币式自动洗衣店
tóubìshì zìdòngxǐyīdiàn
laundromat

照相器材店
zhàoxiàng qìcáidiàn
camera store

绿色食品店
lǜsèshípǐndiàn
health food store

艺术品店
yìshùpǐndiàn
art supply store

旧货商店
jiùhuò shāngdiàn
secondhand store

裁缝店
cáifengdiàn
tailor shop

美发店
měifàdiàn
salon

市场 shìchǎng | market

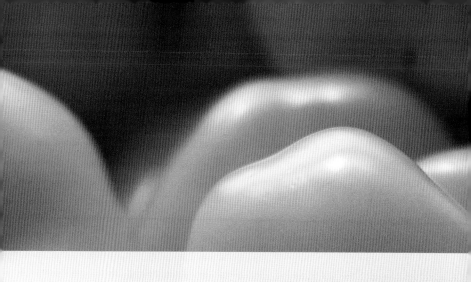

食物 shíwù
food

肉 ròu • meat

羊羔肉
gāoyángròu
lamb

肉店老板
ròudiànlǎobǎn
butcher

吊肉钩
diàoròugōu
meat hook

秤
chèng
scale

磨刀器
módāoqì
knife sharpener

熏肉
xūnròu
bacon

香肠
xiāngcháng
sausages

肝脏
gānzàng
liver

词汇 cíhuì • vocabulary

猪肉 zhūròu pork	野味肉 yěwèiròu venison	下水 xiàshuǐ variety meat	放养的 fàngyǎngde free range	熟肉 shúròu cooked meat
牛肉 niúròu beef	兔肉 tùròu rabbit	腌制的 yānzhìde cured	有机(饲养)的 yǒujī(sìyǎng)de organic	白肉 (指家禽肉、鱼肉等) báiròu (zhǐjiāqínròu, yúròuděng) white meat
小牛肉 xiǎoniúròu veal	牛舌 niúshé tongue	熏制的 xūnzhìde smoked	瘦肉 shòuròu lean meat	红肉 (牛肉、猪肉和羊肉) hóngròu (niúròu, zhūròu hé yángròu) red meat

切块 qiēkuài · cuts

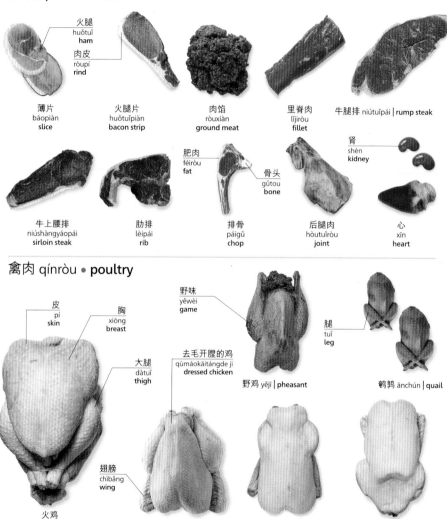

火腿
huǒtuǐ
ham

肉皮
ròupí
rind

薄片
báopiàn
slice

火腿片
huǒtuǐpiàn
bacon strip

肉馅
ròuxiàn
ground meat

里脊肉
lǐjǐròu
fillet

牛腿排 niútuǐpái | **rump steak**

肥肉
féiròu
fat

骨头
gǔtou
bone

肾
shèn
kidney

牛上腰排
niúshàngyāopái
sirloin steak

肋排
lèipái
rib

排骨
páigǔ
chop

后腿肉
hòutuǐròu
joint

心
xīn
heart

禽肉 qínròu · **poultry**

皮
pí
skin

胸
xiōng
breast

野味
yěwèi
game

腿
tuǐ
leg

大腿
dàtuǐ
thigh

去毛开膛的鸡
qùmáokāitángde jī
dressed chicken

野鸡 yějī | **pheasant**

鹌鹑 ānchún | **quail**

翅膀
chìbǎng
wing

火鸡
huǒjī
turkey

鸡 jī | **chicken**

鸭 yā | **duck**

鹅 é | **goose**

鱼 yú • fish

去皮虾
qùpíxiā
peeled shrimp

冰
bīng
ice

羊鱼
yángyú
red mullet

大比目鱼片
dàbǐmùyúpiàn
halibut fillets

虹鳟鱼
hóngzūnyú
rainbow trout

鳐鱼翅
yáoyúchì
skate wings

水产店
shuǐchǎndiàn
fish counter

安康鱼
ānkāngyú
monkfish

鲭鱼
qīngyú
mackerel

鳟鱼
zūnyú
trout

剑鱼
jiànyú
swordfish

鳎鱼
tǎyú
Dover sole

柠檬鲽
níngméngdié
lemon sole

黑线鳕
hēixiànxuě
haddock

沙丁鱼
shādīngyú
sardine

鳐鱼
yáoyú
skate

牙鳕
yáxuě
whiting

海鲈
hǎilú
sea bass

鲑鱼 guīyú | salmon

鳕鱼
xuěyú
cod

鲷鱼
diāoyú
sea bream

金枪鱼
jīnqiāngyú
tuna

中文 zhōngwén • english

海鲜 hǎixiān • seafood

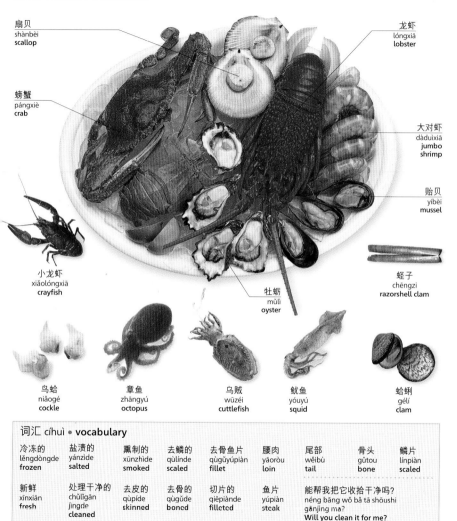

扇贝
shànbèi
scallop

龙虾
lóngxiā
lobster

螃蟹
pángxiè
crab

大对虾
dàduìxiā
jumbo shrimp

贻贝
yíbèi
mussel

小龙虾
xiǎolóngxiā
crayfish

牡蛎
mǔlì
oyster

蛏子
chēngzi
razorshell clam

乌蛤
niǎogé
cockle

章鱼
zhāngyú
octopus

乌贼
wūzéi
cuttlefish

鱿鱼
yóuyú
squid

蛤蜊
gélí
clam

词汇 cíhuì • vocabulary

冷冻的 lěngdòngde frozen	盐渍的 yánzìde salted	熏制的 xūnzhìde smoked	去鳞的 qùlínde scaled	去骨鱼片 qùgǔyúpiàn fillet	腰肉 yāoròu loin	尾部 wěibù tail	骨头 gǔtou bone	鳞片 línpiàn scaled
新鲜 xīnxiān fresh	处理干净的 chǔlǐgān jìngde cleaned	去皮的 qùpíde skinned	去骨的 qùgǔde boned	切片的 qiēpiànde filleted	鱼片 yúpiàn steak	能帮我把它收拾干净吗? néng bāng wǒ bǎ tā shōushi gānjìng ma? Will you clean it for me?		

蔬菜1 shūcài • vegetables 1

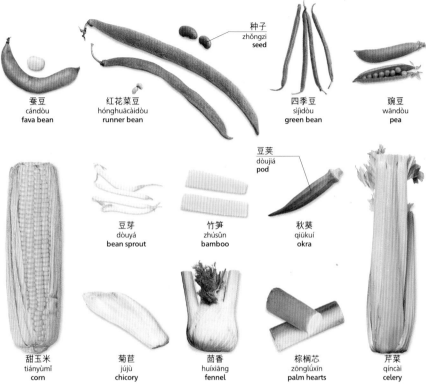

种子
zhǒngzi
seed

蚕豆
cándòu
fava bean

红花菜豆
hónghuācàidòu
runner bean

四季豆
sìjìdòu
green bean

豌豆
wāndòu
pea

豆荚
dòujiá
pod

豆芽
dòuyá
bean sprout

竹笋
zhúsǔn
bamboo

秋葵
qiūkuí
okra

甜玉米
tiányùmǐ
corn

菊苣
jújù
chicory

茴香
huíxiāng
fennel

棕榈芯
zōnglǘxīn
palm hearts

芹菜
qíncài
celery

词汇 cíhuì • vocabulary

叶 yè leaf	小花球 xiǎohuāqiú floret	尖 jiān tip	有机(栽培)的 yǒují(zāipéi)de organic	这儿卖有机蔬菜吗？ zhè'er mài yǒujīshūcài ma? Do you sell organic vegetables?
菜梗 càigěng stalk	果仁 guǒrén kernel	芯 xīn heart	塑料袋 sùliàodài plastic bag	这些是当地产的吗？ zhèxiē shì dāngdìchǎnde ma? Are these grown locally?

芝麻菜
zhīmacài
arugula

豆瓣菜
dòubàncài
watercress

红球菊苣
hóngqiújújù
radicchio

抱子甘蓝
bàozǐgānlán
Brussels sprout

甜叶菜
tiányècài
Swiss chard

羽衣甘蓝
yǔyīgānlán
kale

酸模
suānmó
sorrel

苦苣
kǔjù
endive

菠公英
púgōngyīng
dandelion

菠菜
bōcài
spinach

球茎甘蓝
qiújīnggānlán
kohlrabi

油菜
yóucài
bok choy

莴苣
wōjù
lettuce

西兰花
xīlánhuā
broccoli

卷心菜
juǎnxīncài
cabbage

嫩圆白菜
nènyuánbáicài
spring greens

蔬菜2 shūcài · vegetables 2

萝卜，芜菁
luóbo, wújīng
turnip

小红萝卜
xiǎohóngluóbo
radish

朝鲜蓟
cháoxiǎnjì
artichoke

花椰菜，菜花
huāyēcài, càihuā
cauliflower

芦笋
lúsǔn
asparagus

马铃薯
mǎlíngshǔ
potato

西葫芦
xīhúlu
squash

洋葱
yángcōng
onion

甜椒
tiánjiāo
pepper

辣椒
làjiāo
chili pepper

甜玉米
tiányùmǐ
sweetcorn

词汇 cíhuì · vocabulary

樱桃番茄 yīngtáofānqié **cherry tomato**	块根芹 kuàigēnqín **celeriac**	冷冻的 lěngdòngde **frozen**	苦 kǔ **bitter**
胡萝卜 húluóbo **carrot**	芋头 yùtou **taro root**	生 shēng **raw**	硬 yìng **firm**
面包果 miànbāoguǒ **breadfruit**	木薯 mùshǔ **cassava**	辣 là **hot (spicy)**	果肉 guǒròu **flesh**
嫩马铃薯 nènmǎlíngshǔ **new potato**	荸荠 bíqí **water chestnut**	甜 tián **sweet**	根 gēn **root**

请给我一公斤马铃薯。
qǐng gěi wǒ yì gōngjīn mǎlíngshǔ.
May I have one kilo of potatoes, please?

每公斤多少钱?
měi gōngjīn duōshǎo qián?
What's the price per kilo?

那些叫什么?
nàxiē jiào shénme?
What are those called?

红薯
hóngshǔ
sweet potato

山药
shānyào
yam

甜菜
tiáncài
beet

芜菁甘蓝
wújīnggānlán
rutabaga

菊芋
júyù
Jerusalem artichoke

辣根菜
làgēncài
horseradish

欧洲防风根
ōuzhōufángfēnggēn
parsnip

姜
jiāng
ginger

茄子
qiézi
eggplant

番茄
fānqié
tomato

葱
cōng
scallion

韭葱
jiǔcōng
leek

葱头
cōngtóu
shallot

大蒜
dàsuàn
garlic

蒜瓣儿
suànbàn'er
clove

块菌
kuàijūn
truffle

蘑菇
mógu
mushroom

黄瓜
huángguā
cucumber

密生西葫芦
mìshēngxīhúlu
zucchini

冬南瓜
dōngnánguā
butternut squash

橡果形冬瓜
xiàngguǒxíngdōngguā
acorn squash

南瓜
nánguā
pumpkin

水果1 shuǐguǒyī • fruit 1

柑橘类水果 gānjúlèishuǐguǒ • citrus fruit

有核水果 yǒuhéshuǐguǒ • stone fruit

橙子
chéngzi
orange

细皮小柑橘
xìpíxiǎogānjú
clementine

桃
táo
peach

油桃
yóutáo
nectarine

海绵层
hǎimiáncéng
pith

牙买加丑橘
yámǎijiāchǒujú
ugli fruit

葡萄柚
pútáoyòu
grapefruit

杏
xìng
apricot

李子
lǐzi
plum

樱桃
yīngtáo
cherry

橘瓣儿
júbànr
segment

无核蜜橘
wúhémìjú
satsuma

苹果
píngguǒ
apple

梨
lí
pear

橘子
júzi
tangerine

外皮
wàipí
zest

酸橙
suānchéng
lime

柠檬
níngméng
lemon

金橘
jīnjú
kumquat

果篮 guǒlán | basket of fruit

浆果和甜瓜 jiāngguǒ hé tiánguā · berries and melons

草莓
cǎoméi
strawberry

覆盆子
fùpénzǐ
raspberry

甜瓜
tiánguā
melon

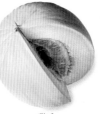

葡萄
pútáo
grapes

黑莓
hēiméi
blackberry

红醋栗
hóngcùlì
red currant

瓜皮
guāpí
rind

蔓越橘
mànyuèjú
cranberry

黑醋栗
hēicùlì
black currant

瓜籽
guāzǐ
seed

瓜瓤
guǎráng
flesh

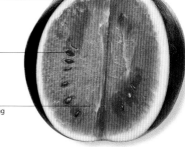

蓝莓
lánméi
blueberry

白醋栗
báicùlì
white currant

西瓜
xīguā
watermelon

罗甘莓
luógānméi
loganberry

醋栗
cùlì
gooseberry

词汇 cíhuì · vocabulary

大黄 dàihuáng rhubarb	酸 suān sour	脆 cuì crisp	汁液 zhīyè juice	它们熟吗？ tāmen shú ma? **Are they ripe?**
纤维 xiànwéi fiber	新鲜 xīnxiān fresh	烂 làn rotten	核 hé core	我可以尝一个吗？ wǒ kěyǐ cháng yígè ma? **Can I try one?**
甜 tián sweet	多汁 duōzhī juicy	果肉 guǒròu pulp	无核 wúhé seedless	它们能放多久？ tāmen néng fàng duōjiǔ? **How long will they keep?**

水果2 shuǐguǒ • fruit 2

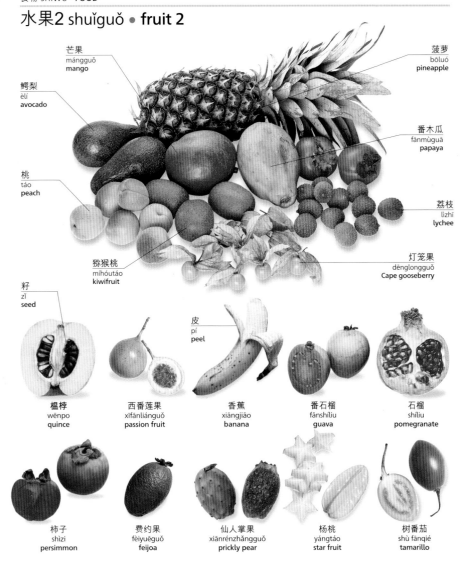

芒果
mángguǒ
mango

鳄梨
èlí
avocado

桃
táo
peach

狝猴桃
míhóutáo
kiwifruit

籽
zǐ
seed

菠萝
bōluó
pineapple

番木瓜
fānmùguā
papaya

荔枝
lìzhī
lychee

灯笼果
dēnglóngguǒ
Cape gooseberry

皮
pí
peel

榅桲
wēnpo
quince

西番莲果
xīfānliánguǒ
passion fruit

香蕉
xiāngjiāo
banana

番石榴
fānshíliu
guava

石榴
shíliu
pomegranate

柿子
shìzi
persimmon

费约果
fèiyuēguǒ
feijoa

仙人掌果
xiānrénzhǎngguǒ
prickly pear

杨桃
yángtáo
star fruit

树番茄
shù fānqié
tamarillo

坚果和干果 jiānguǒ hé gānguǒ • **nuts and dried fruit**

松子
sōngzǐ
pine nut

开心果
kāixīnguǒ
pistachio

腰果
yāoguǒ
cashew

花生
huāshēng
peanut

榛子
zhēnzi
hazelnut

巴西果
bāxīguǒ
Brazil nut

美洲山核桃
měizhōushānhétao
pecan

杏仁
xìngrén
almond

核桃
hétao
walnut

栗子
lìzi
chestnut

澳洲坚果
àozhōujiānguǒ
macadamia

无花果
wúhuāguǒ
fig

椰枣
yēzǎo
date

梅干
méigān
prune

壳
ké
shell

无核葡萄干
wúhépútáogān
sultana

葡萄干
pútáogān
raisin

无核小葡萄干
wúhéxiǎopútáogān
currant

果肉
guǒròu
flesh

椰子
yēzi
coconut

词汇 cíhuì • **vocabulary**

未熟的 wèishúde **green**	硬 yìng **hard**	果仁 guǒrén **kernel**	盐渍的 yánzìde **salted**	烘烤的 hōngkǎode **roasted**	去壳的 qùkéde **shelled**	蜜饯 mìjiàn **candied fruit**
成熟的 chéngshúde **ripe**	软 ruǎn **soft**	脱水的 tuōshuǐde **desiccated**	生 shēng **raw**	应季的 yìngjìde **seasonal**	完整 wánzhěng **whole**	热带水果 rèdàishuǐguǒ **tropical fruit**

谷物及豆类 gǔwùjídòulèi • grains and legumes

谷物 gǔwù • grains

小麦
xiǎomài
wheat

燕麦
yànmài
oats

大麦
dàmài
barley

小米
xiǎomǐ
millet

玉米
yùmǐ
corn

奎奴亚藜
kuínúyàlí
quinoa

词汇 cíhuì • vocabulary		
种子 zhǒngzi seed	香 xiāng fragranced	易烹调的 yìpēngtiáode quick cooking
外壳 wàiké husk	谷类食品 gǔlèishípǐn cereal	长粒 chánglì long-grain
谷粒 gǔlì kernel	整粒 zhěnglì whole-grain	短粒 duǎnlì short-grain
干燥 gānzào dry	浸泡 jìnpào soak (v)	
新鲜 xīnxiān fresh		

米 mǐ • rice

白米
báimǐ
white rice

糙米
cāomǐ
brown rice

菰米
gūmǐ
wild rice

布丁米
bùdīngmǐ
arborio rice

加工过的谷物 jiāgōngguòde gǔwù • processed grains

蒸粗麦粉
zhēngcūmàifěn
couscous

碎粒小麦
suìlìxiǎomài
cracked wheat

粗粒小麦粉
cūlìxiǎomàifěn
semolina

麦麸
màifū
bran

豆类 dòulèi • legumes

棉豆
miándòu
butter beans

菜豆
càidòu
haricot beans

红芸豆
hóngyúndòu
red kidney beans

赤豆
chìdòu
adzuki beans

蚕豆
cándòu
fava beans

大豆
dàdòu
soybeans

黑眼豆
hēiyǎndòu
black-eyed peas

斑豆
bāndòu
pinto beans

绿豆
lǜdòu
mung beans

小(粒)菜豆
xiǎo(lì)càidòu
flageolet beans

褐色小扁豆
hèsèxiǎobiǎndòu
brown lentils

红豆
hóngdòu
red lentils

青豆
qīngdòu
green peas

鹰嘴豆
yīngzuǐdòu
chickpeas

干豌豆瓣
gānwāndòubàn
split peas

种子 zhǒngzi • seeds

南瓜籽
nánguāzǐ
pumpkin seed

芥菜籽
jiècàizǐ
mustard seed

葛缕子籽
gělǚzǐzǐ
caraway

芝麻籽
zhīmazǐ
sesame seed

向日葵籽
xiàngrìkuízǐ
sunflower seed

香草和香辛料 xiāngcǎo hé xiāngxīnliào • herbs and spices

香辛料 xiāngxīnliào • spices

香子兰 xiāngzǐlán | vanilla

肉豆蔻
ròudòukòu
nutmeg

肉豆蔻衣
ròudòukòuyī
mace

姜黄根
jiānghuánggēn
turmeric

枯茗，小茴香
kūmíng, xiǎohuíxiāng
cumin

香料包
xiāngliàobāo
bouquet garni

多香果
duōxiāngguǒ
allspice

胡椒粒
hújiāolì
peppercorn

葫芦巴
húlúbā
fenugreek

辣椒末
làjiāomò
chili powder

颗粒状
kēlìzhuàng
whole

压碎的
yāsuìde
crushed

藏红花
zànghónghuā
saffron

小豆蔻
xiǎodòukòu
cardamom

咖喱粉
gālífěn
curry powder

磨碎的
mósuìde
ground

辣椒粉
làjiāofěn
paprika

片状
piànzhuàng
flakes

大蒜
dàsuàn
garlic

香草 xiāngcǎo • herbs

桂皮
guìpí
sticks

肉桂
ròuguì
cinnamon

茴香籽
huíxiāngzǐ
fennel seeds

茴香
huíxiāng
fennel

月桂叶
yuèguìyè
bay leaf

欧芹
ōuqín
parsley

柠檬草
níngméngcǎo
lemon grass

丁香
dīngxiāng
cloves

细香葱
xìxiāngcōng
chives

薄荷
bòhe
mint

百里香
bǎilǐxiāng
thyme

鼠尾草
shǔwěicǎo
sage

八角，大料
bājiǎo, dàliào
star anise

龙蒿
lónghāo
tarragon

墨角兰
mòjiǎolán
marjoram

罗勒
luólè
basil

姜
jiāng
ginger

牛至
niúzhì
oregano

香菜
xiāngcài
cilantro

莳萝
shíluó
dill

迷迭香
mídiéxiāng
rosemary

瓶装食品 píngzhuāngshípǐn • bottled foods

软木塞
ruǎnmùsāi
cork

葵花籽油
kuíhuāzǐyóu
sunflower oil

核桃油
hétáoyóu
walnut oil

葡萄籽油
pútáozǐyóu
grapeseed oil

杏仁油
xìngrényóu
almond oil

芝麻油
zhīmayóu
sesame seed oil

榛仁油
zhēnrényóu
hazelnut oil

橄榄油
gǎnlǎnyóu
olive oil

香草
xiāngcǎo
herbs

香油
xiāngyóu
flavored oil

油
yóu
oils

甜酱 tiánjiàng • sweet spreads

广口瓶
guǎngkǒupíng
jar

蜜脾
mìpí
honeycomb

固体蜂蜜
gùtǐfēngmì
set honey

柠檬酱
níngméngjiàng
lemon curd

覆盆子酱
fùpénzǐjiàng
raspberry jam

橘子酱
júzijiàng
marmalade

液体蜂蜜
yètǐfēngmì
clear honey

枫糖浆
fēngtángjiàng
maple syrup

酱料和调味品 jiàngliàohétiáowèipǐn · sauces and condiments

瓶
píng
bottle

苹果醋
píngguǒcù
cider vinegar

香脂醋
xiāngzhīcù
balsamic vinegar

蛋黄酱
dànhuángjiàng
mayonnaise

英式芥末酱
yīngshì jièmojiàng
English mustard

番茄酱
fānqiéjiàng
ketchup

法式芥末酱
fǎshì jièmojiàng
French mustard

酸辣酱
suānlàjiàng
chutney

麦芽醋
màiyácù
malt vinegar

醋
cù
vinegar

酒醋
jiǔcù
wine vinegar

调味汁
tiáowèizhī
sauce

颗粒芥末酱
kēlì jièmojiàng
whole-grain mustard

密封瓶
mìfēngpíng
canning jar

花生酱
huāshēngjiàng
peanut butter

巧克力酱
qiǎokèlìjiàng
chocolate spread

罐装水果
guànzhuāngshuǐguǒ
preserved fruit

词汇 cíhuì · vocabulary

玉米油
yùmǐyóu
corn oil

菜籽油
càizǐyóu
canola oil

花生油
huāshēngyóu
peanut oil

冷榨油
lěngzhàyóu
cold-pressed oil

植物油
zhíwùyóu
vegetable oil

乳制品 rǔzhìpǐn · dairy products

奶酪 nǎilào · cheese

碎奶酪
suìnǎilào
grated cheese

奶酪皮
nǎilàopí
rind

半硬奶酪
bànyìngnǎilào
semi-hard cheese

硬奶酪
yìngnǎilào
hard cheese

半软奶酪
bànruǎnnǎilào
semi-soft cheese

白干酪
báigānlào
cottage cheese

奶油干酪
nǎiyóugānlào
cream cheese

蓝纹奶酪
lánwénnǎilào
blue cheese

软奶酪
ruǎnnǎilào
soft cheese

鲜奶酪 xiānnǎilào | fresh cheese

奶 nǎi · milk

全脂奶
quánzhīnǎi
whole milk

半脱脂牛奶
bàntuōzhī niúnǎi
reduced-fat milk

脱脂牛奶
tuōzhī niúnǎi
skim milk

奶盒
nǎihé
milk carton

山羊奶
shānyángnǎi
goat's milk

炼乳
liànrǔ
condensed milk

牛奶 niúnǎi | cow's milk

黄油
huángyóu
butter

人造黄油
rénzàohuángyóu
margarine

奶油
nǎiyóu
cream

稀奶油
xīnǎiyóu
half-and-half

高脂肪奶油
gāozhīfángnǎiyóu
heavy cream

掼奶油
guànnǎiyóu
whipped cream

酸奶油
suānnǎiyóu
sour cream

酸奶
suānnǎi
yogurt

冰激凌
bīngjīlíng
ice cream

蛋 dàn • eggs

蛋黄
dànhuáng
yolk

蛋白
dànbái
egg white

蛋壳
dànké
shell

蛋杯
dànbēi
eggcup

煮鸡蛋 zhǔjīdàn | soft-boiled egg

鸡蛋
jīdàn
hen's egg

鸭蛋
yādàn
duck egg

鹅蛋
édàn
goose egg

鹌鹑蛋
ānchúndàn
quail egg

词汇 cíhuì • vocabulary

已经过巴氏消毒的 yǐ jīngguò bāshìxiāodúde pasteurized	奶昔 nǎixī milk shake	盐渍的 yánzìde salted	绵羊奶 miányángnǎi sheep's milk	乳糖 rǔtáng lactose	均质 jūnzhì homogenized
未经过巴氏消毒的 wèi jīngguò bāshìxiāodúde unpasteurized	冻酸奶 dòngsuānnǎi frozen yogurt	无盐的 wúyánde unsalted	酪乳 làorǔ buttermilk	不含脂肪的 bùhánzhīfángde fat-free	奶粉 nǎifěn powdered milk

面包和面粉 miànbāo hé miànfěn · **breads and flours**

切片面包
qiēpiànmiànbāo
sliced bread

罂粟籽
yīngsùzǐ
poppy seeds

黑面包
hēimiànbāo
rye bread

棍子面包
gùnzimiànbāo
baguette

面包店 miànbāodiàn | **bakery**

制作面包 zhìzuò miànbāo · **making bread**

精白面粉
jīngbáimiànfěn
white flour

黑麦面粉
hēimàimiànfěn
brown flour

全麦面粉
quánmàimiànfěn
whole-wheat flour

酵母
jiàomǔ
yeast

筛撒 shāisǎ | **sift (v)**

搅拌 jiǎobàn | **mix (v)**

生面团
shēng
miàntuán
dough

和面 huómiàn | **knead (v)**

烘制 hōngzhì | **bake (v)**

面包皮
miànbāopí
crust

面包块
miànbāokuài
loaf

切片
qiēpiàn
slice

白面包
báimiànbāo
white bread

黑面包
hēimiànbāo
brown bread

全麦面包
quánmàimiànbāo
whole-wheat bread

麸皮面包
fūpímiànbāo
multigrain bread

玉米面包
yùmǐmiànbāo
corn bread

苏打面包
sūdámiànbāo
soda bread

酸面包
suānmiànbāo
sourdough bread

薄干脆饼
báogāncuìbǐng
flat bread

硬面包圈，百吉饼
yìngmiànbāoquān, bǎijíbǐng
bagel

软面包片
ruǎnmiànbāopiàn | bun

小面包
xiǎomiànbāo | roll

葡萄干面包
pútáogānmiànbāo
fruit bread

撒籽面包
sāzǐmiànbāo
seeded bread

印度式面包
yìndùshìmiànbāo
naan bread

皮塔饼
pítǎbǐng
pita bread

薄脆饼干
báocuìbǐnggān
crispbread

词汇 cíhuì · vocabulary

高筋面粉 gāojīnmiànfěn **bread flour**	发起 fāqǐ **rise (v)**	发酵 fājiào **prove (v)**	面包屑 miànbāoxiè **breadcrumbs**	切片机 qiēpiànjī **slicer**
自发粉 zìfāfěn **self-rising flour**	中筋面粉 zhōngjīnmiànfěn **all-purpose flour**	浇糖 jiāotáng **glaze (v)**	细长形面包 xìchángxíngmiànbāo **flute**	面包师 miànbāoshī **baker**

糕点 gāodiǎn · cakes and desserts

长条奶油夹心点心
chángtiáo nǎiyóu jiāxīn diǎnxīn
éclair

花结酥皮
huājiésūpí
choux pastry

千层饼
qiāncéngbǐng
puff pastry

奶油
nǎiyóu
cream

夹心酥
jiāxīnsū
phyllo dough

夹心
jiāxīn
filling

外覆巧克力
wàifù qiǎokèlì
chocolate-covered

水果蛋糕
shuǐguǒ dàngāo
fruitcake

松饼
sōngbǐng
muffin

水果馅饼
shuǐguǒ xiànbǐng
fruit tart

松糕
sōnggāo
sponge cake

蛋白甜饼
dànbái tiánbǐng
meringue

蛋糕 dàngāo | cakes

词汇 cíhuì · vocabulary

奶油蛋糕
nǎiyóu dàngāo
crème pâtissière

小圆蛋糕
xiǎoyuán dàngāo
bun

面团
miàntuán
pastry

米饭布丁
mǐfàn bùdīng
rice pudding

我可以吃一片吗?
wǒ kěyǐ chī yīpiàn ma?
May I have a slice, please?

巧克力蛋糕
qiǎokèlì dàngāo
chocolate cake

蛋奶糕
dànnǎigāo
custard

切片
qiēpiàn
slice

庆祝会
qìngzhùhuì
celebration

巧克力脆片
qiǎokèlì cuìpiàn
chocolate chip

指形饼干
zhǐxíng bǐnggān
ladyfinger

果仁巧克力脆饼
guǒrén qiǎokèlì
cuìbǐng
Florentine

蜜饯布丁
mìjiàn bùdīng
trifle

饼干 bǐnggān | cookies

奶油冻/慕思
nǎiyóudòng/mùsī
mousse

果汁冰糕
guǒzhī bīnggāo
sherbet

奶油馅饼
nǎiyóu xiànbǐng
cream pie

焦糖蛋奶
jiāotáng dànnǎi
crème caramel

庆祝蛋糕 qìngzhù dàngāo • celebration cakes

顶层
dǐngcéng
top tier

缎带
duàndài
ribbon

底层
dǐcéng
bottom tier

糖霜
tángshuāng
frosting

杏仁糊
xìngrénhú
marzipan

婚礼蛋糕 hūnlǐ dàngāo | wedding cake

装饰
zhuāngshì
decoration

生日蜡烛
shēngrì làzhú
birthday candles

吹熄
chuīxī
blow out (v)

生日蛋糕 shēngrì dàngāo | birthday cake

熟食店 shúshídiàn • delicatessen

辣香肠
làxiāngcháng
spicy sausage

油
yóu
oil

萨拉米香肠
sàlāmǐ
xiāngcháng
salami

醋
cù
vinegar

生肉
shēngròu
uncooked meat

柜台
guìtái
counter

意大利辣香肠
yìdàlìlà
xiāngcháng
pepperoni

果酱饼
guǒjiàngbǐng
quiche

肉酱
ròujiàng
pâté

莫泽雷勒干酪
mòzéléilè gānlào
mozzarella

布里干酪
bùlǐ gānlào
Brie

山羊奶酪
shānyáng nǎilào
goat cheese

切达干酪
qiēdá gānlào
cheddar

外皮
wàipí
rind

帕尔马干酪
pà'ěrmǎ gānlào
Parmesan

卡门贝干酪
kǎménbèi gānlào
Camembert

伊丹奶酪
yīdānnǎilào
Edam

蒙切各干酪
méngqiēgè gānlào
Manchego

西式馅饼/派
xīshì xiànbǐng/pài
potpie

黑橄榄
hēigǎnlǎn
black olive

辣椒
làjiāo
chili pepper

酱
jiàng
sauce

小圆面包
xiǎoyuán miànbāo
bread roll

熟肉
shúròu
cooked meat

绿橄榄
lǜgǎnlǎn
green olive

三明治柜台 sānmíngzhì guìtái | **sandwich counter**

火腿
huǒtuǐ
ham

熏鱼
xūnyú
smoked fish

马槟榔
mǎbīngláng
capers

西班牙香肠
xībānyáxiāngcháng
chorizo

意大利熏火腿
yìdàlì xūnhuǒtuǐ
prosciutto

填馅橄榄
tiánxiàn gǎnlǎn
stuffed olive

词汇 cíhuì • vocabulary

油渍 yóuzì **in oil**	调味汁浸泡的 tiáowèizhījìnpàode **marinated**	熏制的 xūnzhìde **smoked**
卤制 lǔzhì **in brine**	盐渍的 yánzìde **salted**	风干的 fēnggānde **cured**

请拿一个号。
qǐng ná yīgè hào.
Take a number, please.

我能尝尝吗?
wǒ néng chángchang ma?
Can I try some of that, please?

请来6片。
qǐng lái liùpiàn.
May I have six slices of that, please?

饮料 yǐnliào • drinks

水 shuǐ • water

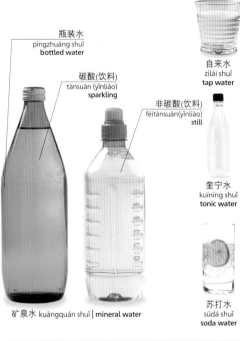

瓶装水
píngzhuāng shuǐ
bottled water

碳酸(饮料)
tànsuān (yǐnliào)
sparkling

非碳酸(饮料)
fēitànsuān(yǐnliào)
still

自来水
zìlái shuǐ
tap water

奎宁水
kuíníng shuǐ
tonic water

苏打水
sūdá shuǐ
soda water

矿泉水 kuàngquán shuǐ | **mineral water**

热饮 rèyǐn • hot drinks

茶包
chábāo
teabag

茶叶
cháyè
loose-leaf tea

茶
chá
tea

咖啡豆
kāfēidòu
beans

咖啡末
kāfēimò
ground coffee

咖啡
kāfēi
coffee

热巧克力
rèqiǎokèlì
hot chocolate

麦芽饮料
màiyáyǐnliào
malted drink

软(不含酒精的)饮料 ruǎn (bùhán jiǔjīngde) yǐnliào • soft drinks

吸管
xīguǎn
straw

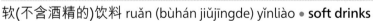

番茄汁
fānqiézhī
tomato juice

葡萄汁
pútáozhī
grape juice

柠檬水
níngméng shuǐ
lemonade

橘子水
júzi shuǐ
orangeade

可乐
kělè
cola

含酒精饮料 hán jiǔjīng yǐnliào • alcoholic drinks

罐
guàn
can

啤酒
píjiǔ
beer

苹果酒
píngguǒjiǔ
hard cider

苦啤酒
kǔpíjiǔ
bitter

浓烈黑啤酒
nóngliè hēipíjiǔ
stout

杜松子酒
dùsōngzǐjiǔ | gin

伏特加酒
fútèjiājiǔ | vodka

威士忌 wēishìjì | whiskey

朗姆酒
lǎngmǔjiǔ
rum

白兰地
báilándì
brandy

无糖份的
wútángfènde
dry

玫瑰红
méiguīhóng
rosé

白
bái
white

红
hóng
red

波尔图葡萄酒
bōěrtú pútáojiǔ
port

雪利酒
xuělìjiǔ
sherry

堪培利酒
kānpéilìjiǔ
Campari

利口酒
likǒujiǔ
liqueur

龙舌兰酒
lóngshélánjiǔ
tequila

香槟酒
xiāngbīnjiǔ
champagne

葡萄酒 pútáojiǔ | wine

外出就餐 wàichū jiùcān
eating out

咖啡馆 kāfēiguǎn · café

遮阳伞
zhēyángsǎn
umbrella

遮阳篷
zhēyángpéng
awning

菜单
càidān
menu

露天咖啡座
lùtiān kāfēizuò
sidewalk café

侍者
shìzhě
server

咖啡机
kāfēijī
coffee machine

桌子
zhuōzi
table

路边咖啡座 lùbiān kāfēizuò | patio café

快餐店 kuàicāndiàn | snack bar

咖啡 kāfēi · coffee

牛奶咖啡
niúnǎi kāfēi
coffee with milk

黑咖啡
hēikāfēi
black coffee

可可粉
kěkěfěn
cocoa powder

泡沫
pàomò
froth

过滤式咖啡
guòlǜshì kāfēi
filter coffee

意式浓缩咖啡
yìshìnóngsuō kāfēi
espresso

卡布奇诺咖啡
kǎbùqínuò kāfēi
cappuccino

冰咖啡
bīngkāfēi
iced coffee

茶 chá • tea

草药茶
cǎoyàochá
herbal tea

菊花茶
júhuāchá
chamomile tea

绿茶
lǜchá
green tea

奶茶
nǎichá
tea with milk

红茶
hóngchá
black tea

柠檬茶
níngméngchá
tea with lemon

薄荷茶
bòhechá
mint tea

冰茶
bīngchá
iced tea

果汁和奶昔 guǒzhī hé nǎixī • juices and milkshakes

橘子汁
júzizhī
orange juice

苹果汁
píngguǒzhī
apple juice

菠萝汁
bōluózhī
pineapple juice

番茄汁
fānqiézhī
tomato juice

巧克力奶昔
qiǎokèlì nǎixī
chocolate milkshake

草莓奶昔
cǎoméi nǎixī
strawberry milkshake

咖啡奶昔
kāfēi nǎixī
coffee milkshake

食物 shíwù • food

黑面包
hēimiànbāo
whole-wheat bread

烤三明治
kǎosānmíngzhì
toasted sandwich

沙拉
shālā
salad

一勺量
yìsháoliàng
scoop

冰激凌
bīngjīlíng
ice cream

油酥点心
yóusūdiǎnxin
pastry

酒吧 jiǔbā • bar

量杯
liángbēi
dispenser

收款机
shōukuǎnjī
cash register

酒保
jiǔbǎo
bartender

啤酒龙头
píjiǔ lóngtóu
beer tap

咖啡机
kāfēijī
coffee machine

玻璃杯
bōlibēi
glasses

冰桶
bīngtǒng
ice bucket

酒吧椅
jiǔbāyǐ
bar stool

烟灰缸
yānhuīgāng
ashtray

杯垫
bēidiàn
coaster

吧台
bātái
bar counter

开瓶器
kāipíngqì
bottle opener

夹钳
jiāqián
tongs

搅拌棒
jiǎobànbàng
stirrer

摇杆
yáogǎn
lever

量杯
liángbēi
measure

拔塞钻 básāizuàn | corkscrew

鸡尾酒调制器 jīwěijiǔ tiáozhìqì
cocktail shaker

水罐
shuǐguàn
pitcher

冰块
bīngkuài
ice cube

奎宁杜松子酒
kuíníng dùsōngzǐjiǔ
gin and tonic

加水威士忌
jiāshuǐ wēishìjì
scotch and water

加可乐朗姆酒
jiākělè lǎngmǔjiǔ
rum and cola

加橙汁伏特加酒
jiāchéngzhī fútèjiājiǔ
screwdriver

马提尼酒
mǎtíníjiǔ
martini

鸡尾酒
jīwěijiǔ
cocktail

葡萄酒
pútáojiǔ
wine

啤酒 píjiǔ | beer

单份
dānfèn
single

双份
shuāngfèn
double

冰和柠檬
bīng hé níngméng
ice and lemon

一小杯
yì xiǎobēi
shot

量杯
liángbēi
measure

不加冰
bù jiābīng
without ice

加冰
jiābīng
with ice

酒吧小吃 jiǔbā xiǎochī · bar snacks

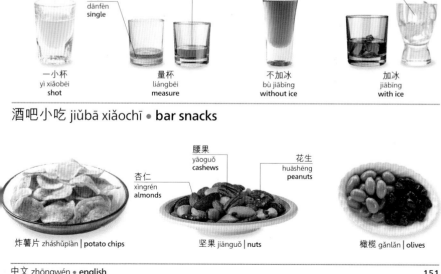

腰果
yāoguǒ
cashews

花生
huāshēng
peanuts

杏仁
xingrén
almonds

炸薯片 zháshǔpiàn | potato chips

坚果 jiānguǒ | nuts

橄榄 gǎnlǎn | olives

餐馆 cānguǎn • restaurant

餐具摆放
cānjù bǎifàng
table setting

助厨
zhùchú
sous chef

主厨
zhǔchú
chef

厨房 chúfáng | kitchen

玻璃杯
bōlibēi
glass

托盘
tuōpán
tray

侍者 shìzhě | server

词汇 cíhuì • vocabulary

晚餐菜单 wǎncān càidān dinner menu	特色菜 tèsècài specials	价格 jiàgé price	小费 xiǎofèi tip	自助餐 zìzhùcān buffet	盐 yán salt
酒单 jiǔdān wine list	按菜单点菜 àn càidān diǎncài à la carte	账单 zhàngdān check	含服务费 hán fúwùfèi service charge included	酒吧 jiǔbā bar	胡椒粉 hújiāofěn pepper
午餐菜单 wǔcān càidān lunch menu	甜食小车 tiánshí xiǎochē dessert cart	收据 shōujù receipt	不含服务费 bùhán fúwùfèi service charge not included	客人 kèrén customer	

中文 zhōngwén • english

菜单
càidān
menu

点菜 diǎncài | order (v)

付账 fùzhàng | pay (v)

儿童套餐
értóng tàocān
child's meal

菜肴 càiyáo • courses

开胃酒
kāiwèijiǔs
apéritif

头盘
tóupán
appetizer

汤
tāng
soup

主菜
zhǔcài
entrée

配菜
pèicài
side order

餐后甜点 cānhòu tiándiǎn
dessert

咖啡 kāfēi
coffee

要一张两人桌。
yào yìzhāng liǎngrénzhuō.
A table for two, please.

能让我看看菜单/酒单吗？
néng ràng wǒ kànkan càidān/jiǔdān ma?
Can I see the menu/wine list please?

有固定价格菜单吗？
yǒu gùdìng jiàgé càidān ma?
Is there a fixed-price menu?

有素食吗？
yǒu sùshí ma?
Do you have any vegetarian dishes?

请给我账单/收据。
qǐng gěi wǒ zhàngdān/shōujù.
Could I have the check/a receipt, please?

我们能分开结账吗？
wǒmen néng fēnkāi jiézhàng ma?
Can we pay separately?

请问卫生间在哪儿？
qǐngwèn wèishēngjiān zàinǎ'er?
Where is the restroom, please?

快餐 kuàicān • fast food

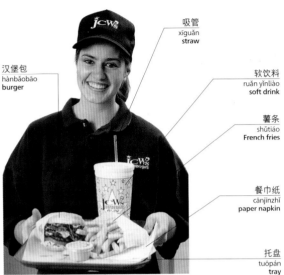

吸管
xīguǎn
straw

汉堡包
hànbǎobāo
burger

软饮料
ruǎn yǐnliào
soft drink

薯条
shǔtiáo
French fries

餐巾纸
cānjīnzhǐ
paper napkin

托盘
tuōpán
tray

汉堡套餐 hànbǎotàocān | burger meal

词汇 cíhuì • vocabulary

比萨饼店
bǐsàbǐngdiàn
pizzeria

快餐店
kuàicāndiàn
burger bar

菜单
càidān
menu

店内用餐
diànnèi yòngcān
eat-in

外带
wàidài
to go

重新加热
chóngxīn jiārè
reheat (v)

番茄酱
fānqiéjiàng
ketchup

我带走吃。
wǒ dàizǒu chī.
Can I have that to go, please?

你们提供送餐服务吗?
nǐmen tígōng sòngcānfúwù ma?
Do you deliver?

比萨饼
bǐsàbǐng
pizza

价目表
jiàmùbiǎo
price list

罐装饮料
guànzhuāng yǐnliào
canned drink

送餐 sòngcān | home delivery

食品摊 shípǐntān | street vendor

中文 zhōngwén • english

小圆面包
xiǎoyuan
miànbāo
bun

芥末
Jièmò
mustard

香肠
xiāngcháng
sausage

汉堡包
hànbǎobāo
hamburger

鸡肉汉堡
jīròu hànbǎo
chicken burger

蔬菜汉堡
shūcài hànbǎo
veggie burger

热狗 règǒu | **hot dog**

馅
xiàn
filling

三明治
sānmíngzhì
sandwich

总汇三明治
zǒnghuì sānmíngzhì
club sandwich

单片三明治
dānpiàn sānmíngzhì
open-faced sandwich

菜卷
càijuǎn
wrap

酱
jiàng
sauce

开胃的
kāiwèide
savory

甜味的
tiánwèide
sweet

装饰配料
zhuāngshìpèiliào
topping

烤肉串
kǎoròuchuàn
kebab

鸡块
jīkuài
chicken nuggets

薄饼卷 báobǐngjuǎn | **crepes**

鱼和薯条
yú hé shǔtiáo
fish and chips

肋排
lèipái
ribs

炸鸡
zhájī
fried chicken

比萨饼
bǐsàbǐng
pizza

早餐 zǎocān • breakfast

牛奶
niúnǎi
milk

谷类食品
gǔlèishípǐn
cereal

果酱
guǒjiàng
jam

干果
gānguǒ
dried fruit

火腿
huǒtuǐ
ham

奶酪
nǎilào
cheese

薄脆饼干
báocuìbǐnggān
crispbread

自助早餐
zizhùzǎocān
breakfast buffet

橘子酱
júzijiàng
marmalade

肉酱
ròujiàng
pâté

黄油
huángyóu
butter

果汁
guǒzhī
fruit juice

咖啡
kāfēi
coffee

热巧克力
rèqiǎokèlì
hot chocolate

羊角面包
yángjiǎo miànbāo
croissant

茶
chá
tea

早餐桌 zǎocānzhuō | breakfast table

饮料 yǐnliào | drinks

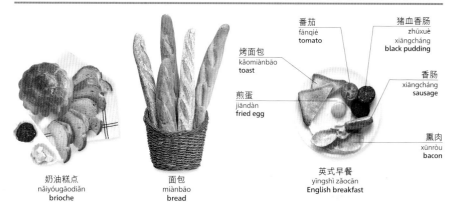

番茄
fānqié
tomato

猪血香肠
zhūxuè
xiāngcháng
black pudding

烤面包
kǎomiànbāo
toast

香肠
xiāngcháng
sausage

煎蛋
jiāndàn
fried egg

熏肉
xūnròu
bacon

奶油糕点
nǎiyóugāodiǎn
brioche

面包
miànbāo
bread

英式早餐
yīngshì zǎocān
English breakfast

蛋黄
dànhuáng
yolk

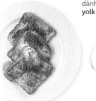

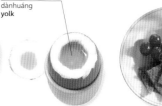

熏鲱鱼
xūnfēiyú
kippers

法式吐司
fǎshìtǔsī
French toast

煮鸡蛋
zhǔjīdàn
soft-boiled egg

炒鸡蛋
chǎojīdàn
scrambled eggs

奶油
nǎiyóu
whipped cream

果味酸奶
guǒwèisuānnǎi
fruit yogurt

薄煎饼
báojiānbǐng
crepes

华夫饼
huáfūbǐng
waffles

麦片粥
màipiànzhōu
oatmeal

鲜果
xiānguǒ
fresh fruit

正餐 zhèngcān ● **dinner**

汤 tāng | soup

肉汤 ròutāng | broth

炖菜 dùncài | stew

咖喱 gālí | curry

烤肉 kǎoròu | roast

馅饼 xiànbǐng | potpie

蛋奶酥 dànnǎisū | soufflé

烤肉串 kǎoròuchuàn
kebab

肉丸 ròuwán | meatballs

煎蛋饼 jiāndànbǐng
omelet

面条
miàntiáo
noodles

炒菜 chǎocài | stir-fry

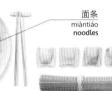

意大利面食 yìdàlì miànshí
pasta

米饭 mǐfàn | rice

什锦沙拉 shíjǐnshālā
tossed salad

蔬菜沙拉 shūcàishālā
green salad

调味汁 tiáowèizhī | dressing

烹调手法 pēngtiáo shǒufǎ • **techniques**

装馅 zhuāngxiàn | stuffed

浇汁 jiāozhī | in sauce

烤制 kǎozhì | grilled

调味汁浸泡的
tiáowèizhījìnpàode | marinated

水煮 shuǐzhǔ | poached

捣成糊状 dǎochénghúzhuàng
mashed

烘制 hōngzhì | baked

煎制 jiānzhì | pan fried

炒制 chǎozhì | fried

腌渍 yānzì | pickled

熏制 xūnzhì | smoked

油炸 yóuzhá | deep-fried

枫糖浸泡 fēngtángjìnpào
in syrup

调味 tiáowèi | dressed

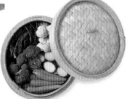

清蒸 qīngzhēng | steamed

风干 fēnggān | cured

学习 xuéxí
study

学校 xuéxiào • school

白板
báibǎn
whiteboard

老师
lǎoshī
teacher

书包
shūbāo
schoolbag

学生
xuéshēng
student

课桌
kèzhuō
desk

教室 jiàoshì | classroom

女生
nǚshēng
schoolgirl

男生
nánshēng
schoolboy

词汇 cíhuì • vocabulary

历史 lìshǐ history	自然科学 zìránkēxué science	物理 wùlǐ physics
语言 yǔyán languages	艺术 yìshù art	化学 huàxué chemistry
文学 wénxué literature	音乐 yīnyuè music	生物学 shēngwùxué biology
地理 dìlǐ geography	数学 shùxué math	体育 tǐyù physical education

学习活动 xuéxí huódòng • activities

读 dú | read (v)

写 xiě | write (v)

拼写 pīnxiě | spell (v)

画 huà | draw (v)

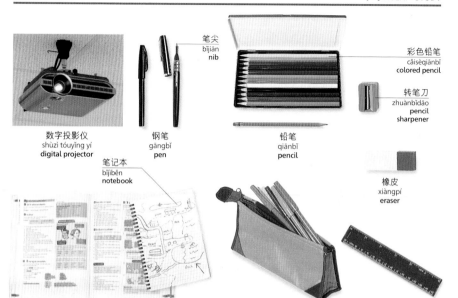

笔尖
bǐjiān
nib

彩色铅笔
cǎisèqiānbǐ
colored pencil

转笔刀
zhuànbǐdāo
pencil sharpener

数字投影仪
shùzì tóuyǐng yí
digital projector

钢笔
gāngbǐ
pen

铅笔
qiānbǐ
pencil

笔记本
bǐjìběn
notebook

橡皮
xiàngpí
eraser

教科书 jiàokēshū | **textbook**

笔袋 bǐdài | **pencil case**

尺子 chǐzi | **ruler**

提问 tíwèn | **question (v)**

回答 huídá | **answer (v)**

讨论 tǎolùn | **discuss (v)**

学习 xuéxí | **learn (v)**

词汇 cíhuì • vocabulary

校长 xiàozhǎng **principal**	答案 dá'àn **answer**	评分 píngfēn **grade**
课 kè **lesson**	作业 zuòyè **homework**	年级 niánjí **year**
问题 wèntí **question**	考试 kǎoshì **test**	字典 zìdiǎn **dictionary**
记笔记 jìbǐjì **take notes (v)**	作文 zuòwén **essay**	百科全书 bǎikēquánshū **encyclopedia**

数学 shùxué · **math**

平面图形 píngmiàntúxíng · **shapes**

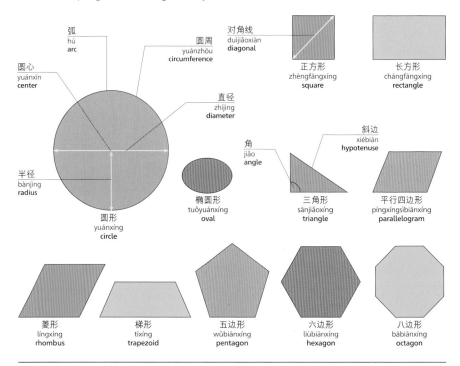

弧
hú
arc

圆周
yuánzhōu
circumference

对角线
duìjiǎoxiàn
diagonal

圆心
yuánxīn
center

直径
zhíjìng
diameter

正方形
zhèngfāngxíng
square

长方形
chángfāngxíng
rectangle

斜边
xiébiàn
hypotenuse

角
jiǎo
angle

半径
bànjìng
radius

椭圆形
tuǒyuánxíng
oval

三角形
sānjiǎoxíng
triangle

平行四边形
píngxíngsìbiānxíng
parallelogram

圆形
yuánxíng
circle

菱形
língxíng
rhombus

梯形
tīxíng
trapezoid

五边形
wǔbiānxíng
pentagon

六边形
liùbiānxíng
hexagon

八边形
bābiānxíng
octagon

立体 lìtǐ · **solids**

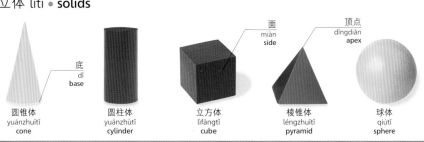

面
miàn
side

顶点
dǐngdiǎn
apex

底
dǐ
base

圆锥体
yuánzhuītǐ
cone

圆柱体
yuánzhùtǐ
cylinder

立方体
lìfāngtǐ
cube

棱锥体
léngzhuītǐ
pyramid

球体
qiútǐ
sphere

线 xiàn · **lines**

平直	平行	垂直	弯曲
píngzhí	píngxíng	chuízhí	wānqū
straight	**parallel**	**perpendicular**	**curved**

度量 dùliàng · **measurements**

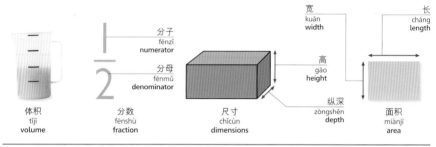

分子
fēnzǐ
numerator

分母
fēnmǔ
denominator

宽
kuān
width

长
cháng
length

高
gāo
height

纵深
zòngshēn
depth

体积	分数	尺寸	面积
tǐjī	fēnshù	chǐcùn	miànjī
volume	**fraction**	**dimensions**	**area**

学习用具 xuéxíyòngjù · **equipment**

三角板	量角器	直尺	圆规	计算器
sānjiǎobǎn	liángjiǎoqì	zhíchǐ	yuánguī	jìsuànqì
triangle	**protractor**	**ruler**	**compass**	**calculator**

词汇 cíhuì · **vocabulary**

几何	正	倍	等于	加	乘	等式
jǐhé	zhèng	bèi	děngyú	jiā	chéng	děngshì
geometry	**plus**	**times**	**equals**	**add (v)**	**multiply (v)**	**equation**

算术	负	除以	计数	减	除	百分比
suànshù	fù	chúyǐ	jìshù	jiǎn	chú	bǎifēnbǐ
arithmetic	**minus**	**divided by**	**count (v)**	**subtract (v)**	**divide (v)**	**percentage**

科学 kēxué • science

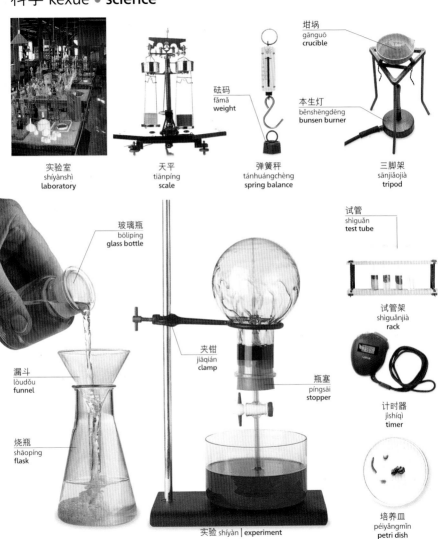

坩埚
gānguō
crucible

砝码
fǎmǎ
weight

本生灯
běnshēngdēng
bunsen burner

实验室
shíyànshì
laboratory

天平
tiānpíng
scale

弹簧秤
tánhuángchèng
spring balance

三脚架
sānjiǎojià
tripod

玻璃瓶
bōlipíng
glass bottle

试管
shìguǎn
test tube

试管架
shìguǎnjià
rack

夹钳
jiāqián
clamp

瓶塞
píngsāi
stopper

漏斗
lòudǒu
funnel

烧瓶
shāopíng
flask

计时器
jìshíqì
timer

培养皿
péiyǎngmǐn
petri dish

实验 shíyàn | experiment

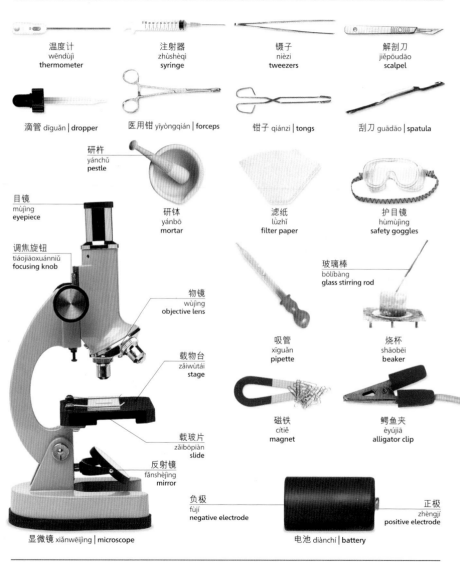

温度计
wēndùjì
thermometer

注射器
zhùshèqì
syringe

镊子
nièzi
tweezers

解剖刀
jiěpōudāo
scalpel

滴管 dīguǎn | dropper

医用钳 yīyòngqián | forceps

钳子 qiánzi | tongs

刮刀 guādāo | spatula

研杵
yánchǔ
pestle

研钵
yánbō
mortar

滤纸
lǜzhǐ
filter paper

护目镜
hùmùjìng
safety goggles

目镜
mùjìng
eyepiece

调焦旋钮
tiáojiāoxuánniǔ
focusing knob

物镜
wùjìng
objective lens

载物台
zǎiwùtái
stage

载玻片
zǎibōpiàn
slide

反射镜
fǎnshèjìng
mirror

玻璃棒
bōlíbàng
glass stirring rod

吸管
xīguǎn
pipette

烧杯
shāobēi
beaker

磁铁
cítiě
magnet

鳄鱼夹
èyújiā
alligator clip

负极
fùjí
negative electrode

正极
zhèngjí
positive electrode

显微镜 xiǎnwēijìng | microscope

电池 diànchí | battery

高等院校 gāoděngyuànxiào · **college**

招生办
zhāoshēngbàn
admissions office

运动场
yùndòngchǎng
playing field

学生食堂
xuéshēngshítáng
cafeteria

学生宿舍
xuéshēngsùshè
residence hall

健康中心
jiànkāngzhōngxīn
health center

校园 xiàoyuán | campus

词汇 cíhuì · vocabulary

借书证 jièshūzhèng **library card**	问询处 wènxúnchù **help desk**	借出 jièchū **loan**
阅览室 yuèlǎnshì **reading room**	借入 jièrù **borrow (v)**	书 shū **book**
推荐书目 tuījiànshūmù **reading list**	预订 yùdìng **reserve (v)**	书名 shūmíng **title**
还书日期 huánshūrìqī **due date**	续借 xùjiè **renew (v)**	走廊 zǒuláng **aisle**

借书处
jièshūchù
circulation desk

图书管理员
túshūguǎnlǐyuán
librarian

书架
shūjià
bookshelf

期刊
qīkān
periodical

杂志
zázhì
journal

图书馆 túshūguǎn | library

大学生
dàxuéshēng
undergraduate

讲师
jiǎngshī
professor

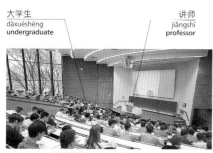

毕业生
biyèshēng
graduate

学位袍
xuéwèipáo
gown

阶梯教室 jiētījiàoshì | lecture hall

毕业典礼 biyèdiǎnlǐ | graduation ceremony

高等专科学校 gāoděngzhuānkē xuéxiào • schools

模特
mótè
model

美术学院 měishùxuéyuàn
art school

音乐学院 yīnyuèxuéyuàn
music school

舞蹈学院 wǔdǎoxuéyuàn
dance school

词汇 cíhuì • vocabulary

奖学金 jiǎngxuéjīn scholarship	研究 yánjiū research	(学位) 论文 (xuéwèi) lùnwén dissertation	医学 yīxué medicine	哲学 zhéxué philosophy
文凭 wénpíng diploma	硕士学位 shuòshìxuéwèi master's	系 xì department	动物学 dòngwùxué zoology	文学 wénxué literature
学位 xuéwèi degree	博士学位 bóshìxuéwèi doctorate	法律 fǎlǜ law	物理学 wùlǐxué physics	艺术史 yìshùshǐ art history
研究生阶段的 yánjiūshēng jiēduànde postgraduate	论文 lùnwén thesis	工程学 gōngchéngxué engineering	政治学 zhèngzhìxué political science	经济学 jīngjìxué economics

工作 gōngzuò
work

办公室1 bàngōngshì · office 1

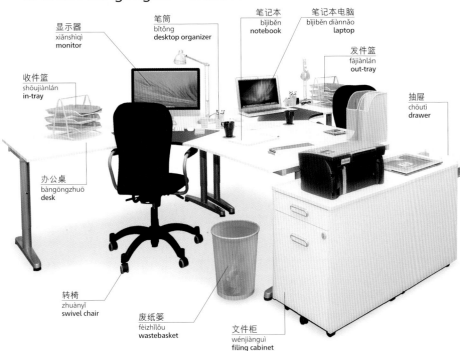

显示器
xiǎnshìqì
monitor

笔筒
bǐtǒng
desktop organizer

笔记本
bǐjìběn
notebook

笔记本电脑
bǐjìběn diànnǎo
laptop

收件篮
shōujiànlán
in-tray

发件篮
fājiànlán
out-tray

抽屉
chōutì
drawer

办公桌
bàngōngzhuō
desk

转椅
zhuànyǐ
swivel chair

废纸篓
fèizhǐlǒu
wastebasket

文件柜
wénjiànguì
filing cabinet

办公设备 bàngōngshèbèi · office equipment

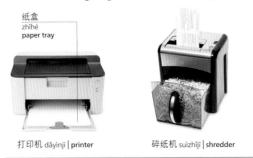

纸盒
zhǐhé
paper tray

打印机 dǎyìnjī | **printer**

碎纸机 suìzhǐjī | **shredder**

词汇 cíhuì · vocabulary

打印
dǎyìn
print (v)

放大
fàngdà
enlarge (v)

复印
fùyìn
copy (v)

缩小
suōxiǎo
reduce (v)

我要复印。
wǒ yào fùyìn.
I need to make some copies.

办公用品 bàngōngyòngpǐn · office supplies

礼帖
lǐtiě
compliments slip

印有笺头的信纸
yìn yǒu jiāntóude xìnzhǐ
letterhead

信封
xìnfēng
envelope

文件盒
wénjiànhé
box file

分隔页
fēngéyè
divider

带纸夹的笔记板
dài zhǐjiāde bǐjìbǎn
clipboard

便笺
biànjiān
notepad

标签
biāoqiān
tab

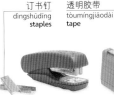

悬挂式文件夹
xuánguàshì wénjiànjiā
hanging file

格式文件夹
géshì wénjiànjiā
expanding file

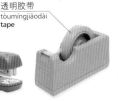

盒式文件夹
héshì wénjiànjiā
binder

备忘录
bèiwànglù
personal organizer

订书钉
dìngshūdīng
staples

透明胶带
tòumíngjiāodài
tape

印台
yìntái
ink pad

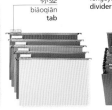

订书机
dìngshūjī
stapler

胶带架
jiāodàijià
tape dispenser

打孔器
dǎkǒngqì
hole punch

橡皮图章
xiàngpítúzhāng
rubber stamp

皮筋
píjīn
rubber band

强力纸夹
qiánglìzhǐjiā
bulldog clip

曲别针
qūbiézhēn
paper clip

图钉
túdīng
thumbtack

公告栏 gōnggàolán
bulletin board

办公室2 bàngōngshì · office 2

活动挂图
huódòngguàtú
flip chart

挂图架
guàtújià
easel

经理
jīnglǐ
manager

提案
tí'àn
proposal

报告
bàogào
report

主管
zhǔguǎn
executive

会议记录
huìyìjìlù
minutes

会议 huìyì | meeting

词汇 cíhuì · vocabulary

会议室
huìyìshì
meeting room

参加
cānjiā
attend (v)

议程
yìchéng
agenda

主持
zhǔchí
chair (v)

什么时候开会?
shénme shíhou kāihuì?
What time is the meeting?

您几点上下班?
nín jǐdiǎn shàngxiàbān?
What are your office hours?

讲解人
jiǎngjiěrén
speaker

介绍 jièshào | presentation

商务 shāngwù · **business**

商人
shāngrén
businessman

女商人
nǚshāngrén
businesswoman

工作午餐 gōngzuòwǔcān | **business lunch**

商务旅行 shāngwùlǚxíng | **business trip**

约会
yuēhuì
appointment

客户
kèhù
client

总经理
zǒngjīnglǐ
CEO

日志 rìzhì | **day planner**

商业交易 shāngyèjiāoyì | **business deal**

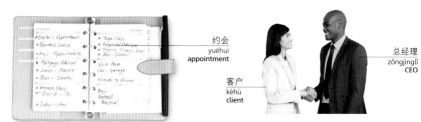

词汇 cíhuì · **vocabulary**

公司
gōngsī
company

员工
yuángōng
staff

会计部
kuàijìbù
accounting department

法律事务部
fǎlǜshìwùbù
legal department

总部，总公司
zǒngbù, zǒnggōngsī
head office

薪水
xīnshuǐ
salary

市场部
shìchǎngbù
marketing department

客户服务部
kèhùfúwùbù
customer service department

分部，分公司
fēnbù, fēngōngsī
regional office

工资单
gōngzīdān
payroll

销售部
xiāoshòubù
sales department

人力资源部
rénlìzīyuánbù
human resources department

计算机 jìsuànjī · computer

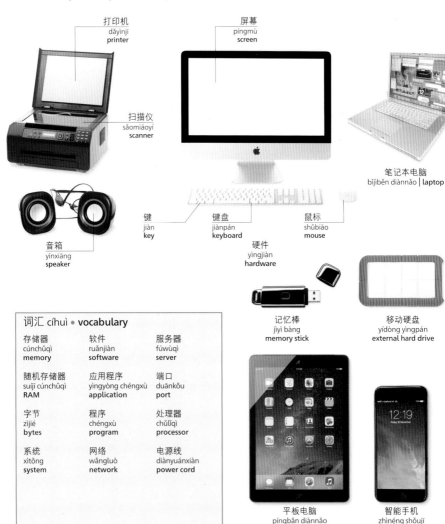

打印机
dǎyìnjī
printer

屏幕
píngmù
screen

扫描仪
sǎomiáoyí
scanner

笔记本电脑
bǐjìběn diànnǎo | laptop

键
jiàn
key

键盘
jiànpán
keyboard

鼠标
shǔbiāo
mouse

硬件
yìngjiàn
hardware

音箱
yīnxiāng
speaker

记忆棒
jìyì bàng
memory stick

移动硬盘
yídòng yìngpán
external hard drive

词汇 cíhuì · vocabulary

存储器 cúnchǔqì memory	软件 ruǎnjiàn software	服务器 fúwùqì server
随机存储器 suíjī cúnchǔqì RAM	应用程序 yìngyòng chéngxù application	端口 duānkǒu port
字节 zìjié bytes	程序 chéngxù program	处理器 chǔlǐqì processor
系统 xìtǒng system	网络 wǎngluò network	电源线 diànyuánxiàn power cord

平板电脑
píngbǎn diànnǎo
tablet

智能手机
zhìnéng shǒujī
smartphone

桌面 zhuōmiàn · desktop

字体
zìtǐ
font

菜单栏
càidānlán
menubar

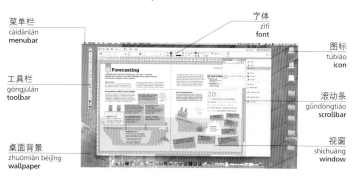

图标
túbiāo
icon

工具栏
gōngjùlán
toolbar

滚动条
gǔndòngtiáo
scrollbar

桌面背景
zhuōmiàn bèijǐng
wallpaper

视窗
shìchuāng
window

文件
wénjiàn
file

文件夹
wénjiànjiā
folder

回收站
huíshōuzhàn
trash

互联网 hùliánwǎng · internet

浏览器
liúlǎnqì
browser

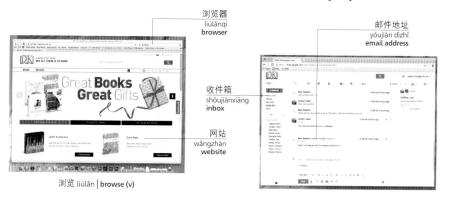

浏览 liúlǎn | browse (v)

电子邮件 diànzǐ yóujiàn · email

邮件地址
yóujiàn dìzhǐ
email address

收件箱
shōujiànxiāng
inbox

网站
wǎngzhàn
website

词汇 cíhuì · vocabulary

连接 liánjiē connect (v)	服务商 fúwùshāng service provider	登录 dēnglù log on (v)	下载 xiàzài download (v)	发送 fāsòng send (v)	保存 bǎocún save (v)
安装 ānzhuāng install (v)	电子邮件账户 diànzǐyóujiàn zhànghù email account	在线 zàixiàn online	附件 fùjiàn attachment	接收 jiēshōu receive (v)	搜索 sōusuǒ search (v)

媒体 méitǐ · media

电视演播室 diànshì yǎnbōshì · television studio

布景
bùjǐng
set

节目主持人
jiémùzhǔchírén
host

照明
zhàomíng
light

摄像机
shèxiàngjī
camera

摄像机升降器
shèxiàngjī shēngjiàngqì
camera crane

摄像师
shèxiàngshī
cameraman

词汇 cíhuì · vocabulary

频道 píndào channel	新闻 xīnwén news	新闻媒体 xīnwénméitǐ press	肥皂剧 féizàojù soap opera	动画片 dònghuàpiàn cartoon	直播 zhíbō live
节目编排 jiémùbiānpái programming	纪录片 jìlùpiàn documentary	电视连续剧 diànshì liánxùjù television series	游戏节目 yóuxìjiémù game show	录播 lùbō prerecorded	播放 bōfàng broadcast (v)

采访记者 cǎifǎngjìzhě
interviewer

记者 jìzhě | reporter

自动提示机 zìdòngtíshìjī
teleprompter

新闻播音员 xīnwénbōyīnyuán
anchor

演员 yǎnyuán | actors

录音吊杆 lùyīndiàogān
sound boom

场记板 chǎngjìbǎn
clapper board

电影布景 diànyǐngbùjǐng
movie set

无线电广播 wúxiàndiànguǎngbō · radio

录音师
lùyīnshī
sound technician

混音台
hùnyīntái
mixing desk

话筒
huàtǒng
microphone

录音室 lùyīnshì | recording studio

词汇 cíhuì · vocabulary

广播电台
guǎngbōdiàntái
radio station

广播
guǎngbō
broadcast

波长
bōcháng
wavelength

长波
chángbō
long wave

短波
duǎnbō
short wave

模拟信号
mónǐxìnhào
analog

中波
zhōngbō
medium wave

频率
pínlǜ
frequency

音量
yīnliàng
volume

调音
tiáoyīn
tune (v)

流行音乐节目主持人
liúxíngyīnyuè jiémù
zhǔchírén
DJ

数字信号
shùzìxìnhào
digital

法律 fǎlǜ · law

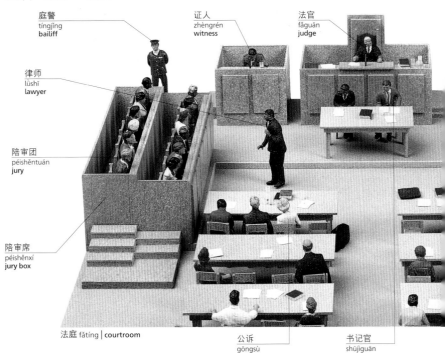

庭警
tíngjǐng
bailiff

证人
zhèngrén
witness

法官
fǎguān
judge

律师
lǜshī
lawyer

陪审团
péishěntuán
jury

陪审席
péishěnxí
jury box

法庭 fǎtíng | courtroom

公诉
gōngsù
prosecution

书记官
shūjìguān
court clerk

词汇 cíhuì · vocabulary

律师事务所 lǜshīshìwùsuǒ **lawyer's office**	传讯 chuánxùn **summons**	传票 chuánpiào **writ**	诉讼案件 sùsòng ànjiàn **court case**
法律咨询 fǎlǜzīxún **legal advice**	陈辞 chéncí **statement**	开庭日 kāitíngrì **court date**	控告 kònggào **charge**
诉讼委托人 sùsòngwěituōrén **client**	逮捕令 dàibǔlìng **warrant**	抗辩 kàngbiàn **plea**	被告 bèigào **accused**

中文 zhōngwén · english

速记员
sùjìyuán
stenographer

嫌疑犯
xiányífàn
suspect

被告人
bèigàorén
defendant

被告律师
bèigàolǜshī
defense

拼凑人像
pīncòurénxiàng
composite sketch

罪犯
zuìfàn
criminal

犯罪记录
fànzuìjìlù | **criminal record**

狱警 yùjǐng | **prison guard**

单人牢房
dānrénláofáng | **cell**

监狱 jiānyù | **prison**

词汇 cíhuì • vocabulary

证据 zhèngjù **evidence**	有罪 yǒuzuì **guilty**	保释金 bǎoshìjīn **bail**	我要见律师。 wǒ yào jiàn lǜshī. **I want to see a lawyer.**
判决 pànjué **verdict**	无罪释放 wúzuìshìfàng **acquitted**	上诉 shàngsù **appeal**	法院在哪儿? fǎyuàn zàinǎ'er? **Where is the courthouse?**
无罪 wúzuì **innocent**	判刑 pànxíng **sentence**	假释 jiǎshì **parole**	我可以保释吗? wǒ kěyǐ bǎoshì ma? **Can I post bail?**

农场1 nóngchǎng · farm 1

农田
nóngtián
farmland

农家场院
nóngjiā chǎngyuàn
farmyard

附属建筑物
fùshǔ jiànzhùwù
outbuilding

农舍
nóngshè
farmhouse

田地
tiándì
field

农民
nóngmín
farmer

谷仓
gǔcāng
barn

菜地
càidì
vegetable
garden

树篱
shùlí
hedge

大门
dàmén
gate

围栏
wéilán
fence

牧场
mùchǎng
pasture

家畜
jiāchù
livestock

中耕机
zhōnggēngjī
cultivator

拖拉机 tuōlājī | tractor

联合收割机 liánhéshōugējī | combine

农场类型 nóngchǎng lèixíng · types of farms

庄稼
zhuāngjia
crop

羊群
yángqún
flock

种植园
zhòngzhíyuán
crop farm

乳牛场
rǔniúchǎng
dairy farm

牧羊场
mùyángchǎng
sheep farm

养鸡场 yǎngjīchǎng
poultry farm

葡萄树
pútáoshù
vine

养猪场
yǎngzhūchǎng
pig farm

养鱼场
yǎngyúchǎng
fish farm

果园
guǒyuán
fruit farm

葡萄园
pútáoyuán
vineyard

农活 nónghuó · actions

犁
lí
furrow

犁地
lídì
plow (v)

播种
bōzhǒng
sow (v)

挤奶
jǐ'nǎi
milk (v)

饲养
sìyǎng
feed (v)

词汇 cíhuì · vocabulary

除草剂 chúcǎojì **herbicide**	牧群 mùqún **herd**	饲料槽 sìliàocáo **trough**
杀虫剂 shāchóngjì **pesticide**	筒仓 tǒngcāng **silo**	种植 zhòngzhí **plant (v)**

灌溉 guàngài | water (v)

收获 shōuhuò | harvest (v)

农场2 nóngchǎng · farm 2

农作物 nóngzuòwù · crops

小麦
xiǎomài
wheat

玉米
yùmǐ
corn

大麦
dàmài
barley

油菜籽
yóucàizǐ
rapeseed

向日葵
xiàngrìkuí
sunflower

捆包
kǔnbāo
bale

干草
gāncǎo
hay

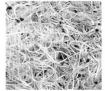
紫花苜蓿
zǐhuāmùxu
alfalfa

烟草
yāncǎo
tobacco

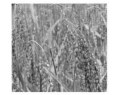
水稻
shuǐdào
rice

茶
chá
tea

咖啡
kāfēi
coffee

亚麻
yàmá
flax

甘蔗
gānzhe
sugarcane

棉花
miánhua
cotton

稻草人
dàocǎorén
scarecrow

家畜 jiāchù • livestock

小猪
xiǎozhū
piglet

猪
zhū
pig

牛犊
niúdú
calf

母牛
mǔniú
cow

公牛
gōngniú
bull

绵羊
miányáng
sheep

小山羊
xiǎoshānyáng
kid

羊羔
yánggāo
lamb

山羊
shānyáng
goat

马驹
mǎjū
foal

马
mǎ
horse

驴
lú
donkey

小鸡
xiǎojī
chick

鸡
jī
chicken

公鸡
gōngjī
rooster

火鸡
huǒjī
turkey

小鸭
xiǎoyā
duckling

鸭
yā
duck

马厩
mǎjiù
stable

家畜圈
jiāchùjuàn
pen

鸡舍
jīshè
chicken coop

猪圈
zhūjuàn
pigsty

建筑 jiànzhù · construction

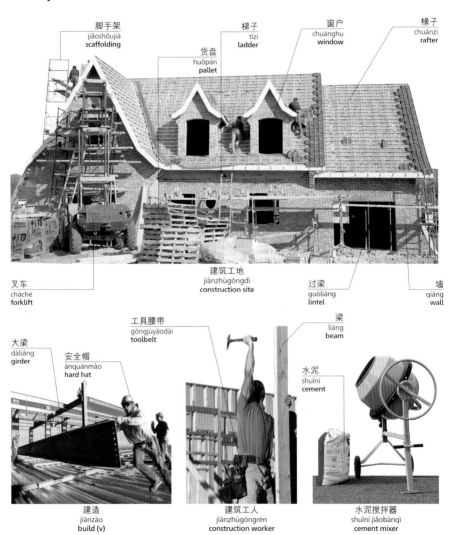

脚手架
jiǎoshǒujià
scaffolding

货盘
huòpán
pallet

梯子
tīzi
ladder

窗户
chuānghu
window

椽子
chuánzi
rafter

叉车
chāchē
forklift

建筑工地
jiànzhùgōngdì
construction site

过梁
guòliáng
lintel

墙
qiáng
wall

大梁
dàliáng
girder

安全帽
ānquánmào
hard hat

工具腰带
gōngjùyāodài
toolbelt

梁
liáng
beam

水泥
shuǐní
cement

建造
jiànzào
build (v)

建筑工人
jiànzhùgōngrén
construction worker

水泥搅拌器
shuǐní jiǎobànqì
cement mixer

建筑材料 jiànzhù cáiliào · **materials**

砖
zhuān
brick

木材
mùcái
lumber

瓦片
wǎpiàn
roof tile

煤渣砌块
méizhāqikuài
cinder block

工具 gōngjù · **tools**

灰浆
huījiāng
mortar

抹刀
mǒdāo
trowel

水准仪
shuǐzhǔnyí
level

柄
bǐng
handle

大锤
dàchuí
sledgehammer

丁字镐
dīngzìgǎo
pickax

铁锹
tiěqiāo
shovel

(工程)机械 (gōngchéng) jīxiè · **machinery**

压路机
yālùjī
road roller

翻斗卡车
fāndǒukǎchē
dump truck

支座
zhīzuò
support

吊钩
diàogōu
hook

起重机 qǐzhòngjī | crane

道路施工 dàolùshīgōng · **roadwork**

柏油路面
bǎiyóulùmiàn
asphalt

锥形隔离墩
zhuīxínggélídūn
cone

风钻
fēngzuàn
jackhammer

重铺路面
chóngpū lùmiàn
resurfacing

挖掘机
wājuéjī
excavator

职业1 zhíyè • occupations 1

木匠
mùjiàng
carpenter

电工
diàngōng
electrician

水暖工
shuǐnuǎngōng
plumber

建筑工人
jiànzhùgōngrén
construction worker

园丁
yuándīng
gardener

吸尘器
xīchénqì
vacuum
cleaner

清洁工
qīngjiégōng
cleaner

机械师
jīxièshī
mechanic

屠户
túhù
butcher

鱼贩
yúfàn
fish seller

蔬菜水果商
shūcài shuǐguǒshāng
produce seller

花商
huāshāng
florist

美发师
měifàshī
hairdresser

理发师
lǐfàshī
barber

珠宝匠
zhūbǎojiàng
jeweler

售货员
shòuhuòyuán
salesperson

房地产商
fángdichǎnshāng
realtor

配镜师
pèijingshī
optometrist

口罩
kǒuzhào
mask

牙医
yáyī
dentist

医生
yīshēng
doctor

药剂师
yàojishī
pharmacist

护士
hùshi
nurse

兽医
shòuyī
veterinarian

农民
nóngmín
farmer

渔民
yúmín
fisherman

徽章
huīzhāng
badge

机枪
jīqiāng
machine gun

制服
zhìfú
uniform

保安
bǎo'ān
security guard

水手
shuǐshǒu
sailor

士兵
shìbīng
soldier

警察
jǐngchá
police officer

消防队员
xiāofángduìyuán
firefighter

职业2 zhíyè · occupations 2

律师
lùshī
lawyer

会计师
kuàijìshī
accountant

模型
móxíng
model

建筑师 jiànzhùshī | architect

科学家
kēxuéjiā
scientist

老师
lǎoshī
teacher

图书管理员
túshūguǎnlǐyuán
librarian

接待员
jiēdàiyuán
receptionist

邮袋
yóudài
mailbag

邮递员
yóudìyuán
mail carrier

公共汽车司机
gōnggòngqìchē sījī
bus driver

卡车司机
kǎchē sījī
truck driver

出租车司机
chūzūchē sījī
taxi driver

飞行员
fēixíngyuán
pilot

空中小姐
kōngzhōngxiǎojiě
flight attendant

旅行代理
lǚxíngdàilǐ
travel agent

厨师帽
chúshīmào
chef's hat

厨师
chúshī
chef

芭蕾舞裙
bālěiwǔqún
tutu

音乐家
yīnyuèjiā
musician

舞蹈演员
wǔdǎoyǎnyuán
dancer

女演员
nǚ yǎnyuán
actress

歌手
gēshǒu
singer

女侍者
nǚshìzhě
waitress

酒保
jiǔbǎo
bartender

运动员
yùndòngyuán
sportsman

雕塑家
diāosùjiā
sculptor

画家
huàjiā
painter

摄影师
shèyǐngshī
photographer

新闻播音员
xīnwén bōyīnyuán
anchor

笔记
bǐjì
notes

新闻记者
xīnwén jìzhě
journalist

编辑
biānjí
editor

设计师
shèjìshī
designer

女缝纫师
nǚféngrènshī
seamstress

裁缝
cáiféng
tailor

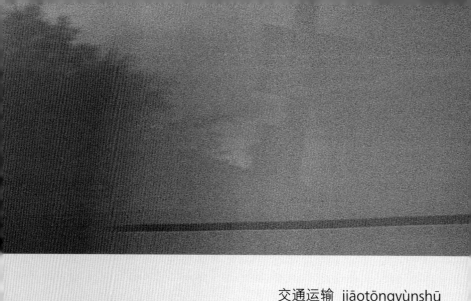

交通运输 jiāotōngyùnshū
transportation

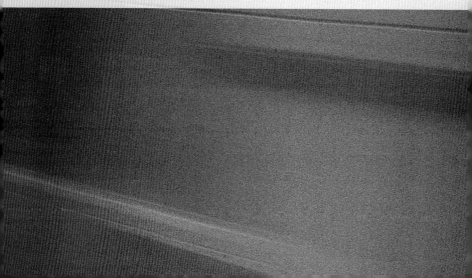

道路 dàolù • roads

高速公路
gāosùgōnglù
freeway

收费站
shōufèizhàn
toll booth

路面标志
lùmiànbiāozhì
road markings

主路入口
zhǔlùrùkǒu
on-ramp

单行道
dānxíngdào
one-way street

隔离带
gélídài
divider

交汇处
jiāohuìchù
interchange

交通信号灯
jiāotōng
xìnhàodēng
traffic light

内车道
nèichēdào
right lane

中央车道
zhōngyāngchēdào
middle lane

外车道
wàichēdào
left lane

出口匝道
chūkǒuzādào
off-ramp

交通
jiāotōng
traffic

立交桥
lìjiāoqiáo
overpass

硬质路肩
yìngzhìlùjiān
shoulder

载重汽车
zàizhòngqìchē
truck

中央分车带
zhōngyāng fēnchēdài
median strip

高架桥下通道
gāojià qiáoxià tōngdào
underpass

求救电话
qiújiù diànhuà
emergency phone

残疾人停车处
cánjírén tíngchēchù
disabled parking

交通堵塞
jiāotōngdǔsè
traffic jam

人行横道
rénxínghéngdào
crosswalk

卫星导航
wèixīng dǎoháng
satnav

停车计时收费器
tíngchē jìshí shōufèiqì
parking meter

交通警察
jiāotōng jǐngchá
traffic policeman

词汇 cíhuì · vocabulary

环岛
huándǎo
roundabout

绕行道路
ràoxíngdàolù
detour

道路施工
dàolùshīgōng
roadwork

防撞护栏
fángzhuànghùlán
guardrail

双程分隔车道
shuāngchéng fēngé chēdào
divided highway

停车
tíngchē
park (v)

驾驶
jiàshǐ
drive (v)

倒车
dàochē
reverse (v)

超车
chāochē
pass (v)

拖走
tuōzǒu
tow away (v)

这是去… 的路吗?
zhèshìqù… de lù ma?
Is this the road to ...?

哪里可以停车?
nǎli kěyǐ tíngchē?
Where can I park?

交通标志 jiāotōng biāozhì · road signs

禁行
jìnxíng
do not enter

限速
xiànsù
speed limit

危险
wēixiǎn
hazard

禁止停车
jìnzhǐ tíngchē
no stopping

禁止右转
jìnzhǐ yòuzhuǎn
no right turn

公共汽车 gōnggòngqìchē · bus

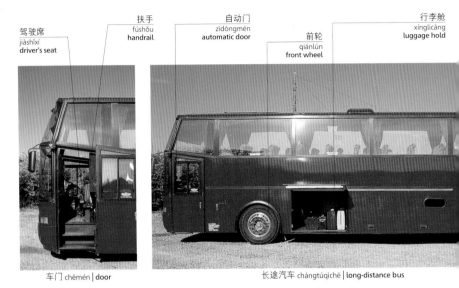

驾驶席
jiàshǐxí
driver's seat

扶手
fúshǒu
handrail

自动门
zìdòngmén
automatic door

前轮
qiánlún
front wheel

行李舱
xínglǐcāng
luggage hold

车门 chēmén | door

长途汽车 chángtúqìchē | long-distance bus

公共汽车种类 gōnggòngqìchē zhǒnglèi · types of buses

公交线路号
gōngjiāoxiànlùhào
route number

司机
sījī
driver

双层公共汽车
shuāngcéng gōnggòngqìchē
double-decker bus

有轨电车
yǒuguǐdiànchē
tram

无轨电车
wúguǐdiànchē
streetcar

校车 xiàochē | school bus

后轮
hòulún
rear wheel

窗户
chuānghu
window

停车按钮
tíngchē ànniǔ
stop button

公共汽车票
gōnggòngqìchēpiào
bus ticket

铃
líng
bell

公共汽车总站
gōnggòngqìchē zǒngzhàn
bus station

公共汽车站
gōnggòngqìchēzhàn
bus stop

词汇 cíhuì · vocabulary

车费
chēfèi
fare

轮椅通道
lúnyǐ tōngdào
wheelchair access

时刻表
shíkèbiǎo
schedule

公共汽车候车亭
gōngqìchē hòuchētíng
bus shelter

您在... 停吗?
nín zài... tíng ma?
Do you stop at …?

哪路车去...?
nǎlù chē qù...?
Which bus goes to …?

小型公共汽车
xiǎoxíng gōnggòngqìchē
minibus

游览车 yóulǎnchē | tour bus

班车 bānchē | shuttle bus

汽车1 qìchēyī · car 1

外部 wàibù · exterior

外后视镜
wàihòushìjìng
side mirror

风挡
fēngdǎng
windshield

内后视镜
nèihòushìjìng
rearview mirror

雨刷
yǔshuā
windshield wiper

车门
chēmén
door

引擎盖
yǐnqínggài
hood

行李箱
xínglixiāng
trunk

转向灯
zhuànxiàngdēng
turn signal

车牌
chēpái
license plate

保险杠
bǎoxiǎngàng
bumper

前灯
qiándēng
headlight

车轮
chēlún
wheel

轮胎
lúntāi
tire

行李
xíngli
luggage

车顶行李架
chēdǐng xínglijià
roof rack

尾部车门
wěibùchēmén
tailgate

安全带
ānquándài
seat belt

儿童座椅
értóngzuòyǐ
car seat

种类 zhǒnglèi · types

电动汽车
diàndòng qìchē
electric car

揭背式轿车
jiēbèishì jiàochē
hatchback

家庭轿车，三厢车
jiātíng jiàochē, sānxiāngchē
sedan

客货两用车
kèhuò liǎngyòngchē
station wagon

敞篷车
chǎngpéngchē
convertible

跑车
pǎochē
sports car

六座厢式车
liùzuò xiāngshìchē
minivan

四轮驱动(车)
sìlúnqūdòng(chē)
four-wheel drive

老式汽车
lǎoshìqìchē
vintage

大型高级轿车
dàxínggāojí jiàochē
limousine

加油站 jiāyóuzhàn · gas station

汽油泵
qìyóubèng
gas pump

价格
jiàgé
price

加油处
jiāyóuchù
forecourt

词汇 cíhuì · vocabulary

油 yóu **oil**	含铅 hánqiān **leaded**	自动洗车站 zìdòngxǐchēzhàn **car wash**
汽油 qìyóu **gasoline**	柴油 cháiyóu **diesel**	防冻液 fángdòngyè **antifreeze**
无铅 wúqiān **unleaded**	汽车修理站 qìchē xiūlǐzhàn **garage**	喷水器 pēnshuǐqì **windshield washer fluid**

请加满油。
qǐng jiāmǎn yóu.
Fill it up, please.

汽车2 qìchē · car 2

内部 nèibù · interior

座椅头枕
zuòyǐ tóuzhěn
headrest

门锁
ménsuǒ
door lock

车门把手
chēmén
bǎshou
handle

后座
hòuzuò
backseat

扶手
fúshǒu
armrest

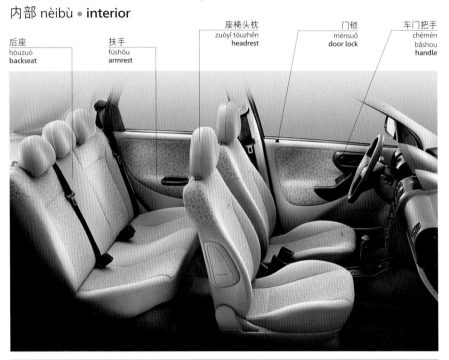

词汇 cíhuì · vocabulary

双门	四门	自动	刹车	加速器, 油门
shuāngmén	sìmén	zìdòng	shāchē	jiāsùqì, yóumén
two-door	**four-door**	**automatic**	**brake**	**accelerator**

三门	手动	点火	离合器	空调
sānmén	shǒudòng	diǎnhuǒ	líhéqì	kōngtiáo
hatchback	**manual**	**ignition**	**clutch**	**air-conditioning**

您能告诉我去...的路吗?
nín néng gàosù wǒ qù...de lù ma?
Can you tell me the way to …?

停车场在哪里?
tíngchēchǎng zàinǎli?
Where is the parking lot?

这儿可以停车吗?
zhè'er kěyǐ tíngchē ma?
Can I park here?

操作装置 cāozuòzhuāngzhì · **controls**

方向盘
fāngxiàngpán
steering
wheel

喇叭
lǎba
horn

仪表盘
yíbiǎopán
dashboard

警示灯
jǐngshìdēng
hazard lights

卫星导航仪
wèixīng dǎohángyí
satellite navigation

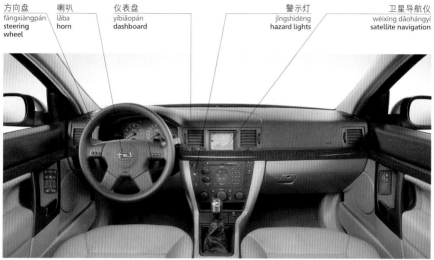

左侧驾驶 zuǒcèjiàshǐ | left-hand drive

温度计
wēndùjì
temperature gauge

转速表
zhuànsùbiǎo
tachometer

车速表
chēsùbiǎo
speedometer

油量表
yóuliàngbiǎo
fuel gauge

汽车音响
qìchē
yīnxiǎng
car stereo

车灯开关
chēdēng kāiguān
light switch

暖风开关
nuǎnfēng kāiguān
heater controls

里程表
lǐchéngbiǎo
odometer

安全气囊
ānquánqìnáng
air bag

变速杆
biànsùgǎn
gearshift

右侧驾驶 yòucèjiàshǐ | right-hand drive

汽车3 qìchē · car 3

机械构造 jīxiègòuzào · mechanics

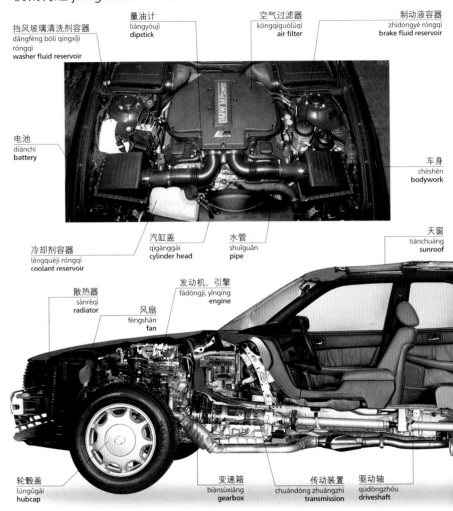

挡风玻璃清洗剂容器
dǎngfēng bōli qīngxǐjì
róngqì
washer fluid reservoir

量油计
liángyóujì
dipstick

空气过滤器
kōngqìguòlǜqì
air filter

制动液容器
zhìdòngyè róngqì
brake fluid reservoir

电池
diànchí
battery

车身
chēshēn
bodywork

冷却剂容器
lěngquèjì róngqì
coolant reservoir

汽缸盖
qìgānggài
cylinder head

水管
shuǐguǎn
pipe

天窗
tiānchuāng
sunroof

散热器
sànrèqì
radiator

风扇
fēngshàn
fan

发动机，引擎
fādòngjī, yǐnqíng
engine

轮毂盖
lúngǔgài
hubcap

变速箱
biànsùxiāng
gearbox

传动装置
chuándòng zhuāngzhì
transmission

驱动轴
qūdòngzhóu
driveshaft

爆胎 bàotāi • flat tire

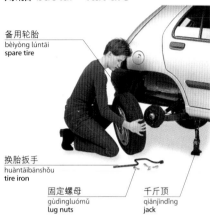

备用轮胎
bèiyòng lúntāi
spare tire

换胎扳手
huàntāibānshǒu
tire iron

固定螺母
gùdìngluómǔ
lug nuts

千斤顶
qiānjīndǐng
jack

更换轮胎
gēnghuàn lúntāi
change a tire (v)

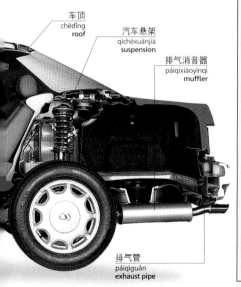

车顶
chēdǐng
roof

汽车悬架
qìchēxuánjià
suspension

排气消音器
páiqìxiāoyīnqì
muffler

排气管
páiqìguǎn
exhaust pipe

词汇 cíhuì • vocabulary

车祸
chēhuò
car accident

故障
gùzhàng
breakdown

保险
bǎoxiǎn
insurance

拖车
tuōchē
tow truck

机械师
jīxièshī
mechanic

胎压
tāiyā
tire pressure

保险盒
bǎoxiǎnhé
fuse box

火花塞
huǒhuāsāi
spark plug

风扇皮带
fēngshànpídài
fan belt

油箱
yóuxiāng
gas tank

点火定时
diǎnhuǒdìngshí
timing

涡轮增压器
wōlúnzēngyāqì
turbocharger

配电器
pèidiànqì
distributor

底盘
dǐpán
chassis

手刹车
shǒushāchē
parking brake

交流发电机
jiāoliúfādiànjī
alternator

轮轴皮带
lúnzhóupídài
cam belt

我的车坏了。
wǒ de chē huàile.
My car has broken down.

我的车发动不起来。
wǒ de chē fādòng bù qǐlái.
My car won't start.

摩托车 mótuōchē · **motorcycle**

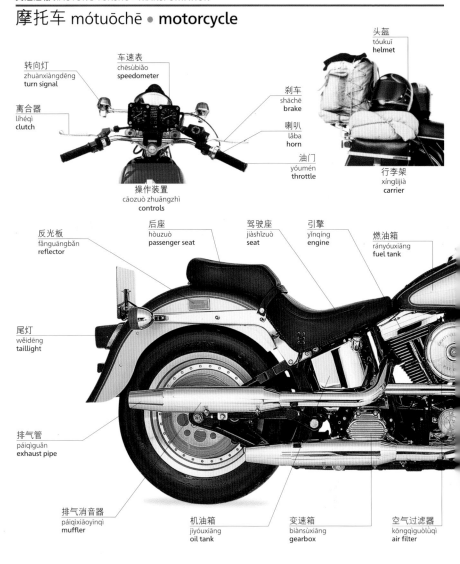

头盔
tóukuī
helmet

转向灯
zhuǎnxiàngdēng
turn signal

车速表
chēsùbiǎo
speedometer

刹车
shāchē
brake

离合器
líhéqì
clutch

喇叭
lǎba
horn

油门
yóumén
throttle

操作装置
cāozuò zhuāngzhì
controls

行李架
xínglijià
carrier

反光板
fǎnguāngbǎn
reflector

后座
hòuzuò
passenger seat

驾驶座
jiàshǐzuò
seat

引擎
yǐnqíng
engine

燃油箱
rányóuxiāng
fuel tank

尾灯
wěidēng
taillight

排气管
páiqìguǎn
exhaust pipe

排气消音器
páiqìxiāoyīnqì
muffler

机油箱
jīyóuxiāng
oil tank

变速箱
biànsùxiāng
gearbox

空气过滤器
kōngqìguòlǜqì
air filter

种类 zhǒnglèi • types

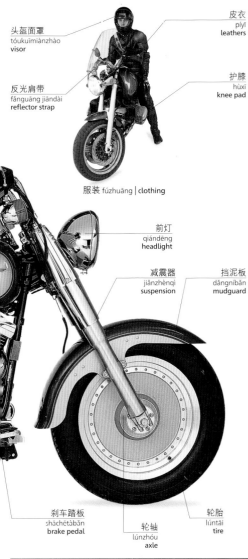

头盔面罩
tóukuīmiànzhào
visor

皮衣
píyī
leathers

护膝
hùxī
knee pad

反光肩带
fǎnguāng jiāndài
reflector strap

服装 fúzhuāng | clothing

前灯
qiándēng
headlight

减震器
jiǎnzhènqì
suspension

挡泥板
dǎngníbǎn
mudguard

刹车踏板
shāchētàbǎn
brake pedal

轮轴
lúnzhóu
axle

轮胎
lúntāi
tire

赛车 sàichē | racing bike

风挡
fēngdǎng
windshield

旅行摩托 lǚxíngmótuō | tourer

越野摩托 yuèyěmótuō | dirt bike

支架
zhījià
stand

小轮摩托 xiǎolúnmótuō | scooter

自行车 zìxíngchē · **bicycle**

车座
chēzuò
saddle

座杆
zuògǎn
seat post

水瓶
shuǐpíng
water bottle

车架
chējià
frame

刹车
shāchē
brake

轮毂
lúngǔ
hub

齿轮
chǐlún
gears

轮圈
lúnquān
rim

轮胎
lúntāi
tire

车链
chēliàn
chain

脚蹬
jiǎodēng
pedal

链盘
liànpán
cog

双座自行车 shuāngzuò zìxíngchē
tandem

赛车
sàichē
racing bike

山地车
shāndìchē
mountain bike

旅行车
lǚxíngchē
touring bike

头盔
tóukuī
helmet

公路车
gōnglùchē
road bike

自行车道 zìxíngchēdào | bike lane

横梁
héngliáng
crossbar

车把
chēbǎ
handlebar

变速杆
biànsùgǎn
gear lever

轮胎撬杆
lúntāi qiàogǎn
tire lever

补胎片
bǔtāipiàn
patch

车闸
chēzhá
brake lever

修理工具箱 xiūlǐ gōngjùxiāng
repair kit

前叉
qiánchā
fork

钥匙
yàoshi
key

辐条
fútiáo
spoke

气筒
qìtǒng
pump

车锁
chēsuǒ
lock

车轮
chēlún
wheel

气门
qìmén
valve

胎面
tāimiàn
tread

内胎
nèitāi
inner tube

儿童座椅
értóngzuòyǐ
child seat

词汇 cíhuì • vocabulary

车灯 chēdēng **headlight**	支架 zhījià **kickstand**	刹车片 shāchēpiàn **brake block**	车筐 chēkuāng **basket**	踏脚套 tàjiǎotào **toe clip**	刹车 shāchē **brake (v)**
尾灯 wěidēng **rear light**	自行车支架 zìxíngchē zhījià **bike rack**	绳索 shéngsuǒ **cable**	发电机 fādiànjī **dynamo**	趾带 zhǐdài **toe strap**	骑车 qíchē **cycle (v)**
反光镜 fǎnguāngjìng **reflector**	稳定轮 wěndìnglún **training wheels**	扣链齿 kòuliànchǐ **sprocket**	爆胎 bàotāi **flat tire**	蹬踏 dēngtà **pedal (v)**	变速 biànsù **change gears (v)**

列车 lièchē · train

客车厢
kèchēxiāng
railcar

站台号
zhàntáihào
platform number

站台
zhàntái
platform

旅客
lǚkè
commuter

手推车
shǒutuīchē
cart

火车站 huǒchēzhàn | train station

列车种类 lièchē zhǒnglèi · types of train

火车头
huǒchētóu
engine

驾驶室
jiàshǐshì
engineer's cab

铁轨
tiěguǐ
rail

蒸汽机车
zhēngqìjīchē
steam train

柴油机车 cháiyóujīchē | diesel train

电力机车
diànlìjīchē
electric train

高速列车
gāosùlièchē
high-speed train

单轨列车
dānguǐlièchē
monorail

地铁
dìtiě
subway

有轨电车
yǒuguǐdiànchē
tram

货车
huòchē
freight train

行李架
xínglijià
luggage rack

车窗
chēchuāng
window

轨道
guǐdào
track

门
mén
door

座位
zuòwèi
seat

检票口 jiǎnpiàokǒu | ticket gates

车厢隔间
chēxiānggéjiān
compartment

扩音器
kuòyīnqì
public address system

列车时刻表
lièchē
shíkèbiǎo
schedule

车票
chēpiào
ticket

餐车 cānchē | dining car

车站大厅 chēzhàndàtīng | concourse

卧铺车厢
wòpùchēxiāng
sleeping compartment

词汇 cíhuì • vocabulary

铁路网
tiělùwǎng
railroad network

城际列车
chéngjì lièchē
express train

上下班高峰期
shàngxiàbān gāofēngqī
rush hour

地铁线路图
dìtiě xiànlùtú
subway map

晚点
wǎndiǎn
delay

车费
chēfèi
fare

售票处
shòupiàochù
ticket office

检票员
jiǎnpiàoyuán
ticket inspector

换乘
huànchéng
transfer (v)

载电轨
zàidiànguǐ
live rail

信号
xìnhào
signal

紧急刹车闸
jǐnjí shāchēzhá
emergency lever

飞机 fēijī · **aircraft**

班机 bānjī · **airliner**

机头
jītóu
nose

驾驶舱
jiàshǐcāng
cockpit

引擎
yǐnqíng
engine

机身
jīshēn
fuselage

机翼
jīyì
wing

尾翼
wěiyì
tail

方向舵
fāngxiàngduò
rudder

舱门
cāngmén
exit

头部机轮
tóubùjīlún
nosewheel

起落架
qǐluòjià
landing gear

副翼
fùyì
aileron

垂直尾翼
chuízhíwěiyì
fin

水平尾翼
shuǐpíngwěiyì
tailplane

机舱 jīcāng · **cabin**

紧急出口
jǐnjí chūkǒu
emergency exit

空乘人员
kōngchéng rényuán
flight attendant

头顶锁柜
tóudǐng suǒguì
overhead bin

通风口
tōngfēngkǒu
air vent

窗户
chuānghu
window

阅读灯
yuèdúdēng
reading light

座位
zuòwèi
seat

排
pái
row

搁板
gēbǎn
tray-table

扶手
fúshǒu
armrest

走廊
zǒuláng
aisle

椅背
yǐbèi
seat back

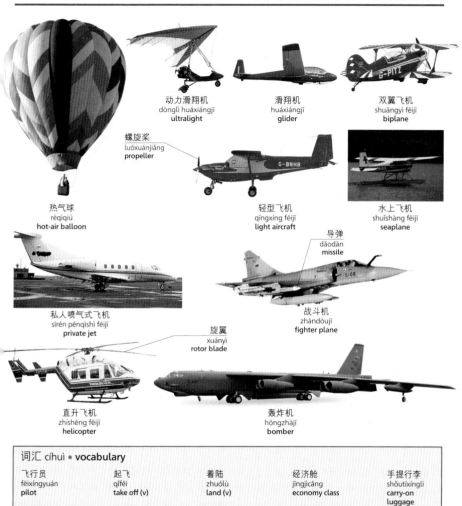

动力滑翔机
dònglì huáxiángjī
ultralight

滑翔机
huáxiángjī
glider

双翼飞机
shuāngyì fēijī
biplane

螺旋桨
luóxuánjiǎng
propeller

热气球
rèqìqiú
hot-air balloon

轻型飞机
qīngxíng fēijī
light aircraft

水上飞机
shuǐshàng fēijī
seaplane

导弹
dǎodàn
missile

私人喷气式飞机
sīrén pēnqìshì fēijī
private jet

战斗机
zhàndòujī
fighter plane

旋翼
xuányì
rotor blade

直升飞机
zhíshēng fēijī
helicopter

轰炸机
hōngzhàjī
bomber

词汇 cíhuì • vocabulary

飞行员 fēixíngyuán **pilot**	起飞 qǐfēi **take off (v)**	着陆 zhuólù **land (v)**	经济舱 jīngjìcāng **economy class**	手提行李 shǒutíxíngli **carry-on luggage**
副驾驶员 fùjiàshǐyuán **copilot**	飞行 fēixíng **fly (v)**	高度 gāodù **altitude**	商务舱 shāngwùcāng **business class**	安全带 ānquándài **seat belt**

机场 jīchǎng · airport

停机坪
tíngjīpíng
apron

行李拖车
xínglǐtuōchē
baggage trailer

候机楼
hòujīlóu
terminal

服务车
fúwùchē
service vehicle

登机通道
dēngjītōngdào
jetway

班机 bānjī | airliner

词汇 cíhuì · vocabulary

跑道 pǎodào **runway**	航班号 hángbānhào **flight number**	行李传送带 xínglǐ chuánsòngdài **baggage carousel**	假日 jiàrì **vacation**
国际航线 guójì hángxiàn **international flight**	入境检查 rùjìngjiǎnchá **immigration**	安全 ānquán **security**	办理登机手续 bànlǐ dēngjī shǒuxù **check in (v)**
国内航线 guónèi hángxiàn **domestic flight**	海关 hǎiguān **customs**	X光行李检查机 Xguāng xínglǐ jiǎnchájī **X-ray machine**	控制塔 kòngzhìtǎ **control tower**
联运 liányùn **connection**	超重行李 chāozhòng xínglǐ **excess baggage**	假日指南 jiàrì zhǐnán **travel brochure**	订机票 dìngjīpiào **book a flight (v)**

手提行李
shǒutí xíngli
carry-on luggage

(大件)行李
(dàjiàn) xíngli
luggage

行李推车
xíngli tuīchē
cart

办理登机手续处
bànlǐ dēngjī shǒuxùchù
check-in desk

签证
qiānzhèng
visa

护照 hùzhào | **passport**

护照检查处
hùzhào jiǎncháchù
passport control

登机牌
dēngjīpái
boarding pass

机票
jīpiào
ticket

登机门号
dēngjīménhào
gate number

出发
chūfā
departures

候机大厅
hòujīdàtīng
departure lounge

目的地
mùdìdì
destination

抵达
dǐdá
arrivals

信息屏
xìnxīpíng
information screen

免税商店
miǎnshuì shāngdiàn
duty-free shop

领取行李处
lǐngqǔ xínglichù
baggage claim

出租车站
chūzūchēzhàn
taxi stand

租车处
zūchēchù
car rental

船 chuán • ship

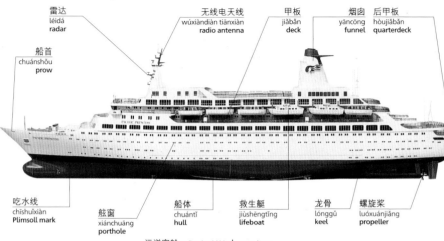

雷达
léidá
radar

无线电天线
wúxiàndiàn tiānxiàn
radio antenna

甲板
jiǎbǎn
deck

烟囱
yāncōng
funnel

后甲板
hòujiǎbǎn
quarterdeck

船首
chuánshǒu
prow

吃水线
chīshuǐxiàn
Plimsoll mark

舷窗
xiánchuāng
porthole

船体
chuántǐ
hull

救生艇
jiùshēngtǐng
lifeboat

龙骨
lónggǔ
keel

螺旋桨
luóxuánjiǎng
propeller

远洋客轮 yuǎnyángkèlún | ocean liner

驾驶台
jiàshǐtái
bridge

轮机舱
lúnjīcāng
engine room

客舱
kècāng
cabin

船上厨房
chuánshàng chúfáng
galley

词汇 cíhuì • vocabulary

船坞 chuánwù dock	卷扬机 juǎnyángjī windlass
港口 gǎngkǒu port	船长 chuánzhǎng captain
舷梯 xiántī gangway	快艇 kuàitǐng speedboat
锚 máo anchor	划桨船 huájiǎngchuán rowboat
岸边缆桩 ànbiānlánzhuāng bollard	独木舟 dúmùzhōu canoe

其他船型 qítāchuánxíng · other ships

渡船
dùchuán
ferry

舷外马达
xiánwàimǎdá
outboard motor

充气式橡皮艇
chōngqìshi xiàngpítíng
inflatable dinghy

水翼艇
shuǐyìtíng
hydrofoil

游艇
yóutǐng
yacht

双体船
shuāngtǐchuán
catamaran

拖船
tuōchuán
tugboat

气垫船
qìdiànchuán
hovercraft

帆缆
fānlǎn
rigging

货舱
huòcāng
hold

集装箱船
jízhuāngxiāng chuán
container ship

帆船
fānchuán
sailboat

货船
huòchuán
freighter

指挥塔
zhǐhuītǎ
conning tower

油轮
yóulún
oil tanker

航空母舰
hángkōng mǔjiàn
aircraft carrier

战舰
zhànjiàn
battleship

潜水艇
qiánshuǐtíng
submarine

港口 gǎngkǒu · **port**

仓库
cāngkù
warehouse

起重机
qǐzhòngjī
crane

叉车
chāchē
forklift

出入港通道
chūrùgǎng tōngdào
access road

海关
hǎiguān
customs house

船坞
chuánwù
dock

集装箱
jízhuāngxiāng
container

码头
mǎtóu
quay

货物
huòwù
cargo

渡船码头
dùchuán mǎtóu
ferry terminal

渡船
dùchuán
ferry

售票处
shòupiàochù
ticket office

乘客
chéngkè
passenger

集装箱港口 jízhuāngxiāng gǎngkǒu | **container port**

客运码头 kèyùn mǎtóu | **passenger port**

渔网
yúwǎng
net

渔船
yúchuán
fishing boat

缆绳
lǎnshéng
mooring

小船停靠区 xiǎochuántíngkàoqū | marina

渔港 yúgǎng | fishing port

港口 gǎngkǒu | harbor

栈桥 zhànqiáo | pier

防波堤
fángbōdī
jetty

船厂
chuánchǎng
shipyard

塔灯
tǎdēng
lamp

灯塔
dēngtǎ
lighthouse

浮标
fúbiāo
buoy

词汇 cíhuì • vocabulary

海岸警卫队
hǎi'àn jǐngwèiduì
coast guard

港务局长
gǎngwù júzhǎng
harbor master

抛锚
pāomáo
drop anchor (v)

干船坞
gānchuánwù
dry dock

停泊
tíngbó
moor (v)

进入船坞
jìnrùchuánwù
dock (v)

上船
shàngchuán
board (v)

离船登岸
líchuándēngàn
disembark (v)

起航
qǐháng
set sail (v)

体育运动 tǐyùyùndòng
sports

美式橄榄球 měishì gǎnlǎnqiú · football

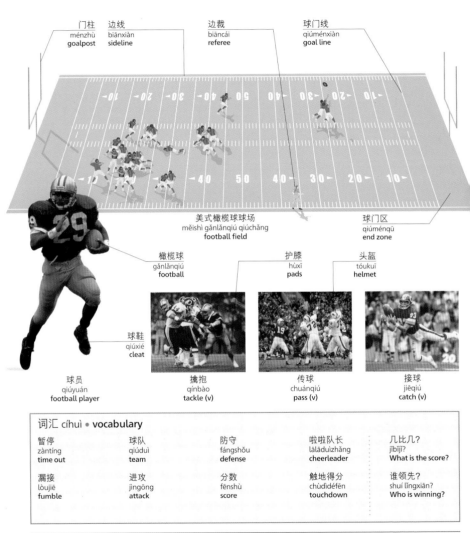

门柱
ménzhù
goalpost

边线
biānxiàn
sideline

边裁
biāncái
referee

球门线
qiúménxiàn
goal line

美式橄榄球球场
měishì gǎnlǎnqiú qiúchǎng
football field

球门区
qiúménqū
end zone

橄榄球
gǎnlǎnqiú
football

护膝
hùxī
pads

头盔
tóukuī
helmet

球鞋
qiúxié
cleat

球员
qiúyuán
football player

擒抱
qínbào
tackle (v)

传球
chuánqiú
pass (v)

接球
jiēqiú
catch (v)

词汇 cíhuì · vocabulary

暂停 zàntíng time out	球队 qiúduì team	防守 fángshǒu defense	啦啦队长 lāláduìzhǎng cheerleader	几比几? jǐbǐjǐ? What is the score?
漏接 lòujiē fumble	进攻 jìngōng attack	分数 fēnshù score	触地得分 chùdìdéfēn touchdown	谁领先? shuí lǐngxiān? Who is winning?

英式橄榄球 yīngshì gǎnlǎnqiú • rugby

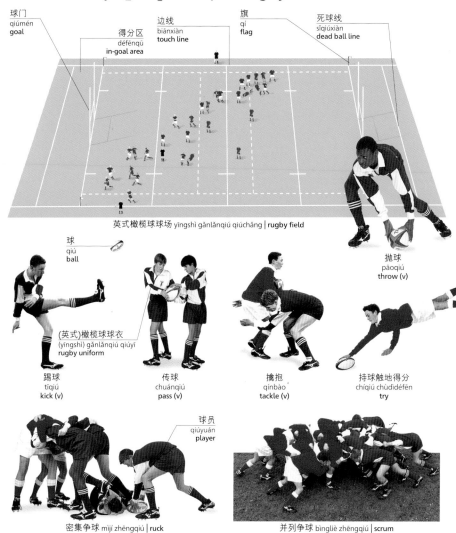

球门
qiúmén
goal

得分区
défēnqū
in-goal area

边线
biānxiàn
touch line

旗
qí
flag

死球线
sǐqiúxiàn
dead ball line

英式橄榄球球场 yīngshì gǎnlǎnqiú qiúchǎng | rugby field

球
qiú
ball

抛球
pāoqiú
throw (v)

(英式)橄榄球球衣
(yīngshì) gǎnlǎnqiú qiúyī
rugby uniform

踢球
tīqiú
kick (v)

传球
chuánqiú
pass (v)

擒抱
qínbào
tackle (v)

持球触地得分
chíqiú chùdìdéfēn
try

球员
qiúyuán
player

密集争球 mìjí zhēngqiú | ruck

并列争球 bìngliè zhēngqiú | scrum

足球 zúqiú • soccer

足球
zúqiú
soccer ball

守门员
shǒuményuán
goalkeeper

足球球衣
zúqiú qiúyī
soccer uniform

足球球员
zúqiú qiúyuán
soccer player

前锋
qiánfēng
forward

主裁判
zhǔcáipàn
referee

中圈
zhōngquān
center circle

足球场
zúqiúchǎng
soccer field

门柱
ménzhù
goalpost

球网
qiúwǎng
net

球门横梁
qiúmén héngliáng
crossbar

球门 qiúmén | **goal**

带球 dàiqiú | **dribble (v)**

头球
tóuqiú
head (v)

人墙
rénqiáng
wall

任意球 rènyìqiú | **free kick**

罚球区
fáqiúqū
penalty area

球门线
qiúmén xiàn
goal line

球门区
qiúmén qū
goal area

球门
qiúmén
goal

防守队员
fángshǒuduìyuán
defender

边裁
biāncái
linesman

角旗
jiǎoqí
corner flag

掷界外球 zhìjièwàiqiú
throw-in

踢球 tīqiú
kick (v)

球鞋
qiúxié
cleat

传球
chuánqiú
pass (v)

射门 shèmén | shoot (v)

救球
jiùqiú
save (v)

铲球
chǎnqiú
tackle (v)

词汇 cíhuì • vocabulary

体育场 tǐyùchǎng stadium	犯规 fànguī foul	黄牌 huángpái yellow card	联赛 liánsài league	加时 jiāshí extra time
进球得分 jìnqiúdéfēn score a goal (v)	角球 jiǎoqiú corner	越位 yuèwèi offside	平局 píngjú tie	替补队员 tìbǔduìyuán substitute
罚点球 fádiǎnqiú penalty	红牌 hóngpái red card	罚出场外 fáchūchǎngwài send off	半场 bànchǎng halftime	换人 huànrén substitution

曲棍类运动 qǔgùnlèi yùndòng · hockey

冰球 bīngqiú · ice hockey

防守区
fángshǒuqū
defending zone

球门线
qiúmén xiàn
goal line

进攻区
jìngōngqū
attack zone

中场
zhōngchǎng
neutral zone

守门员
shǒuményuán
goalkeeper

球门
qiúmén
goal

争球圈
zhēngqiúquān
face-off circle

中圈
zhōngquān
center circle

手套
shǒutào
glove

护肩
hùjiān
pad

冰球场
bīngqiú chǎng
ice hockey rink

球杆
qiúgān
stick

冰鞋
bīngxié
ice skate

曲棍球 qūgùnqiú · field hockey

曲棍球棒
qūgùnqiú bàng
hockey stick

曲棍球
qūgùnqiú
ball

冰球
bīngqiú
puck

冰球球员 bīngqiú qiúyuán
ice hockey player

滑行
huáxíng
skate (v)

击球
jīqiú
hit (v)

中文 zhōngwén · english

板球 bǎnqiú · cricket

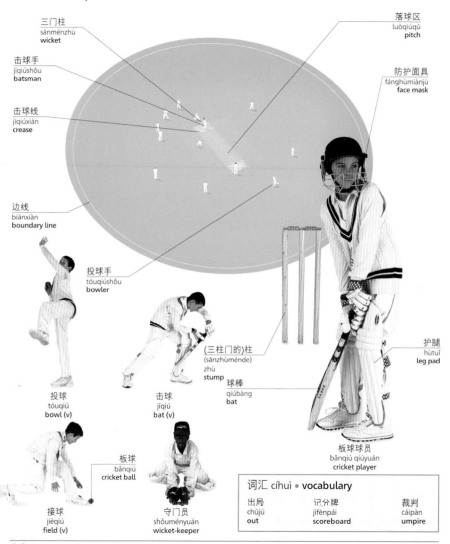

三门柱
sānménzhù
wicket

击球手
jīqiúshǒu
batsman

击球线
jīqiúxiàn
crease

边线
biānxiàn
boundary line

落球区
luòqiúqū
pitch

防护面具
fánghùmiànjù
face mask

投球手
tóuqiúshǒu
bowler

(三柱门的)柱
(sānzhùménde)
zhù
stump

球棒
qiúbàng
bat

护腿
hùtuǐ
leg pad

投球
tóuqiú
bowl (v)

击球
jīqiú
bat (v)

板球球员
bǎnqiú qiúyuán
cricket player

板球
bǎnqiú
cricket ball

接球
jiēqiú
field (v)

守门员
shǒuményuán
wicket-keeper

词汇 cíhuì · vocabulary

出局	记分牌	裁判
chūjú	jìfēnpái	cáipàn
out	scoreboard	umpire

篮球 lánqiú • basketball

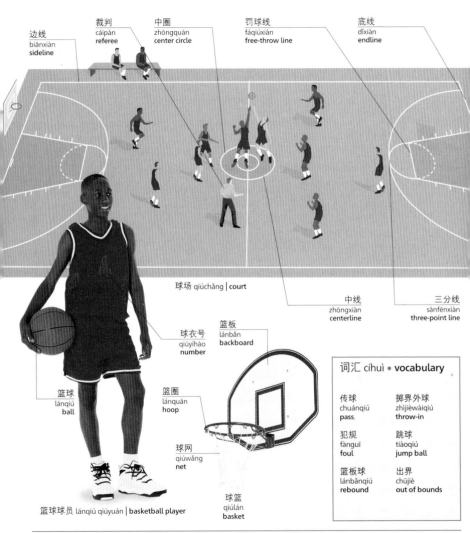

边线
biānxiàn
sideline

裁判
cáipàn
referee

中圈
zhōngquān
center circle

罚球线
fáqiúxiàn
free-throw line

底线
dǐxiàn
endline

球场 qiúchǎng | court

中线
zhōngxiàn
centerline

三分线
sānfēnxiàn
three-point line

球衣号
qiúyīhào
number

篮板
lánbǎn
backboard

篮球
lánqiú
ball

篮圈
lánquān
hoop

球网
qiúwǎng
net

篮球球员 lánqiú qiúyuán | basketball player

球篮
qiúlán
basket

词汇 cíhuì • vocabulary

传球 chuánqiú **pass**	掷界外球 zhíjièwàiqiú **throw-in**
犯规 fànguī **foul**	跳球 tiàoqiú **jump ball**
篮板球 lánbǎnqiú **rebound**	出界 chūjiè **out of bounds**

中文 zhōngwén • **english**

动作 dòngzuò · actions

掷球
zhìqiú
throw (v)

接球
jiēqiú
catch (v)

投篮
tóulán
shoot (v)

跳投
tiàotóu
jump (v)

盯人
dīngrén
mark (v)

阻挡
zǔdǎng
block (v)

运球
yùnqiú
dribble (v)

灌篮
guànlán
dunk (v)

排球 páiqiú · volleyball

拦网
lánwǎng
block (v)

球网
qiúwǎng
net

垫球
diànqiú
dig (v)

裁判
cáipàn
referee

护膝
hùxī
knee support

球场 qiúchǎng | court

棒球 bàngqiú · baseball

球场 qiúchǎng · field

左外野
zuǒwàiyě
left field

内野
nèiyě
infield

中外野
zhōngwàiyě
center field

球棒
qiúbàng
bat

头盔
tóukuī
helmet

守垒员
shǒulěiyuán
baseman

投球区土墩
tóuqiúqū tǔdūn
pitcher's mound

本垒
běnlěi
home plate

击球手 jīqiúshǒu | batter

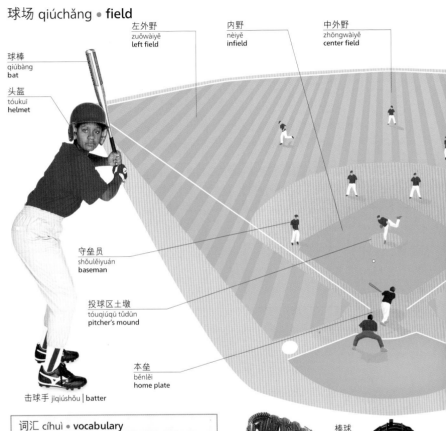

词汇 cíhuì · vocabulary

击球局 jīqiújú inning	安全上垒 ānquánshànglěi safe	界外球 jièwàiqiú foul ball
得分 défēn run	出局 chūjú out	好球 hǎoqiú strike

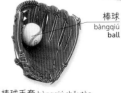

棒球手套 bàngqiú shǒutào
glove

棒球
bàngqiú
ball

防护面具 fánghùmiànjù
mask

动作 dòngzuò · actions

投球 tóuqiú | throw (v)

接球 jiēqiú | catch (v)

外野
wàiyě
outfield

右外野
yòuwàiyě
right field

边线
biānxiàn
foul line

球队
qiúduì
team

队员席
duìyuánxí
dugout

跑垒
pǎolěi
run (v)

守球 shǒuqiú | field (v)

滑垒
huálěi
slide (v)

触杀
chùshā
tag (v)

投球
tóuqiú
pitch (v)

击球
jīqiú
bat (v)

裁判
cáipàn
umpire

接球手 jiēqiúshǒu | catcher

投球手 tóuqiúshǒu | pitcher

比赛 bǐsài | play (v)

网球 wǎngqiú • tennis

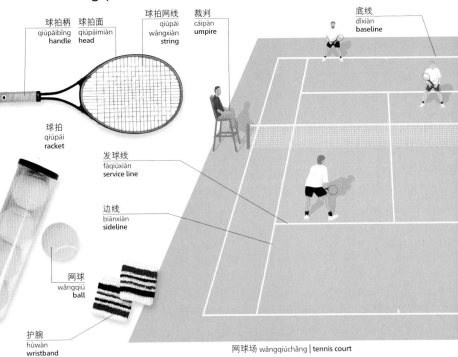

球拍柄
qiúpāibǐng
handle

球拍面
qiúpāimiàn
head

球拍网线
qiúpāi
wǎngxiàn
string

裁判
cáipàn
umpire

底线
dǐxiàn
baseline

球拍
qiúpāi
racket

发球线
fāqiúxiàn
service line

边线
biānxiàn
sideline

网球
wǎngqiú
ball

护腕
hùwàn
wristband

网球场 wǎngqiúchǎng | tennis court

词汇 cíhuì • vocabulary

单打 dāndǎ **singles**	盘，局 pán, jú **set**	零分 língfēn **love**	发球失误 fāqiúshīwù **fault**	削球 xiāoqiú **slice**	边裁 biāncái **linesman**
双打 shuāngdǎ **doubles**	比赛 bǐsài **match**	平分 píngfēn **deuce**	发球得分 fāqiúdéfēn **ace**	连续对打 liánxùduìdǎ **rally**	锦标赛 jǐnbiāosài **championship**
比赛 bǐsài **game**	抢七局 qiǎngqījú **tiebreaker**	发球方占先 fāqiúfāng zhànxiān **advantage**	近网短球 jìnwǎng duǎnqiú **dropshot**	触网! chùwǎng! **let!**	(球在空中)旋转 (qiúzàikōngzhōng) xuánzhuǎn **spin**

击球动作 jīqiúdòngzuò • strokes

发球
fāqiú
serve

拦击球
lánjīqiú
volley

回球
huíqiú
return

吊高球
diàogāoqiú
lob

正手
zhèngshǒu
forehand

反手
fǎnshǒu
backhand

球网
qiúwǎng
net

扣球
kòuqiú
smash

球童
qiútóng
ball boy

发球
fāqiú
serve (v)

网球鞋
wǎngqiúxié
tennis shoes

网球手 wǎngqiúshǒu | player

拍类运动 pāilèi yùndòng • racket games

羽毛球
yǔmáoqiú
shuttlecock

乒乓球拍
pīngpāngqiúpāi
paddle

羽毛球(运动)
yǔmáoqiú (yùndòng)
badminton

乒乓球
pīngpāngqiú
table tennis

壁球
bìqiú
squash

短拍壁球
duǎnpāibìqiú
racquetball

高尔夫球 gāo'ěrfūqiú ● golf

果岭
guǒlǐng
green

沙坑
shākēng
bunker

旗
qí
flag

发球区
fāqiúqū
teeing ground

球洞
qiúdòng
hole

挥杆
huīgān
swing (v)

球道
qiúdào
fairway

长草区
chángcǎoqū
rough

水障碍
shuǐzhàng'ài
water hazard

高尔夫球场
gāo'ěrfū qiúchǎng
golf course

短途小车
duǎntú xiǎochē
golf cart

站位
zhànwèi
stance

高尔夫球员 gāo'ěrfū qiúyuán | golfer

会所 huìsuǒ | clubhouse

球具 qiújù · equipment

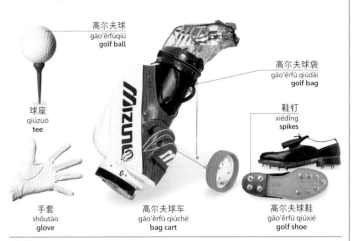

高尔夫球
gāo'ěrfūqiú
golf ball

球座
qiúzuò
tee

高尔夫球袋
gāo'ěrfū qiúdài
golf bag

鞋钉
xiédīng
spikes

手套
shǒutào
glove

高尔夫球车
gāo'ěrfū qiúchē
bag cart

高尔夫球鞋
gāo'ěrfū qiúxié
golf shoe

高尔夫球杆 gāo'ěrfū qiúgān · golf clubs

木杆
mùgān
wood

推杆
tuīgān
putter

铁杆
tiěgān
iron

挖起杆
wāqǐgān
wedge

动作 dòngzuò · actions

开球
kāiqiú
tee-off (v)

远打
yuǎndǎ
drive (v)

轻击
qīngjī
putt (v)

切击
qiējī
chip (v)

词汇 cíhuì · vocabulary

一杆入洞 yīgān rùdòng hole in one	标准杆数 biāozhǔn gānshù par	差点 chàdiǎn handicap	球童 qiútóng caddy	向后挥杆 xiàng hòu huīgān backswing	击球 jīqiú stroke
低于标准杆数 dīyú biāozhǔn gānshù under par	高于标准杆数 gāoyú biāozhǔn gānshù over par	巡回赛 xúnhuísài tournament	观众 guānzhòng spectators	练习挥杆 liànxí huīgān practice swing	打球线 dǎqiúxiàn line of play

田径运动 tiánjìng yùndòng • track and field

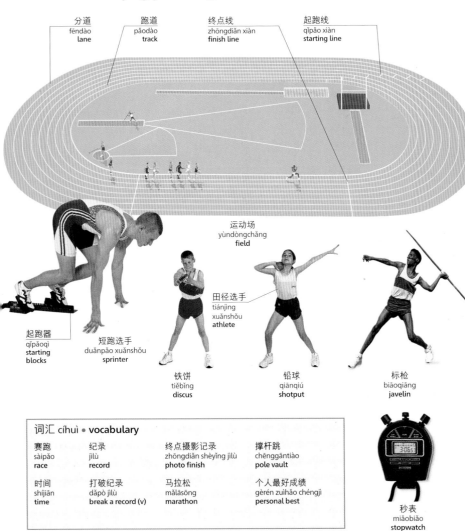

分道
fēndào
lane

跑道
pǎodào
track

终点线
zhōngdiǎn xiàn
finish line

起跑线
qǐpǎo xiàn
starting line

运动场
yùndòngchǎng
field

田径选手
tiánjìng
xuǎnshǒu
athlete

起跑器
qǐpǎoqì
starting
blocks

短跑选手
duǎnpǎo xuǎnshǒu
sprinter

铁饼
tiěbǐng
discus

铅球
qiānqiú
shotput

标枪
biāoqiāng
javelin

词汇 cíhuì • vocabulary

赛跑
sàipǎo
race

纪录
jìlù
record

终点摄影记录
zhōngdiǎn shèyǐng jìlù
photo finish

撑杆跳
chēnggāntiào
pole vault

时间
shíjiān
time

打破纪录
dǎpò jìlù
break a record (v)

马拉松
mǎlāsōng
marathon

个人最好成绩
gèrén zuìhǎo chéngjì
personal best

秒表
miǎobiǎo
stopwatch

接力棒
jiēlìbàng
baton

横杆
hénggǎn
crossbar

接力
jiēlì
relay race

跳高
tiàogāo
high jump

跳远
tiàoyuǎn
long jump

跨栏
kuàlán
hurdles

体操 tǐcāo • **gymnastics**

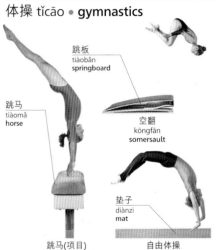

跳板
tiàobǎn
springboard

体操选手
tǐcāo xuǎnshǒu
gymnast

跳马
tiàomǎ
horse

空翻
kōngfān
somersault

平衡木 pínghéngmù | **beam**

丝带
sīdài
ribbon

垫子
diànzi
mat

跳马(项目)
tiàomǎ (xiàngmù)
vault

自由体操
zìyóutǐcāo
floor exercises

侧手翻
cèshǒufān
cartwheel

艺术体操
yìshù tǐcāo
rhythmic gymnastics

词汇 cíhuì • **vocabulary**

单杠 dāngàng **horizontal bar**	鞍马 ānmǎ **pommel horse**	吊环 diàohuán **rings**	奖牌 jiǎngpái **medals**	银牌 yínpái **silver**
双杠 shuānggàng **parallel bars**	高低杠 gāodīgàng **asymmetric bars**	领奖台 lǐngjiǎngtái **podium**	金牌 jīnpái **gold**	铜牌 tóngpái **bronze**

格斗运动 gédòu yùndòng ● combat sports

对手
duìshǒu
opponent

护盔
hùkuī
guard

手套
shǒutào
glove

腰带
yāodài
belt

空手道 kōngshǒudào | karate

跆拳道 táiquándào | tae kwon do

防护面具
fánghùmiànjù
mask

柔道 róudào | judo

竹剑
zhújiàn
sword

合气道 héqìdào | aikido

剑道 jiàndào | kendo

中国武术 zhōngguówǔshù
kung fu

泰拳 tàiquán | kickboxing

摔跤 shuāijiāo | wrestling

拳击 quánjī | boxing

动作 dòngzuò · actions

摔倒 shuāidǎo | fall

抓握 zhuāwò | hold

摔 shuāi | throw

压倒 yādǎo | pin

侧踢 cètī | kick

出拳 chūquán | punch

击打 jīdǎ | strike

跳踢 tiàotī | jump

挡 dǎng | block

劈 pī | chop

词汇 cíhuì · vocabulary

拳击台 quánjī tái **boxing ring**	回合 huíhé **round**	拳头 quántóu **fist**	黑带 hēidài **black belt**	卡波卫勒舞 kǎbōwèilèwǔ **capoeira**
拳击手套 quánjī shǒutào **boxing gloves**	拳击比赛 quánjī bǐsài **bout**	击倒 (对手) jīdǎo (duìshǒu) **knockout**	自卫 zìwèi **self-defense**	相扑 xiāngpū **sumo wrestling**
护齿 hùchǐ **mouth guard**	拳击练习 quánjī liànxí **sparring**	沙袋 shādài **punching bag**	武术 wǔshù **martial arts**	太极拳 tàijíquán **tai chi**

游泳 yóuyǒng ● swimming
泳具 yǒngjù ● equipment

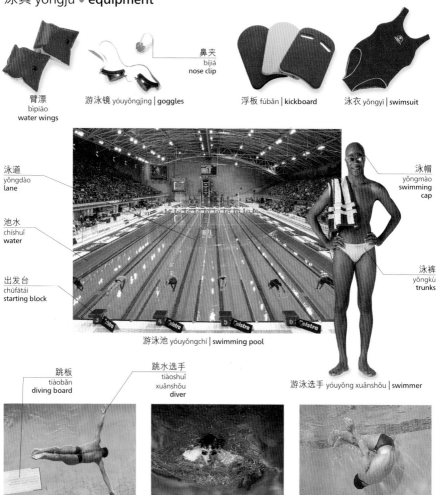

臂漂
bìpiāo
water wings

游泳镜 yóuyǒngjìng | goggles

鼻夹
bíjiá
nose clip

浮板 fúbǎn | kickboard

泳衣 yǒngyī | swimsuit

泳道
yǒngdào
lane

池水
chíshuǐ
water

出发台
chūfātái
starting block

泳帽
yǒngmào
swimming cap

泳裤
yǒngkù
trunks

游泳池 yóuyǒngchí | swimming pool

游泳选手 yóuyǒng xuǎnshǒu | swimmer

跳板
tiàobǎn
diving board

跳水选手
tiàoshuǐ
xuǎnshǒu
diver

跳水 tiàoshuǐ | dive (v)

游泳 yóuyǒng | swim (v)

转身 zhuǎnshēn | turn

泳姿 yǒngzī ● styles

自由泳 zìyóuyǒng | front crawl

蛙泳 wāyǒng | breaststroke

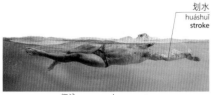

划水
huáshuǐ
stroke

仰泳 yǎngyǒng | backstroke

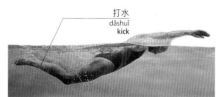

打水
dǎshuǐ
kick

蝶泳 diéyǒng | butterfly

水肺潜水 shuǐfèi qiánshuǐ ● scuba diving

氧气瓶
yǎngqìpíng
air cylinder

潜水服
qiánshuǐfú
wetsuit

潜水面罩
qiánshuǐ miànzhào
mask

脚蹼
jiǎopǔ
fin

呼吸调节器
hūxītiáojié qì
regulator

负重腰带
fùzhòng yāodài
weight belt

水下呼吸管
shuǐxià hūxīguǎn
snorkel

词汇 cíhuì ● vocabulary

跳水 tiàoshuǐ dive	踩水 cǎishuǐ tread water (v)	锁柜 suǒguì lockers	水球 shuǐqiú water polo	浅水区 qiǎnshuǐqū shallow end	抽筋 chōujīn cramp
高台跳水 gāotái tiàoshuǐ high dive	出发跳水 chūfā tiàoshuǐ racing dive	救生员 jiùshēngyuán lifeguard	深水区 shēnshuǐqū deep end	花样游泳 huāyàng yóuyǒng synchronized swimming	溺水 nìshuǐ drown (v)

帆船运动 fānchuán yùndòng • sailing

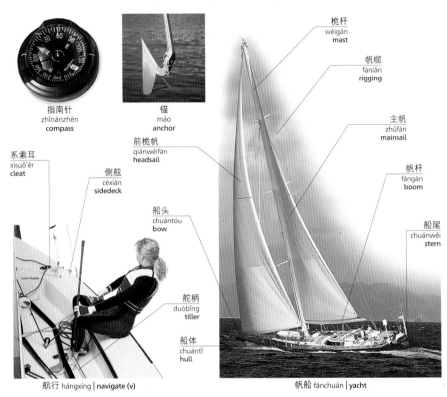

指南针
zhǐnánzhēn
compass

锚
máo
anchor

前桅帆
qiánwéifān
headsail

桅杆
wéigān
mast

帆缆
fānlǎn
rigging

主帆
zhǔfān
mainsail

帆杆
fāngān
boom

船尾
chuánwěi
stern

系索耳
xìsuǒ'ěr
cleat

侧舷
cèxián
sidedeck

船头
chuántóu
bow

舵柄
duòbǐng
tiller

船体
chuántǐ
hull

航行 hángxíng | navigate (v)

帆船 fānchuán | yacht

救生器具 jiùshēngqìjù • safety

照明弹
zhàomíngdàn
flare

救生圈
jiùshēngquān
life buoy

救生衣
jiùshēngyī
life jacket

救生筏
jiùshēngfá
life raft

水上运动 shuǐshàng yùndòng · watersports

桨手
jiǎngshǒu
rower

桨
jiǎng
oar

皮筏
pífá
kayak

双叶桨
shuāngyèjiǎng
paddle

划船 huáchuán | row (v)

划独木舟
huádúmùzhōu
kayaking

帆
fān
sail

冲浪板
chōnglàngbǎn
surfboard

滑水橇
huáshuǐqiāo
ski

帆板运动员
fānbǎn
yùndòngyuán
windsurfer

冲浪
chōnglàng
surfing

滑水
huáshuǐ
waterskiing

快艇
kuàitǐng
speedboating

帆板
fānbǎn
board

套脚带
tàojiǎodài
footstrap

帆板运动 fānbǎn yùndòng | windsurfing

皮划艇
píhuátǐng
rafting

水上摩托
shuǐshàng mótuō
jet skiing

词汇 cíhuì · vocabulary

滑水者 huáshuǐzhě waterskier	艇员 tǐngyuán crew	风 fēng wind	浪花 lànghuā surf	帆脚索 fānjiǎosuǒ sheet	稳向板 wěnxiàngbǎn centerboard
冲浪运动员 chōnglàng yùndòngyuán surfer	抢风航行 qiǎngfēng hángxíng tack (v)	波浪 bōlàng wave	激流 jīliú rapids	舵 duò rudder	(船)倾覆 (chuán) qīngfù capsize (v)

马上运动 mǎshàng yùndòng • horseback riding

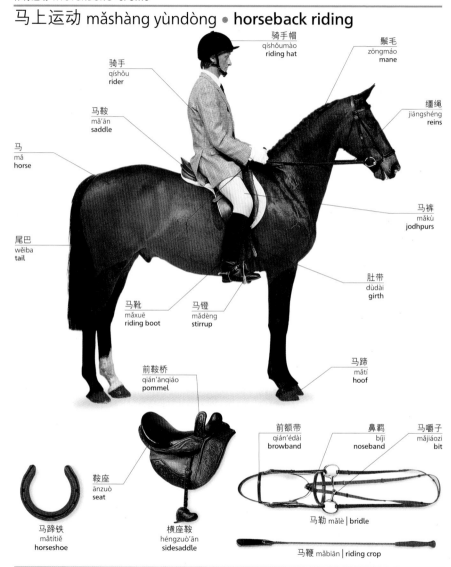

骑手帽
qíshǒumào
riding hat

鬃毛
zōngmáo
mane

骑手
qíshǒu
rider

马鞍
mǎ'ān
saddle

缰绳
jiāngshéng
reins

马
mǎ
horse

马裤
mǎkù
jodhpurs

尾巴
wěiba
tail

肚带
dùdài
girth

马靴
mǎxuē
riding boot

马镫
mǎdèng
stirrup

马蹄
mǎtí
hoof

前鞍桥
qián'ānqiáo
pommel

前额带
qián'édài
browband

鼻羁
bíjī
noseband

马嚼子
mǎjiáozi
bit

鞍座
ānzuò
seat

马勒 mǎlè | bridle

马蹄铁
mǎtítiě
horseshoe

横座鞍
héngzuò'ān
sidesaddle

马鞭 mǎbiān | riding crop

赛事 sàishì • events

赛马
sàimǎ
racehorse

障碍
zhàng'ài
fence

赛马(比赛)
sàimǎ (bǐsài)
horse race

障碍赛
zhàng'àisài
steeplechase

轻驾车赛
qīngjiàchēsài
harness race

牛仔竞技表演
niúzǎijìngjì biǎoyǎn
rodeo

越障碍赛
yuèzhàng'àisài
showjumping

双套马车赛
shuāngtào mǎchēsài
carriage race

长途旅行 chángtú lǚxíng | trail riding

花式骑术 huāshìqíshù | dressage

马球 mǎqiú | polo

词汇 cíhuì • vocabulary

慢步 mànbù walk	慢跑 mànpǎo canter	跳跃 tiàoyuè jump	笼头 lóngtou halter	围场 wéichǎng paddock	无障碍赛马 wúzhàng'àisàimǎ flat race
小跑 xiǎopǎo trot	疾驰 jíchí gallop	马夫 mǎfū groom	马厩 mǎjiù stable	竞技场 jìngjìchǎng arena	赛马场 sàimǎchǎng racecourse

钓鱼 diàoyú • **fishing**

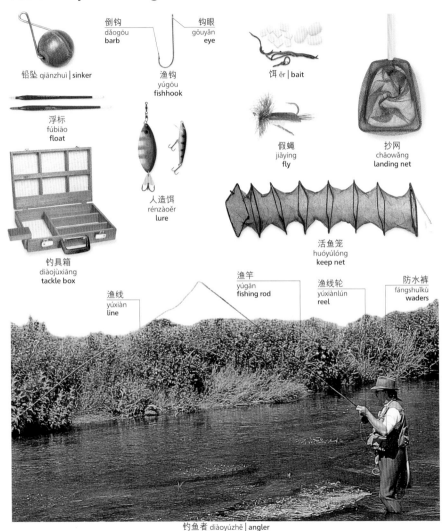

铅坠 qiānzhuì | sinker

倒钩
dǎogōu
barb

钩眼
gōuyǎn
eye

渔钩
yúgōu
fishhook

饵 ěr | bait

浮标
fúbiāo
float

假蝇
jiǎyíng
fly

抄网
chāowǎng
landing net

人造饵
rénzàoěr
lure

钓具箱
diàojùxiāng
tackle box

活鱼笼
huóyúlóng
keep net

渔线
yúxiàn
line

渔竿
yúgān
fishing rod

渔线轮
yúxiànlún
reel

防水裤
fángshuǐkù
waders

钓鱼者 diàoyúzhě | angler

垂钓种类 chuídiào zhǒnglèi · **types of fishing**

淡水垂钓
dànshuǐ chuídiào
freshwater fishing

假蝇垂钓
jiǎyíng chuídiào
fly fishing

休闲垂钓
xiūxián chuídiào
sport fishing

深海垂钓
shēnhǎi chuídiào
deep sea fishing

激浪投钓
jīlàng tóudiào
surfcasting

活动 huódòng · **activities**

撒网
sāwǎng
cast (v)

捕捉
bǔzhuō
catch (v)

收线
shōuxiàn
reel in (v)

网捕
wǎngbǔ
net (v)

放生
fàngshēng
release (v)

词汇 cíhuì · **vocabulary**

装饵 zhuāng'ěr **bait (v)**	钓具 diàojù **tackle**	雨衣 yǔyī **rain gear**	钓鱼许可证 diàoyú xǔkězhèng **fishing license**	渔篓 yúlǒu **creel**
咬钩 yǎogōu **bite (v)**	线轴 xiànzhóu **spool**	杆 gān **pole**	海洋捕捞 hǎiyáng bǔlāo **marine fishing**	渔叉捕鱼 yúchābǔyú **spearfishing**

滑雪 huáxuě • skiing

滑雪坡道
huáxuě pōdào
ski slope

缆车吊椅
lǎnchē diàoyǐ
chairlift

缆车
lǎnchē
cable car

雪道
xuědào
ski run

安全护栏
ānquánhùlán
safety barrier

滑雪杖
huáxuězhàng
ski pole

手套
shǒutào
glove

板边
bǎnbiān
edge

板尖
bǎnjiān
tip

滑雪板
huáxuěbǎn
ski

滑雪靴
huáxuēxuē
ski boot

滑雪者
huáxuězhě
skier

滑雪衫
huáxuěshān
ski jacket

项目 xiàngmù • events

高山速降
gāoshān sùjiàng
downhill skiing

旗门杆
qíméngǎn
gate

小回转
xiǎohuízhuǎn
slalom

跳台滑雪
tiàotái huáxuě
ski jump

越野滑雪
yuèyě huáxuě
cross-country skiing

冬季运动 dōngjì yùndòng • winter sports

攀冰
pānbīng
ice climbing

溜冰
liūbīng
ice-skating

花样滑冰
huāyàng huábīng
figure skating

滑雪镜
huáxuějìng
goggles

冰鞋
bīngxié
skate

单板滑雪
dānbǎn huáxuě
snowboarding

长橇滑雪
chángqiāo huáxuě
bobsled

小型橇
xiǎoxíngqiāo
luge

机动雪橇
jīdòng xuěqiāo
snowmobile

乘橇滑行
chéngqiāo huáxíng
sledding

词汇 cíhuì • vocabulary

高山滑雪 gāoshān huáxuě **alpine skiing**	狗拉雪橇 gǒulā xuěqiāo **dogsledding**
大回转 dàhuízhuǎn **giant slalom**	速滑 sùhuá **speed skating**
雪道外 xuědàowài **off-piste**	冬季两项 dōngjì liǎngxiàng **biathlon**
冰上溜石 bīngshàng liúshí **curling**	雪崩 xuěbēng **avalanche**

其他运动 qítāyùndòng • **other sports**

滑翔机
huáxiángjī
glider

悬挂式滑翔机
xuánguàshì
huáxiángjī
hang-glider

滑翔
huáxiáng
gliding

降落伞
jiàngluòsǎn
parachute

悬挂滑翔
xuánguà huáxiáng
hang-gliding

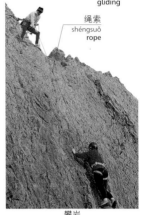

绳索
shéngsuǒ
rope

攀岩
pānyán
rock climbing

跳伞
tiàosǎn
parachuting

滑翔伞
huáxiángsǎn
paragliding

特技跳伞
tèjìtiàosǎn
skydiving

悬绳下降
xuánshéng xiàjiàng
rappelling

蹦极
bèngjí
bungee jumping

汽车拉力赛
qìchē lālìsài
rally driving

赛车手
sàicheshou
race-car driver

赛车
sàichē
auto racing

摩托车越野赛
mótuōchē yuèyěsài
motocross

摩托车赛
mótuōchēsài
motorcycle racing

滑板
huábǎn
skateboard

滑板运动
huábǎn yùndòng
skateboarding

轮滑
lúnhuá
inline skating

球棒
qiúbàng
stick

长曲棍球
cháng qūgùnqiú
lacrosse

面具
miànjù
mask

花剑
huājiàn
foil

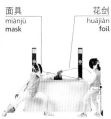
击剑
jījiàn
fencing

保龄球瓶
bǎolíngqiú píng
pin

弓
gōng
bow

箭
jiàn
arrow

箭袋
jiàndài
quiver

射箭
shèjiàn
archery

靶
bǎ
target

射击
shèjī
target shooting

保龄球
bǎolíngqiú
bowling ball

保龄球运动
bǎolíngqiú yùndòng
bowling

美式台球
měishìtáiqiú
pool

斯诺克台球
sīnuòkètáiqiú
snooker

健身 jiànshēn • fitness

健身车
jiànshēnchē
exercise bike

健身器械
jiànshēn qìxiè
gym machine

长椅
chángyǐ
bench

力量训练器
lìliàng xùnliànqì
free weights

横杠
hénggàng
bar

健身房
jiànshēnfáng
gym

划船机
huáchuánjī
rowing machine

跑步机
pǎobùjī
treadmill

交叉训练器
jiāochā xùnliànqì
elliptical trainer

私人教练
sīrén jiàoliàn
personal trainer

踏步机
tàbùjī
stair machine

游泳池
yóuyǒngchí
swimming pool

桑拿浴
sāngnáyù
sauna

锻炼 duànliàn · exercises

伸展腿
shēnzhǎntuǐ
stretch

弓箭步压腿
gōngjiànbù yātuǐ
lunge

紧身衣
jǐnshēnyī
tights

俯卧撑
fǔwòchēng
push-up

哑铃
yǎlíng
dumbbell

蹲起
dūnqǐ
squat

仰卧起坐
yǎngwòqǐzuò
sit-up

二头肌训练
èrtóujī xùnliàn
bicep curl

蹬腿
dēngtuǐ
leg press

杠铃横杆
gànglíng
hénggān
weight bar

运动鞋
yùndòngxié
sneakers

扩胸
kuòxiōng
chest press

重量训练
zhòngliàng xùnliàn
weight training

慢跑
mànpǎo
jogging

普拉提
pǔlātí
Pilates

词汇 cíhuì · vocabulary

训练 xùnliàn train (v)	原地跑 yuándìpǎo jog in place (v)	伸展 shēnzhǎn extend (v)	跳绳 tiàoshéng jumping rope	循环训练法 xúnhuán xùnliànfǎ circuit training
热身 rèshēn warm up (v)	弯曲(四肢) wānqū (sìzhī) flex (v)	引体向上 yǐntǐ xiàngshàng pull up (v)	搏击操 bójīcāo boxercise	

休闲 xiūxián
leisure

剧院 jùyuàn · theater

幕
mù
curtain

舞台侧翼
wǔtáicèyì
wings

布景
bùjǐng
set

观众
guānzhòng
audience

乐队
yuèduì
orchestra

舞台 wǔtái | stage

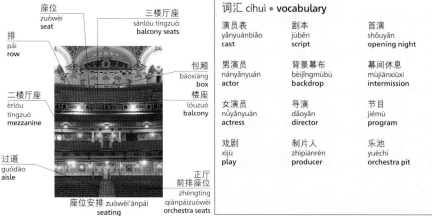

座位
zuòwèi
seat

排
pái
row

三楼厅座
sānlóu tīngzuò
balcony seats

包厢
bāoxiāng
box

楼座
lóuzuò
balcony

二楼厅座
èrlóu
tīngzuò
mezzanine

过道
guòdào
aisle

正厅
前排座位
zhèngtīng
qiánpáizuòwèi
orchestra seats

座位安排 zuòwèi'ānpái
seating

词汇 cíhuì · vocabulary

演员表 yǎnyuánbiǎo cast	剧本 jùběn script	首演 shǒuyǎn opening night
男演员 nányǎnyuán actor	背景幕布 bèijǐngmùbù backdrop	幕间休息 mùjiānxiūxi intermission
女演员 nǚyǎnyuán actress	导演 dǎoyǎn director	节目 jiémù program
戏剧 xìjù play	制片人 zhìpiānrén producer	乐池 yuèchí orchestra pit

音乐会 yīnyuèhuì | concert

音乐剧 yīnyuèjù | musical

戏装
xìzhuāng
costume

芭蕾舞 bālěiwǔ | ballet

词汇 cíhuì • vocabulary

引座员
yǐnzuòyuán
usher

古典音乐
gǔdiǎn yīnyuè
classical music

乐谱
yuèpǔ
musical score

声带
shēngdài
soundtrack

鼓掌喝彩
gǔzhǎnghècǎi
applaud (v)

再来一次
zàiláiyícì
encore

演出什么时候开始?
yǎnchū shénme shíhou kāishǐ?
What time does it start?

我想要两张今晚演出的票。
wǒ xiǎng yào liǎngzhāng jīnwǎn
yǎnchūde piào.
**I'd like two tickets for tonight's
performance.**

歌剧 gējù | opera

电影院 diànyǐngyuàn • movies

爆米花
bàomǐhuā
popcorn

大厅
dàtīng
lobby

售票处
shòupiàochù
box office

海报
hǎibào
poster

电影放映厅
diànyǐng fàngyìngtīng
movie theater

银幕
yínmù
screen

词汇 cíhuì • vocabulary

喜剧片
xǐjùpiàn
comedy

惊险片
jīngxiǎnpiàn
thriller

恐怖片
kǒngbùpiàn
horror movie

西部片
xībùpiàn
Western

爱情片
àiqíngpiàn
romance

科幻片
kēhuànpiàn
science fiction movie

冒险片
màoxiǎnpiàn
adventure movie

动画片
dònghuàpiàn
animated movie

乐队 yuèduì · orchestra

弦乐器 xiányuèqì · strings

竖琴
shùqín
harp

指挥
zhǐhuī
conductor

低音提琴
dīyīntíqín
double bass

小提琴
xiǎotíqín
violin

指挥台
zhǐhuītái
podium

中提琴
zhōngtíqín
viola

大提琴
dàtíqín
cello

乐谱
yuèpǔ
score

钢琴 gāngqín | piano

高音谱号
gāoyīn pǔhào
treble clef

音符
yīnfú
note

五线谱
wǔxiànpǔ
staff

低音谱号
dīyīn pǔhào
bass clef

Andante

rit.

记谱法 jìpǔfǎ | notation

词汇 cíhuì · vocabulary

序曲
xùqǔ
overture

奏鸣曲
zòumíngqǔ
sonata

休止符
xiūzhǐfú
rest

升号
shēnghào
sharp

本位号
běnwèihào
natural

音阶
yīnjiē
scale

交响乐
jiāoxiǎngyuè
symphony

乐器
yuèqì
instruments

音高
yīngāo
pitch

降号
jiànghào
flat

小节线
xiǎojiéxiàn
bar

指挥棒
zhǐhuībàng
baton

木管乐器 mùguǎnyuèqì · **woodwind**

短笛
duǎndí
piccolo

长笛
chángdí
flute

双簧管
shuānghuángguǎn
oboe

英国管
yīngguóguǎn
English horn

单簧管
dānhuángguǎn
clarinet

低音单簧管
dīyīn dānhuángguǎn
bass clarinet

巴松管
bāsōngguǎn
bassoon

倍低音管
bèidīyīnguǎn
double bassoon

萨克斯管
sàkèsīguǎn
saxophone

打击乐器 dǎjīyuèqì · **percussion**

颤音琴
chànyīnqín
vibraphone

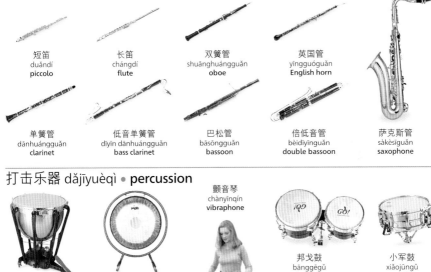

邦戈鼓
bānggēgǔ
bongos

小军鼓
xiǎojūngǔ
snare drum

定音鼓
dìngyīngǔ
kettledrum

锣
luó
gong

钹
bó
cymbals

铃鼓
línggǔ
tambourine

脚踏板
jiǎotàbǎn
foot pedal

三角铁
sānjiǎotiě
triangle

沙锤
shāchuí
maracas

铜管乐器 tóngguǎn yuèqì · **brass**

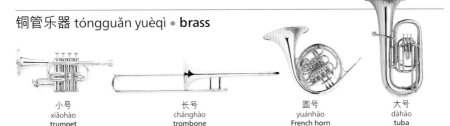

小号
xiǎohào
trumpet

长号
chánghào
trombone

圆号
yuánhào
French horn

大号
dàhào
tuba

音乐会 yīnyuèhuì • concert

吉他手
jítāshǒu
guitarist

主唱
zhǔchàng
lead singer

鼓手
gǔshǒu
drummer

麦克风
màikèfēng
microphone

扩音器
kuòyīnqì
speaker

歌迷
gēmí
fans

摇滚音乐会 yáogǔn yīnyuèhuì | rock concert

乐器 yuèqì • instruments

拾音器
shíyīnqì
pickup

琴颈
qínjǐng
neck

琴衍
qínyǎn
fret

弦轴
xiánzhóu
tuning peg

弦
xián
string

琴马
qínmǎ
bridge

鼓
gǔ
drum

低音吉他
dīyīn jítā
bass guitar

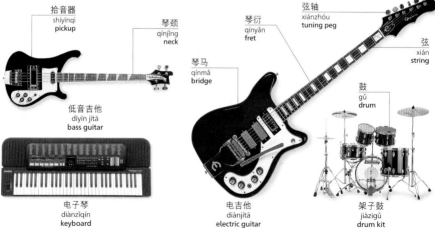

电子琴
diànzǐqín
keyboard

电吉他
diànjítā
electric guitar

架子鼓
jiàzigǔ
drum kit

音乐风格 yīnyuè fēnggé • musical styles

爵士乐 juéshìyuè | jazz

蓝调音乐 lándiào yīnyuè | blues

朋克音乐 péngkè yīnyuè | punk

民间音乐 mínjiān yīnyuè | folk music

流行音乐 liúxíng yīnyuè | pop

舞曲 wǔqǔ | dance

说唱音乐 shuōchàng yīnyuè
rap

重金属摇滚 zhòngjīnshǔyáogǔn
heavy metal

古典音乐 gǔdiǎn yīnyuè
classical music

词汇 cíhuì • vocabulary

歌曲	歌词	旋律	节拍	雷盖音乐	乡村音乐	聚光灯
gēqǔ	gēcí	xuánlǜ	jiépāi	léigài yīnyuè	xiāngcūn yīnyuè	jùguāngdēng
song	lyrics	melody	beat	reggae	country	spotlight

观光 guānguāng • sightseeing

旅行路线
lǚxíng lùxiàn
itinerary

敞篷
chǎngpéng
open-top

This is an official London Sightseeing Bus.

LONDON PRIDE

观光巴士 guānguāngbāshì | tour bus

游客
yóukè
tourist

游览胜地 yóulǎn shèngdì | tourist attraction

导游
dǎoyóu
tour guide

团体旅游
tuántǐlǚyóu
guided tour

小雕像
xiǎodiāoxiàng
figurine

纪念品
jìniànpǐn
souvenirs

词汇 cíhuì • vocabulary

开门 kāimén open	旅行指南 lǚxíngzhǐnán guidebook	便携式摄像机 biànxiéshì shèxiàngjī camcorder	左 zuǒ left	...在哪里? ...zàinǎli? Where is ...?
关门 guānmén closed	胶片 jiāopiàn film	照相机 zhàoxiàngjī camera	右 yòu right	我迷路了。 wǒ mílùle. I'm lost.
入场费 rùchǎngfèi entrance fee	电池 diànchí batteries	(行路的)指引 (xínglùde) zhǐyǐn directions	直行 zhíxíng straight ahead	你能告诉我到...的路吗? nǐ néng gàosù wǒ dào...delù ma? Can you tell me the way to ...?

名胜 míngshèng · attractions

绘画
huìhuà
painting

展品
zhǎnpǐn
exhibit

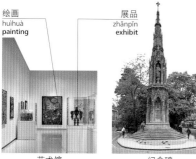

展览
zhǎnlǎn
exhibition

古迹
gǔjì
famous ruin

艺术馆
yìshùguǎn
art gallery

纪念碑
jìniànbēi
monument

博物馆
bówùguǎn
museum

历史建筑
lìshǐ jiànzhù
historic building

赌场
dǔchǎng
casino

庭园
tíngyuán
gardens

国家公园
guójiā gōngyuán
national park

游览信息 yóulǎnxìnxī · information

日程
richéng
times

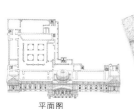

平面图
píngmiàntú
floor plan

地图
dìtú
map

时刻表
shíkèbiǎo
schedule

旅游问询处
lǚyóu wènxúnchù
tourist information

户外活动 hùwàihuódòng · **outdoor activities**

小道
xiǎodào
footpath

日晷
rìguǐ
sundial

咖啡馆
kāfēiguǎn
café

公园 gōngyuán | park

草坪
cǎopíng
grass

长椅
chángyǐ
bench

法式花园
fǎshì huāyuán
formal gardens

过山车
guòshānchē
roller coaster

游乐园
yóulèyuán
fairground

主题公园
zhǔtí gōngyuán
theme park

野生动物园
yěshēng dòngwùyuán
safari park

动物园
dòngwùyuán
zoo

活动 huódòng • activities

骑自行车
qízíxíngchē
cycling

慢跑
mànpǎo
jogging

滑板
huábǎn
skateboarding

滚轴溜冰
gǔnzhóu liūbīng
rollerblading

骑马专用道
qímǎ zhuānyòngdào
bridle path

观鸟
guānniǎo
bird-watching

骑马
qímǎ
horseback riding

远足
yuǎnzú
hiking

食物篮
shíwùlán
hamper

野餐
yěcān
picnic

游乐场 yóulèchǎng • playground

沙坑
shākēng
sandbox

儿童戏水池
értóng xìshuǐchí
wading pool

秋千
qiūqiān
swing

跷跷板 qiāoqiāobǎn | seesaw

滑梯 huátī | slide

攀登架 pāndēngjià | climbing frame

海滩 hǎitān ● **beach**

旅馆 lǚguǎn **hotel**	遮阳伞 zhēyángsǎn **beach umbrella**	海滩小屋 hǎitān xiǎowū **beach hut**	沙 shā **sand**	海浪 hǎilàng **wave**	海 hǎi **sea**

海滨游泳袋
hǎibīn yóuyǒngdài
beach bag

比基尼泳装
bǐjīníyǒngzhuāng
bikini

晒日光浴 shài rìguāngyù | **sunbathe (v)**

救生员
jiùshēngyuán
lifeguard

救生瞭望塔
jiùshēng liàowàngtǎ
lifeguard tower

防风屏
fángfēngpíng
windbreak

海滨步道
hǎibīn bùdào
boardwalk

轻便折叠躺椅
qīngbiàn zhédiétǎngyǐ
deck chair

太阳镜
tàiyángjìng
sunglasses

遮阳帽
zhēyángmào
sun hat

防晒油
fángshàiyóu
suntan lotion

防晒液
fángshàiyè
sunblock

浮水气球
fúshuǐqìqiú
beach ball

游泳圈
yóuyǒngquān
inflatable ring

游泳衣
yóuyǒngyī
swimsuit

铲子
chǎnzi
shovel

桶
tǒng
pail

海滩浴巾
hǎitān yùjīn
beach towel

沙堡
shābǎo
sandcastle

贝壳
bèiké
shell

露营 lùyíng • camping

卫生间
wèishēngjiān
restrooms

垃圾箱
lājīxiāng
waste disposal

浴室
yùshì
shower block

接电装置
jiēdiàn zhuāngzhì
electric hookup

防雨罩
fángyǔzhào
flysheet

地钉
dìdīng
tent peg

防风绳
fángfēng shéng
guy rope

旅行拖车
lǚxíng tuōchē
camper

露营地 lùyíngdì | campground

词汇 cíhuì • vocabulary

露营 lùyíng **camp (v)**	宿营地 sùyíngdì **site**	野餐长椅 yěcān chángyǐ **picnic bench**	木炭 mùtàn **charcoal**
营地管理处 yíngdì guǎnlǐchù **site manager's office**	支帐篷 zhīzhàngpeng **pitch a tent (v)**	吊床 diàochuáng **hammock**	引火物 yǐnhuǒwù **firelighter**
自由宿营地 zìyóu sùyíngdì **sites available**	帐篷杆 zhàngpenggān **tent pole**	野营车 yěyíngchē **camper van**	点火 diǎnhuǒ **light a fire (v)**
满 mǎn **full**	行军床 xíngjūn chuáng **camp bed**	拖车 tuōchē **trailer**	营火 yínghuǒ **campfire**

支架
zhījià
frame

铺地防潮布
pūdì fángcháobù
ground sheet

背包
bèibāo
backpack

保温瓶
bǎowēnpíng
vacuum flask

水瓶
shuǐpíng
water bottle

帐篷
zhàngpeng
tent

驱虫剂
qūchóngjì
insect repellent

营地灯
yíngdìdēng
flashlight

蚊帐
wénzhàng
mosquito net

保暖内衣
bǎonuǎn nèiyī
thermal underwear

徒步靴
túbùxuē
hiking boots

雨衣
yǔyī
rain gear

睡袋
shuìdài
sleeping bag

睡垫
shuìdiàn
sleeping mat

野营炉
yěyínglú
camping stove

烧烤架
shāokǎojià
barbecue grill

充气床垫 chōngqì chuángdiàn | air mattress

家庭娱乐 jiātíngyúlè · **home entertainment**

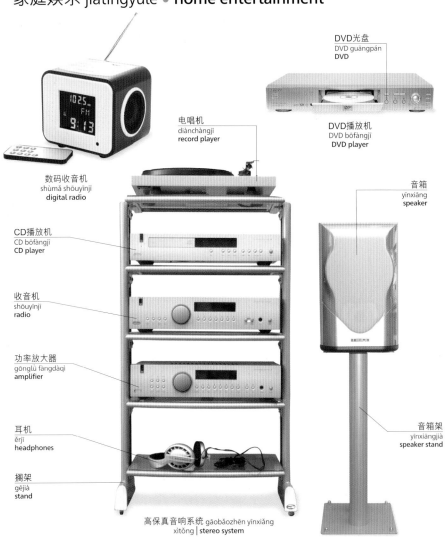

DVD光盘
DVD guāngpán
DVD

DVD播放机
DVD bōfàngjī
DVD player

电唱机
diànchàngjī
record player

数码收音机
shùmǎ shōuyīnjī
digital radio

音箱
yīnxiāng
speaker

CD播放机
CD bōfàngjī
CD player

收音机
shōuyīnjī
radio

功率放大器
gōnglǜ fàngdàqì
amplifier

耳机
ěrjī
headphones

搁架
gējià
stand

音箱架
yīnxiāngjià
speaker stand

高保真音响系统 gāobǎozhēn yīnxiǎng xìtǒng | **stereo system**

显示屏
xiǎnshìpíng
screen

接目杯
jiēmùbēi
eyecup

电视机顶盒
diànshì jīdǐnghé
DTV converter box

便携式摄像机
biànxiéshì shèxiàngjī
camcorder

卫星电视天线
wèixīng diànshì tiānxiàn
satellite dish

平板电视
píngbǎn diànshì
flatscreen TV

控制台
kòngzhìtái
console

快进
kuàijìn
fast-forward

暂停
zàntíng
pause

录制
lùzhì
record

音量
yīnliàng
volume

倒带
dàodài
rewind

播放
bōfàng
play

停止
tíngzhǐ
stop

操纵手柄
cāozòng shǒubǐng
controller

视频游戏 shìpín yóuxì | video game

遥控器 yáokòngqì | remote control

词汇 cíhuì · vocabulary

激光唱盘 jīguāng chàngpán **CD**	故事片 gùshìpiàn **feature film**	节目 jiémù **program**	收费频道 shōufèi píndào **pay-per-view channel**	看电视 kàndiànshì **watch television (v)**
盒式录音带 héshì lùyīndài **cassette tape**	广告 guǎnggào **advertisement**	立体声 lìtǐshēng **stereo**	换频道 huàn píndào **change channel (v)**	关电视 guāndiànshì **turn off the television (v)**
盒式磁带录音机 héshì cídàilùyīnjī **cassette player**	数字式 shùzìshì **digital**	有线电视 yǒuxiàn diànshì **cable television**	调收音机 tiáoshōuyīnjī **tune the radio (v)**	开电视 kāidiànshì **turn on the television (v)**
流媒体 liúméitǐ **streaming**	高清晰度 gāo qīngxī dù **high-definition**	无线网络 wúxiàn wǎngluò **Wi-Fi**		

摄影 shèyǐng · photography

快门键
kuàimén jiàn
shutter release

光圈调节环
guāngquān tiáojiéhuán
aperture dial

镜头
jìngtóu
lens

滤镜
lǜjìng
filter

镜头盖
jìngtóugài
lens cap

单镜头反光照相机 dānjìngtóu fǎnguāngzhàoxiàngjī | SLR camera

闪光灯
shǎnguāngdēng
flash gun

曝光表
bàoguāngbiǎo
light meter

变焦镜头
biànjiāo jìngtóu
zoom lens

三脚架
sānjiǎojià
tripod

相机种类 xiàngjī zhǒnglèi · types of camera

宝丽来相机
bǎolìlái xiàngjī
Polaroid camera

闪光灯
shǎnguāngdēng
flash

数码相机
shùmǎ xiàngjī
digital camera

照相手机
zhàoxiàng shǒujī
camera phone

一次性相机
yícìxìng xiàngjī
disposable camera

照相 zhàoxiàng · photograph (v)

胶卷
jiāojuǎn
film roll

胶片
jiāopiàn
film

调焦
tiáojiāo
focus (v)

冲洗
chōngxǐ
develop (v)

底片
dǐpiàn
negative

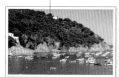

全景照
quánjǐngzhào
landscape

人像照
rénxiàngzhào
portrait

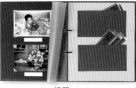

相片 xiàngpiàn | photograph

相册
xiàngcè
photo album

相框
xiàngkuàng
picture frame

问题 wèntí · problems

曝光不足
pùguāng bùzú
underexposed

曝光过度
pùguāng guòdù
overexposed

调焦不准
tiáojiāo bùzhǔn
out of focus

红眼
hóngyǎn
red eye

词汇 cíhuì · vocabulary

取景器
qǔjǐngqì
viewfinder

相机盒
xiàngjīhé
camera case

曝光
pùguāng
exposure

暗室
ànshì
darkroom

样片
yàngpiàn
print

无光泽
wúguāngzé
matte

有光泽
yǒuguāngzé
gloss

放大
fàngdà
enlargement

请冲洗这个胶卷。
qǐng chōngxǐ zhège jiāojuǎn.
I'd like this film processed.

游戏 yóuxì · games

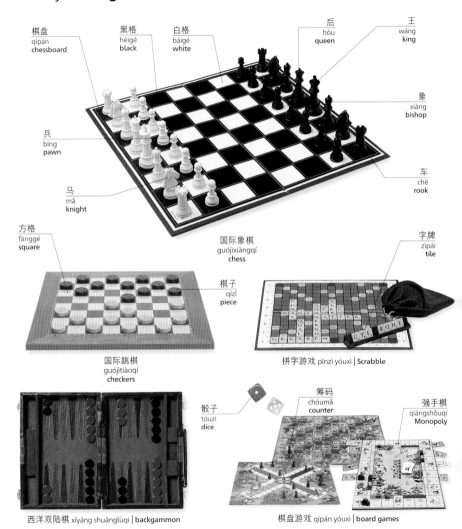

棋盘
qípán
chessboard

黑格
hēigé
black

白格
báigé
white

后
hòu
queen

王
wáng
king

象
xiàng
bishop

兵
bīng
pawn

车
chē
rook

马
mǎ
knight

方格
fānggé
square

国际象棋
guójìxiàngqí
chess

字牌
zìpái
tile

棋子
qízǐ
piece

国际跳棋
guójìtiàoqí
checkers

拼字游戏 pīnzì yóuxì | Scrabble

骰子
tóuzi
dice

筹码
chóumǎ
counter

强手棋
qiángshǒuqí
Monopoly

西洋双陆棋 xīyáng shuānglùqí | backgammon

棋盘游戏 qípán yóuxì | board games

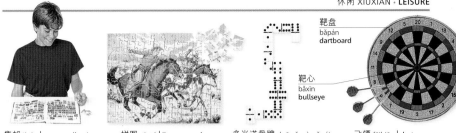

集邮 jíyóu | stamp collecting

拼图 pīntú | jigsaw puzzle

靶盘
bǎpán
dartboard

靶心
bǎxīn
bullseye

多米诺骨牌 duōmǐnuò gǔpái
dominoes

飞镖 fēibiāo | **darts**

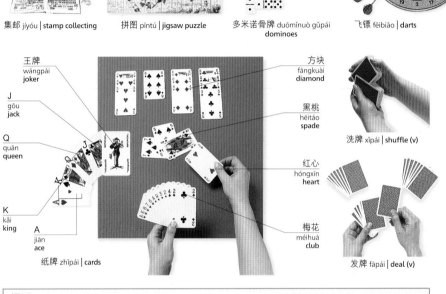

王牌
wángpái
joker

方块
fāngkuài
diamond

J
gōu
jack

黑桃
hēitáo
spade

Q
quān
queen

洗牌 xǐpái | shuffle (v)

红心
hóngxīn
heart

K
kǎi
king

A
jiān
ace

梅花
méihuā
club

纸牌 zhǐpái | cards

发牌 fāpái | deal (v)

词汇 cíhuì • vocabulary

走棋 zǒuqí move	赢 yíng win (v)	输家 shūjiā loser	点 diǎn point	桥牌 qiáopái bridge	掷骰子。 zhìtóuzi. Roll the dice.
玩 wán play (v)	赢家 yíngjiā winner	游戏 yóuxì game	得分 défēn score	一副牌 yìfùpái deck of cards	该谁了？ gāishuíle? Whose turn is it?
玩家 wánjiā player	输 shū lose (v)	赌注 dǔzhù bet	扑克牌 pūkèpái poker	同花 tónghuā suit	该你了。 gāinǐle. It's your move.

工艺美术 1 gōngyìměishù • arts and crafts 1

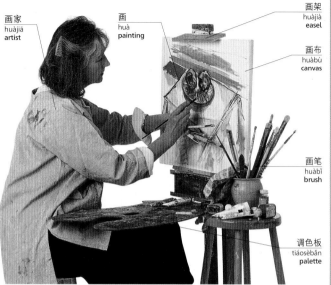

画家
huàjiā
artist

画
huà
painting

画架
huàjià
easel

画布
huàbù
canvas

画笔
huàbǐ
brush

调色板
tiáosèbǎn
palette

(用颜料等)绘画 (yòng yánliào děng) huìhuà | painting

颜料 yánliào • paints

油画颜料
yóuhuà yánliào
oil paint

水彩画颜料
shuǐcǎi huàyánliào
watercolor paint

彩色蜡笔
cǎisèlàbǐ
pastels

丙烯颜料
bǐngxī yánliào
acrylic paint

广告颜料 guǎnggào yánliào
poster paint

颜色 yánsè • colors

红色 hóngsè | red

蓝色 lánsè | blue

黄色 huángsè
yellow

绿色 lǜsè | green

橘色 júsè | orange

紫色 zǐsè | purple

白色 báisè | white

黑色 hēisè | black

灰色 huīsè | gray

粉红色 fěnhóngsè
pink

褐色 hèsè | brown

靛青色 diànqīngsè
indigo

其他工艺 qítā gōngyì • other crafts

素描簿
sùmiáobù
sketch pad

铅笔
qiānbǐ
pencil

草图
cǎotú
sketch

油墨
yóumò
ink

炭笔
tànbǐ
charcoal

素描 sùmiáo | drawing

印刷 yìnshuā | printing

版画 bǎnhuà | engraving

石头
shítou
stone

木槌
mùchuí
mallet

凿子
záozi
chisel

木头
mùtou
wood

刮刀
guādāo
modeling tool

陶工转盘
táogōng zhuànpán
potter's wheel

雕刻
diāokè
sculpting

木工
mùgōng
woodworking

黏土
niántǔ
clay

胶
jiāo
glue

纸板
zhǐbǎn
cardboard

拼贴 pīntiē | collage

陶艺 táoyì | pottery

珠宝制作
zhūbǎo zhizuò
jewelry-making

纸板制型
zhǐbǎnzhixíng
papier-mâché

折纸
zhézhǐ
origami

模型制作
móxíng zhizuò
model-making

工艺美术 2 gōngyìměishù · arts and crafts 2

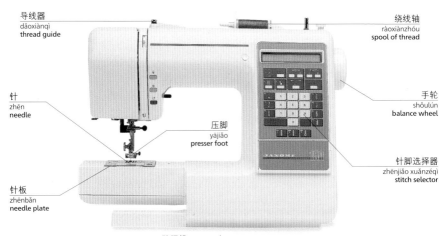

导线器
dǎoxiànqì
thread guide

绕线轴
ràoxiànzhóu
spool of thread

针
zhēn
needle

手轮
shǒulún
balance wheel

压脚
yājiǎo
presser foot

针脚选择器
zhēnjiǎo xuǎnzéqì
stitch selector

针板
zhēnbǎn
needle plate

缝纫机 féngrènjī | sewing machine

剪刀
jiǎndāo
scissors

纸样
zhǐyàng
pattern

针垫
zhēndiàn
pincushion

卷尺
juǎnchǐ
tape measure

布料
bùliào
material

大头针
dàtóuzhēn
pin

针线筐 zhēnxiànkuāng
sewing basket

线
xiàn
thread

领钩环
lǐnggōuhuán
eye

线轴
xiànzhóu
bobbin

领钩
lǐnggōu
hook

顶针
dǐngzhēn
thimble

划粉
huáfěn
tailor's chalk

人体模型
réntǐ móxíng
tailor's dummy

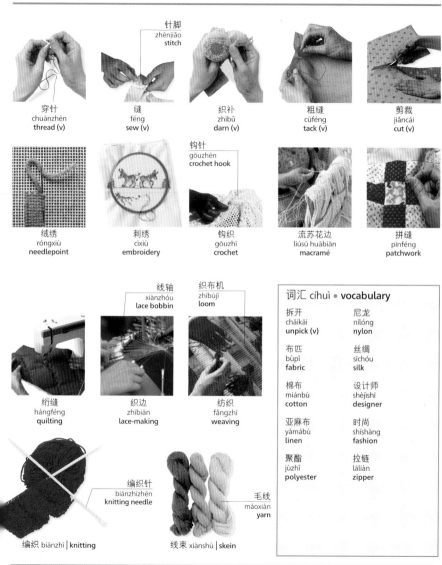

针脚
zhēnjiǎo
stitch

穿针
chuānzhēn
thread (v)

缝
féng
sew (v)

织补
zhībǔ
darn (v)

粗缝
cūféng
tack (v)

剪裁
jiǎncái
cut (v)

绒绣
róngxiù
needlepoint

刺绣
cìxiù
embroidery

钩针
gōuzhēn
crochet hook

钩织
gōuzhī
crochet

流苏花边
liúsū huābiān
macramé

拼缝
pīnféng
patchwork

线轴
xiànzhóu
lace bobbin

织布机
zhībùjī
loom

绗缝
hángféng
quilting

织边
zhībiān
lace-making

纺织
fǎngzhī
weaving

编织针
biānzhīzhēn
knitting needle

毛线
máoxiàn
yarn

编织 biānzhī | knitting

线束 xiànshù | skein

词汇 cíhuì • vocabulary

拆开 chāikāi unpick (v)	尼龙 nílóng nylon
布匹 bùpǐ fabric	丝绸 sīchóu silk
棉布 miánbù cotton	设计师 shèjìshī designer
亚麻布 yàmábù linen	时尚 shíshàng fashion
聚酯 jùzhǐ polyester	拉链 lāliàn zipper

环境 huánjìng
environment

宇宙空间 yǔzhòukōngjiān • space

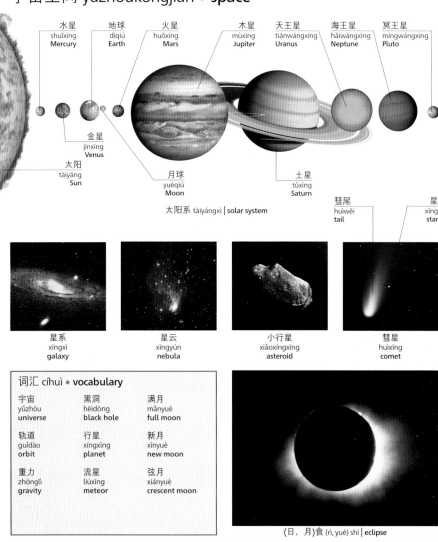

水星
shuǐxīng
Mercury

地球
dìqiú
Earth

火星
huǒxīng
Mars

木星
mùxīng
Jupiter

天王星
tiānwángxīng
Uranus

海王星
hǎiwángxīng
Neptune

冥王星
míngwángxīng
Pluto

金星
jīnxīng
Venus

太阳
tàiyáng
Sun

月球
yuèqiú
Moon

土星
tǔxīng
Saturn

太阳系 tàiyángxì | solar system

彗尾
huìwěi
tail

星
xīng
star

星系
xīngxì
galaxy

星云
xīngyún
nebula

小行星
xiǎoxíngxīng
asteroid

彗星
huìxīng
comet

词汇 cíhuì • vocabulary

宇宙
yǔzhòu
universe

轨道
guǐdào
orbit

重力
zhònglì
gravity

黑洞
hēidòng
black hole

行星
xíngxīng
planet

流星
liúxīng
meteor

满月
mǎnyuè
full moon

新月
xīnyuè
new moon

弦月
xiányuè
crescent moon

(日、月)食 (rì, yuè) shí | eclipse

太空探索 tàikōngfú · space exploration

雷达
léidá
radar

助推器
zhùtuīqì
thruster

舱门
cāngmén
crew hatch

航天飞机
hángtiān fēijī
space shuttle

太空服
tàikōngfú
space suit

推进器
tuījìnqì
booster

宇航员 yǔhángyuán
astronaut

登月舱 dēngyuècāng | lunar module

发射架
fāshèjià
launch pad

发射
fāshè
launch

人造卫星
rénzàowèixīng
satellite

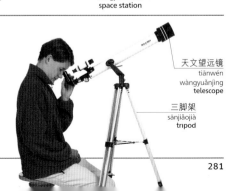

空间站
kōngjiān zhàn
space station

天文学 tiānwénxué · astronomy

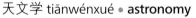

星座
xīngzuò
constellation

双筒望远镜
shuāngtǒng wàngyuǎnjìng
binoculars

天文望远镜
tiānwén wàngyuǎnjìng
telescope

三脚架
sānjiǎojià
tripod

地球 dìqiú • Earth

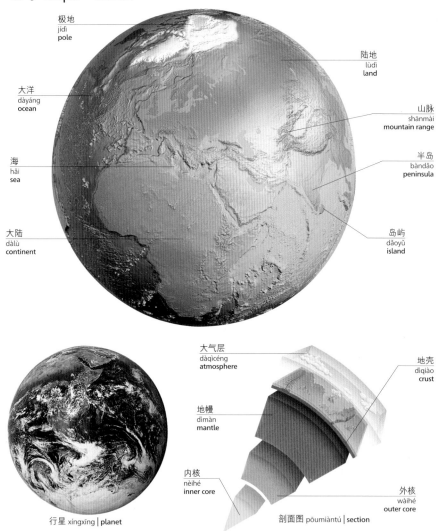

极地
jídì
pole

陆地
lùdì
land

大洋
dàyáng
ocean

山脉
shānmài
mountain range

海
hǎi
sea

半岛
bàndǎo
peninsula

大陆
dàlù
continent

岛屿
dǎoyǔ
island

大气层
dàqìcéng
atmosphere

地壳
dìqiào
crust

地幔
dìmàn
mantle

内核
nèihé
inner core

外核
wàihé
outer core

行星 xíngxīng | planet

剖面图 pōumiàntú | section

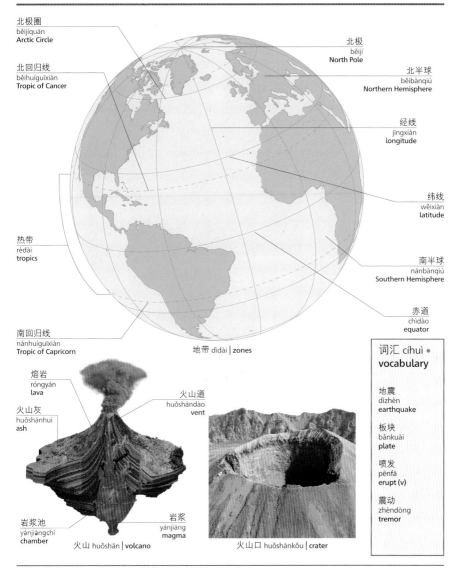

北极圈
běijíquān
Arctic Circle

北极
běijí
North Pole

北回归线
běihuíguīxiàn
Tropic of Cancer

北半球
běibànqiú
Northern Hemisphere

经线
jīngxiàn
longitude

纬线
wěixiàn
latitude

热带
rèdài
tropics

南半球
nánbànqiú
Southern Hemisphere

赤道
chìdào
equator

南回归线
nánhuíguīxiàn
Tropic of Capricorn

地带 dìdài | zones

熔岩
róngyán
lava

火山道
huǒshāndào
vent

火山灰
huǒshānhuī
ash

岩浆池
yánjiāngchí
chamber

岩浆
yánjiāng
magma

火山 huǒshān | volcano

火山口 huǒshānkǒu | crater

词汇 cíhuì ·
vocabulary

地震
dìzhèn
earthquake

板块
bǎnkuài
plate

喷发
pēnfā
erupt (v)

震动
zhèndòng
tremor

地貌 dìmào · landscape

山
shān
mountain

山坡
shānpō
slope

河岸
hé'àn
bank

河流
héliú
river

急流
jíliú
rapids

岩石
yánshí
rocks

冰河 bīnghé | glacier

山谷 shāngǔ | valley

丘陵
qiūlíng
hill

高原
gāoyuán
plateau

峡谷
xiágǔ
gorge

岩洞
yándòng
cave

平原 píngyuán | plain

沙漠 shāmò | desert

森林 sēnlín | forest

树林 shùlín | woods

雨林
yǔlín
rain forest

沼泽
zhǎozé
swamp

草场
cǎochǎng
meadow

草原
cǎoyuán
grassland

瀑布
pùbù
waterfall

溪流
xīliú
stream

湖
hú
lake

间歇喷泉
jiànxiē pēnquán
geyser

海岸
hǎi'àn
coast

悬崖
xuányá
cliff

珊瑚礁
shānhújiāo
coral reef

河口
hékǒu
estuary

天气 tiānqì · **weather**

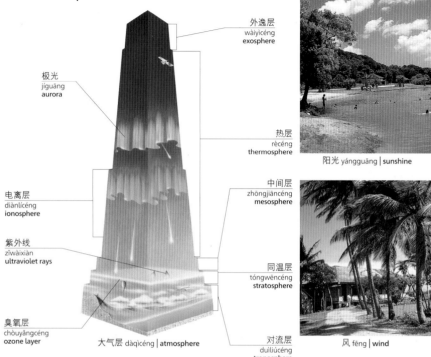

外逸层
wàiyìcéng
exosphere

极光
jíguāng
aurora

热层
rècéng
thermosphere

阳光 yángguāng | sunshine

电离层
diànlícéng
ionosphere

中间层
zhōngjiāncéng
mesosphere

紫外线
zǐwàixiàn
ultraviolet rays

同温层
tóngwēncéng
stratosphere

臭氧层
chòuyǎngcéng
ozone layer

风 fēng | wind

大气层 dàqìcéng | atmosphere

对流层
duìliúcéng
troposphere

词汇 cíhuì · **vocabulary**

雨夹雪 yǔjiáxuě sleet	阵雨 zhènyǔ shower	热 rè hot	干燥 gānzào dry	多风 duōfēng windy	我热/冷。 wǒ rè/lěng. I'm hot/cold.
冰雹 bīngbáo hail	阳光明媚 yángguāng míngmèi sunny	冷 lěng cold	潮 cháo wet	狂风 kuángfēng gale	正在下雨。 zhèngzài xiàyǔ. It's raining.
雷 léi thunder	多云 duōyún cloudy	温暖 wēnnuǎn warm	湿润 shīrùn humid	温度 wēndù temperature	...度 ...dù It's ... degrees.

闪电 shǎndiàn lightning

云 yún | cloud

雨 yǔ | rain

暴风雨 bàofēngyǔ | storm

霭 ǎi | mist

雾 wù | fog

彩虹 cǎihóng | rainbow

雪 xuě | snow

霜 shuāng | frost

冰 bīng | ice

冰柱 bīngzhù icicle

结冰 jiébīng | freeze

飓风 jùfēng | hurricane

龙卷风 lóngjuǎnfēng tornado

季风 jìfēng | monsoon

洪水 hóngshuǐ | flood

岩石 yánshí • rocks

火成岩 huǒchéngyán • igneous

花岗岩
huāgāngyán
granite

黑曜岩
hēiyàoyán
obsidian

玄武岩
xuánwǔyán
basalt

浮石
fúshí
pumice

沉积岩 chénjīyán • sedimentary

砂岩
shāyán
sandstone

石灰岩
shíhuīyán
limestone

白垩
bái'è
chalk

燧石
suìshí
flint

砾岩
lìyán
conglomerate

煤
méi
coal

变质岩 biànzhìyán • metamorphic

板岩
bǎnyán
slate

页岩
yèyán
schist

片麻岩
piànmáyán
gneiss

大理石
dàlǐshí
marble

宝石 bǎoshí • gems

红宝石
hóngbǎoshí
ruby

海蓝宝石
hǎilánbǎoshí
aquamarine

紫水晶
zǐshuǐjīng
amethyst

钻石
zuànshí
diamond

玉石
yùshí
jade

黑玉
hēiyù
jet

绿宝石
lǜbǎoshí
emerald

蛋白石
dànbáishí
opal

蓝宝石
lánbǎoshí
sapphire

月长石
yuèchángshí
moonstone

石榴石
shíliúshí
garnet

黄玉
huángyù
topaz

电气石
diànqìshí
tourmaline

矿物 kuàngwù · minerals

石英
shíyīng
quartz

云母
yúnmǔ
mica

硫磺
liúhuáng
sulfur

赤铁矿
chìtiěkuàng
hematite

方解石
fāngjiěshí
calcite

孔雀石
kǒngquèshí
malachite

绿松石
lǜsōngshí
turquoise

缟玛瑙
gǎomǎnǎo
onyx

玛瑙
mǎnǎo
agate

石墨
shímò
graphite

金属 jīnshǔ · metals

金
jīn
gold

银
yín
silver

铂
bó
platinum

镍
niè
nickel

铁
tiě
iron

铜
tóng
copper

锡
xī
tin

铝
lǚ
aluminium

汞
gǒng
mercury

锌
xīn
zinc

动物1 dòngwùyī • animals 1
哺乳动物 bǔrǔ dòngwù • mammals

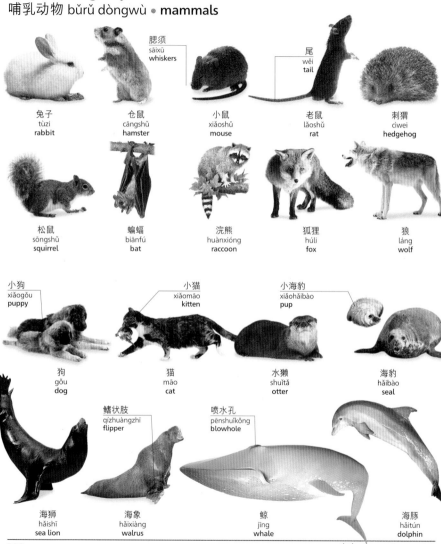

腮须
sāixū
whiskers

尾
wěi
tail

兔子
tùzi
rabbit

仓鼠
cāngshǔ
hamster

小鼠
xiǎoshǔ
mouse

老鼠
lǎoshǔ
rat

刺猬
cìwei
hedgehog

松鼠
sōngshǔ
squirrel

蝙蝠
biānfú
bat

浣熊
huànxióng
raccoon

狐狸
húli
fox

狼
láng
wolf

小狗
xiǎogǒu
puppy

小猫
xiǎomāo
kitten

小海豹
xiǎohǎibào
pup

狗
gǒu
dog

猫
māo
cat

水獭
shuǐtǎ
otter

海豹
hǎibào
seal

鳍状肢
qízhuàngzhī
flipper

喷水孔
pēnshuǐkǒng
blowhole

海狮
hǎishī
sea lion

海象
hǎixiàng
walrus

鲸
jīng
whale

海豚
hǎitún
dolphin

鹿角
lùjiǎo
antler

鬃毛
zōngmáo
mane

蹄
tí
hoof

驼峰
tuófēng
hump

鹿
lù
deer

斑马
bānmǎ
zebra

长颈鹿
chángjǐnglù
giraffe

骆驼
luòtuo
camel

象鼻
xiàngbí
trunk

长牙
chángyá
tusk

角
jiǎo
horn

河马
hémǎ
hippopotamus

象
xiàng
elephant

犀牛
xīniú
rhinoceros

虎
hǔ
tiger

鬃毛
zōngmáo
mane

狮子
shīzi
lion

猴子
hóuzi
monkey

大猩猩
dàxīngxing
gorilla

树袋熊
shùdài xióng
koala

育儿袋
yù'érdài
pouch

熊猫
xióngmāo
panda

爪
zhǎo
claw

袋鼠
dàishǔ
kangaroo

熊
xióng
bear

北极熊
běijí xióng
polar bear

动物 2 dòngwù · animals 2

鸟 niǎo · birds

尾
wěi
tail

金丝雀
jīnsīquè
canary

麻雀
máquè
sparrow

蜂鸟
fēngniǎo
hummingbird

燕子
yànzi
swallow

乌鸦
wūyā
crow

鸽子
gēzi
pigeon

啄木鸟
zhuómùniǎo
woodpecker

隼
sǔn
falcon

猫头鹰
māotóuyīng
owl

海鸥
hǎi'ōu
gull

鹰
yīng
eagle

鹈鹕
tíhú
pelican

火烈鸟
huǒlièniǎo
flamingo

鹳
guàn
stork

鹤
hè
crane

企鹅
qǐ'é
penguin

鸵鸟
tuóniǎo
ostrich

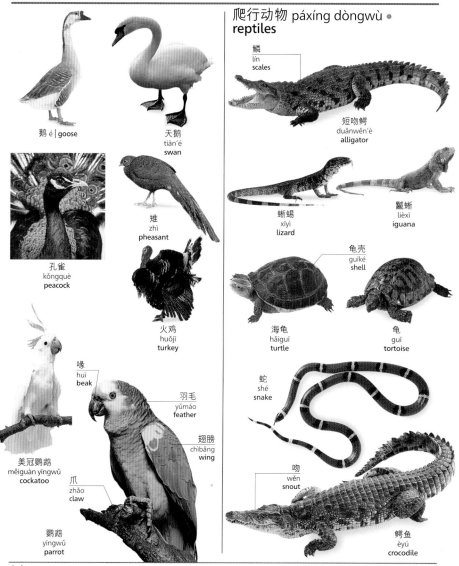

鹅 é | goose

天鹅
tiān'é
swan

孔雀
kǒngquè
peacock

雉
zhì
pheasant

火鸡
huǒjī
turkey

喙
huì
beak

羽毛
yǔmáo
feather

翅膀
chìbǎng
wing

爪
zhǎo
claw

美冠鹦鹉
měiguàn yīngwǔ
cockatoo

鹦鹉
yīngwǔ
parrot

爬行动物 páxíng dòngwù ·
reptiles

鳞
lín
scales

短吻鳄
duǎnwěn'è
alligator

蜥蜴
xīyì
lizard

鬣蜥
lièxī
iguana

龟壳
guīké
shell

海龟
hǎiguī
turtle

龟
guī
tortoise

蛇
shé
snake

吻
wěn
snout

鳄鱼
èyú
crocodile

动物 3 dòngwù · animals 3

两栖动物 liǎngqī dòngwù · amphibians

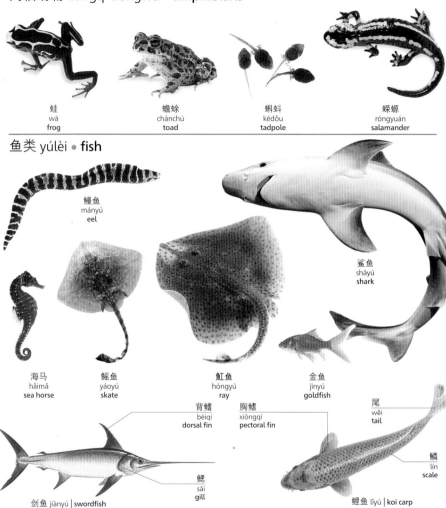

蛙
wā
frog

蟾蜍
chánchú
toad

蝌蚪
kēdǒu
tadpole

蝾螈
róngyuán
salamander

鱼类 yúlèi · fish

鳗鱼
mányú
eel

鲨鱼
shāyú
shark

海马
hǎimǎ
sea horse

鳐鱼
yáoyú
skate

魟鱼
hóngyú
ray

金鱼
jīnyú
goldfish

背鳍
bèiqí
dorsal fin

胸鳍
xiōngqí
pectoral fin

尾
wěi
tail

鳃
sāi
gill

鳞
lín
scale

剑鱼 jiànyú | swordfish

鲤鱼 lǐyú | koi carp

无脊椎动物 wújǐzhuī dòngwù · invertebrates

蚂蚁
mǎyǐ
ant

白蚁
báiyǐ
termite

蜜蜂
mìfēng
bee

黄蜂
huángfēng
wasp

甲壳虫
jiǎqiàochóng
beetle

蟑螂
zhāngláng
cockroach

蛾
é
moth

触角
chùjiǎo
antenna

蝴蝶
húdié
butterfly

茧
jiǎn
cocoon

毛虫
máochóng
caterpillar

蟋蟀 xīshuài | cricket

蚱蜢
zhàměng
grasshopper

螳螂
tángláng
praying mantis

蜇针
zhēzhēn
sting

蝎子
xiēzi
scorpion

蜈蚣
wúgōng
centipede

蜻蜓
qīngtíng
dragonfly

苍蝇
cāngyíng
fly

蚊子
wénzi
mosquito

瓢虫
piáochóng
ladybug

蜘蛛
zhīzhū
spider

蛞蝓
kuòyú
slug

蜗牛
wōniú
snail

蚯蚓 qiūyǐn | worm

海星
hǎixīng
starfish

贻贝
yíbèi
mussel

螃蟹 pángxiè | crab

龙虾 lóngxiā | lobster

章鱼 zhāngyú | octopus

鱿鱼 yóuyú | squid

水母 shuǐmǔ | jellyfish

植物 zhíwù · **plants**

树 shù · **tree**

树枝
shùzhī
branch

叶
yè
leaf

细枝
xìzhī
twig

树皮
shùpí
bark

柳树
liǔshù
willow

根
gēn
root

树干
shùgàn
trunk

橡树 xiàngshù | oak

白杨
báiyáng
poplar

桉树
ānshù
eucalyptus

落叶松
luòyèsōng
larch

山毛榉
shānmáojǔ
beech

桦树
huàshù
birch

松树
sōngshù
pine

雪松
xuěsōng
cedar

枫树
fēngshù
maple

榆树
yúshù
elm

椴树
duànshù
lime

冬青树
dōngqīngshù
holly

浆果
jiāngguǒ
berry

棕榈树
zōnglǘshù
palm

显花植物 xiǎnhuā zhíwù · flowering plant

花
huā
flower

花萼
huā'è
calyx

花蕾
huālěi
bud

雄蕊
xióngruǐ
stamen

花瓣
huābàn
petal

叶梗
yègěng
stalk

主茎
zhǔjīng
stem

毛茛
máogèn
buttercup

雏菊
chújú
daisy

蓟
jì
thistle

蒲公英
púgōngyīng
dandelion

石南花
shínánhuā
heather

罂粟
yīngsù
poppy

毛地黄
máodìhuáng
foxglove

忍冬
rěndōng
honeysuckle

向日葵
xiàngrìkuí
sunflower

苜蓿
mùxu
clover

野风信子
yěfēngxìnzǐ
bluebells

樱草
yīngcǎo
primrose

羽扇豆
yǔshàndòu
lupines

荨麻
qiánmá
nettle

市区 shìqū · city

街道
jiēdào
street

路沿
lùyán
curb

街角
jiējiǎo
street corner

商店
shāngdiàn
store

十字路口
shízìlùkǒu
intersection

单行道
dānxíngdào
one-way system

人行道
rénxíngdào
sidewalk

办公楼
bàngōnglóu
office building

公寓楼
gōngyùlóu
apartment
building

小巷
xiǎoxiàng
alley

停车场
tíngchēchǎng
parking lot

路标
lùbiāo
street sign

安全岛护栏
ānquán
dǎohùlán
barrier

路灯
lùdēng
streetlight

建筑物 jiànzhùwù · buildings

市政厅
shìzhèngtīng
town hall

图书馆
túshūguǎn
library

电影院
diànyǐngyuàn
movie theater

剧院
jùyuàn
theater

大学
dàxué
university

摩天大楼
mótiān dàlóu
skyscraper

区域 qūyù · areas

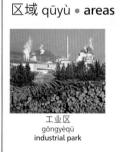
工业区
gōngyèqū
industrial park

市区
shìqū
city

学校
xuéxiào
school

郊区
jiāoqū
suburb

村庄
cūnzhuāng
village

词汇 cíhuì · vocabulary

步行区 bùxíngqū pedestrian zone	小街 xiǎojiē side street	检修井 jiǎnxiūjǐng manhole	排水沟 páishuǐgōu gutter	教堂 jiàotáng church
林阴道 línyīndào avenue	广场 guǎngchǎng square	公共汽车站 gōnggòngqìchē zhàn bus stop	工厂 gōngchǎng factory	下水道 xiàshuǐdào drain

建筑 jiànzhù · architecture

建筑与结构 jiànzhù yǔ jiégòu · buildings and structures

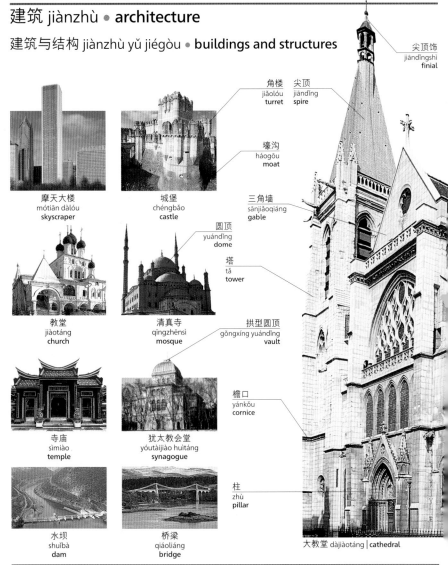

摩天大楼
mótiān dàlóu
skyscraper

城堡
chéngbǎo
castle

角楼
jiǎolóu
turret

尖顶
jiàndǐng
spire

尖顶饰
jiāndǐngshì
finial

壕沟
háogōu
moat

三角墙
sānjiǎoqiáng
gable

圆顶
yuándǐng
dome

塔
tǎ
tower

教堂
jiàotáng
church

清真寺
qīngzhēnsì
mosque

拱型圆顶
gǒngxíng yuándǐng
vault

檐口
yánkǒu
cornice

寺庙
sìmiào
temple

犹太教会堂
yóutàijiào huìtáng
synagogue

柱
zhù
pillar

水坝
shuǐbà
dam

桥梁
qiáoliáng
bridge

大教堂 dàjiàotáng | cathedral

建筑风格 jiànzhù fēnggé · styles

哥特式 gètèshì | Gothic

柱顶楣梁
zhùdǐng méiliáng
architrave

文艺复兴时期风格
wényìfùxīng shíqī fēnggé
Renaissance

巴洛克式
bāluòkèshì
Baroque

拱
gǒng
arch

檐壁
yánbì
frieze

圣坛
shèngtán
choir

洛可可式
luòkěkěshì
Rococo

三角楣
sānjiǎoméi
pediment

新古典主义风格
xīn gǔdiǎnzhǔyì fēnggé
Neoclassical

扶墙
fúqiáng
buttress

新艺术风格
xīn yìshù fēnggé
Art Nouveau

装饰艺术风格
zhuāngshìyìshù fēnggé
Art Deco

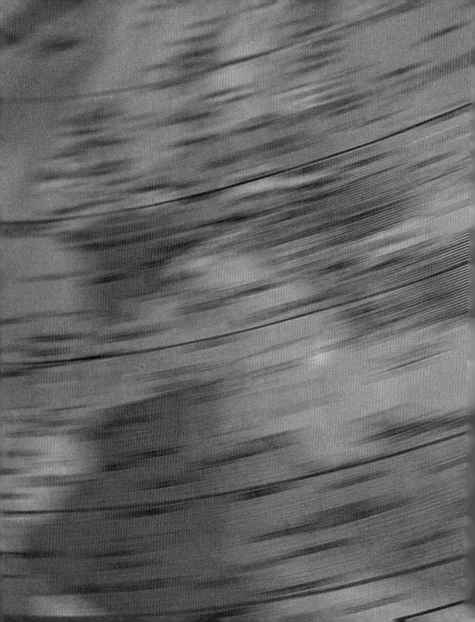

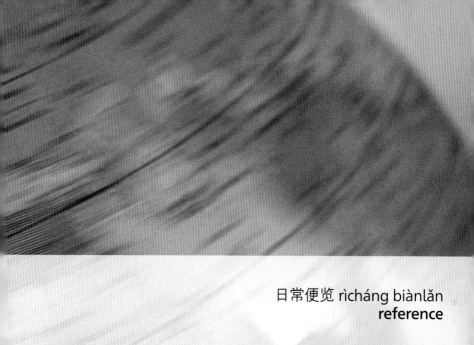

日常便览 rìcháng biànlǎn
reference

时间 shíjiān · **time**

分针
fēnzhēn
minute hand

时针
shízhēn
hour hand

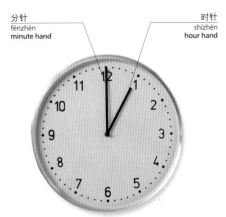

钟表
zhōngbiǎo
clock

词汇 cíhuì · **vocabulary**

秒 miǎo **second**	现在 xiànzài **now**	一刻钟 yí kèzhōng **a quarter of an hour**
分钟 fēnzhōng **minute**	以后 yǐhòu **later**	二十分钟 èrshí fēnzhōng **twenty minutes**
小时 xiǎoshí **hour**	半小时 bàn xiǎoshí **half an hour**	四十分钟 sìshí fēnzhōng **forty minutes**

几点了?
jǐ diǎn le?
What time is it?

三点了。
sāndiǎn le.
It's three o'clock.

一点五分
yìdiǎn wǔ fēn
five past one

一点十分
yìdiǎn shí fēn
ten past one

一点十五分
yìdiǎn shíwǔ fēn
quarter past one

一点二十分
yìdiǎn èrshí fēn
twenty past one

秒针
miǎozhēn
second hand

一点二十五分
yìdiǎn èrshíwǔ fēn
twenty-five past one

一点半
yìdiǎnbàn
one thirty

一点三十五分
yìdiǎn sānshíwǔ fēn
twenty-five to two

一点四十分
yìdiǎn sìshí fēn
twenty to two

一点四十五分
yìdiǎn sānshíwǔ fēn
quarter to two

一点五十分
yìdiǎn wǔshí fēn
ten to two

一点五十五分
yìdiǎn wǔshíwǔ fēn
five to two

两点钟
liǎngdiǎn zhōng
two o'clock

昼夜 zhòuyè · night and day

午夜 wǔyè | midnight

日出 rìchū | sunrise

拂晓 fúxiǎo | dawn

早晨 zǎochén | morning

日落
rìluò
sunset

正午
zhèngwǔ
noon

黄昏 huánghūn | dusk

傍晚 bàngwǎn | evening

下午 xiàwǔ | afternoon

词汇 cíhuì · vocabulary

早
zǎo
early

准时
zhǔnshí
on time

迟
chí
late

你来早了。
nǐ lái zǎo le.
You're early.

你迟到了。
nǐ chídào le.
You're late.

我马上就到。
wǒ mǎshàng jiùdào.
I'll be there soon.

请准时些。
qǐng zhǔnshí xiē.
Please be on time.

待会儿见。
dàihuìer jiàn.
I'll see you later.

几点开始?
jǐdiǎn kāishǐ?
What time does it start?

几点结束?
jǐdiǎn jiéshù?
What time does it end?

天晚了。
tiān wǎnle.
It's getting late.

会持续多久?
huì chíxù duōjiǔ?
How long will it last?

日历 rìlì • calendar

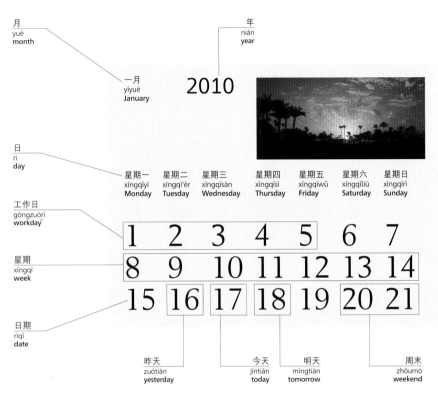

月
yuè
month

年
nián
year

一月
yīyuè
January

2010

日
rì
day

星期一 xīngqīyī Monday	星期二 xīngqī'èr Tuesday	星期三 xīngqīsān Wednesday	星期四 xīngqīsì Thursday	星期五 xīngqīwǔ Friday	星期六 xīngqīliù Saturday	星期日 xīngqīrì Sunday

工作日
gōngzuòrì
workday

星期
xīngqī
week

日期
rìqī
date

1	2	3	4	5	6	7
8	9	10	11	12	13	14
15	16	17	18	19	20	21

昨天
zuótiān
yesterday

今天
jīntiān
today

明天
míngtiān
tomorrow

周末
zhōumò
weekend

词汇 cíhuì • vocabulary

一月 yīyuè January	三月 sānyuè March	五月 wǔyuè May	七月 qīyuè July	九月 jiǔyuè September	十一月 shíyīyuè November
二月 èryuè February	四月 sìyuè April	六月 liùyuè June	八月 bāyuè August	十月 shíyuè October	十二月 shí'èryuè December

中文 zhōngwén • english

年 nián · **years**

1900 一九〇〇年 yījiǔlínglíng nián · nineteen hundred

1901 一九〇一年 yījiǔlíngyī nián · nineteen hundred and one

1910 一九一〇年 yījiǔyīlíng nián · nineteen ten

2000 二〇〇〇年 èrlínglíng nián · two thousand

2001 二〇〇一年 èrlínglíngyī nián · two thousand and one

季节 jìjié · **seasons**

春天
chūntiān
spring

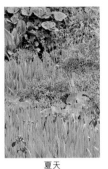

夏天
xiàtiān
summer

秋天
qiūtiān
fall

冬天
dōngtiān
winter

词汇 cíhuì · **vocabulary**

世纪 shìjì century	本周 běnzhōu this week	后天 hòutiān the day after tomorrow	今天几号? jīntiān jǐhào? What's the date today?
十年 shínián decade	上周 shàngzhōu last week	每周 měizhōu weekly	今天是二〇一七年二月七日。 jīntiān shì èrlíngyīqī nián èryuè qīrì. It's February seventh, two thousand and seventeen.
千年 qiānnián millennium	下周 xiàzhōu next week	每月 měiyuè monthly	
两周 liǎngzhōu two weeks	前天 qiántiān the day before yesterday	每年 měinián annual	

数字 shùzì · numbers

0	零 líng · zero		20	二十 èrshí · twenty
1	一 yī · one		21	二十一 èrshíyī · twenty-one
2	二 èr · two		22	二十二 èrshí'èr · twenty-two
3	三 sān · three		30	三十 sānshí · thirty
4	四 sì · four		40	四十 sìshí · forty
5	五 wǔ · five		50	五十 wǔshí · fifty
6	六 liù · six		60	六十 liùshí · sixty
7	七 qī · seven		70	七十 qīshí · seventy
8	八 bā · eight		80	八十 bāshí · eighty
9	九 jiǔ · nine		90	九十 jiǔshí · ninety
10	十 shí · ten		100	一百 yībǎi · one hundred
11	十一 shíyī · eleven		110	一百一十 yībǎiyīshí · one hundred and ten
12	十二 shí'èr · twelve		200	二百 èrbǎi · two hundred
13	十三 shísān · thirteen		300	三百 sānbǎi · three hundred
14	十四 shísì · fourteen		400	四百 sìbǎi · four hundred
15	十五 shíwǔ · fifteen		500	五百 wǔbǎi · five hundred
16	十六 shíliù · sixteen		600	六百 liùbǎi · six hundred
17	十七 shíqī · seventeen		700	七百 qībǎi · seven hundred
18	十八 shíbā · eighteen		800	八百 bābǎi · eight hundred
19	十九 shíjiǔ · nineteen		900	九百 jiǔbǎi · nine hundred

1,000	一千 yìqiān • one thousand
10,000	一万 yīwàn • ten thousand
20,000	两万 liǎngwàn • twenty thousand
50,000	五万 wǔwàn • fifty thousand
55,500	五万五千五百 wǔwàn wǔqiān wǔbǎi • fifty-five thousand five hundred
100,000	十万 shíwàn • one hundred thousand
1,000,000	一百万 yìbǎiwàn • one million
1,000,000,000	十亿 shíyì • one billion

第一 dìyī first

第二 dì'èr second

第三 dìsān third

第四 dìsì • fourth

第五 dìwǔ • fifth

第六 dìliù • sixth

第七 dìqī • seventh

第八 dìbā • eighth

第九 dìjiǔ • ninth

第十 dìshí • tenth

第十一 dìshíyī • eleventh

第十二 dìshí'èr • twelfth

第十三 dìshísān • thirteenth

第十四 dìshísì • fourteenth

第十五 dìshíwǔ • fifteenth

第十六 dìshíliù • sixteenth

第十七 dìshíqī • seventeenth

第十八 dìshíbā • eighteenth

第十九 dìshíjiǔ • nineteenth

第二十 dì'èrshí • twentieth

第二十一 dì'èrshíyī • twenty-first

第二十二 dì'èrshí'èr • twenty-second

第二十三 dì'èrshísān • twenty-third

第三十 dìsānshí • thirtieth

第四十 dìsìshí • fortieth

第五十 dìwǔshí • fiftieth

第六十 dìliùshí • sixtieth

第七十 dìqīshí • seventieth

第八十 dìbāshí • eightieth

第九十 dìjiǔshí • ninetieth

第一百 dìyībǎi • (one) hundredth

度量衡 dùliánghéng • **weights and measures**

面积 miànjī • **area**

平方英尺
píngfāng
yīngchǐ
square foot

平方米
píngfāng mǐ
square meter

距离 jùlí • **distance**

公里
gōnglǐ
kilometer

英里
yīnglǐ
mile

秤盘
chēngpán
pan

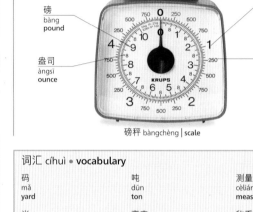

磅
bàng
pound

盎司
àngsī
ounce

千克
qiānkè
kilogram

克
kè
gram

磅秤 bàngchèng | **scale**

词汇 cíhuì • **vocabulary**

码 mǎ **yard**	吨 dūn **ton**	测量 cèliáng **measure (v)**
米 mǐ **meter**	毫克 háokè **milligram**	称重量 chēng zhòngliàng **weigh (v)**

长度 chángdù • **length**

英尺
yīngchǐ
foot

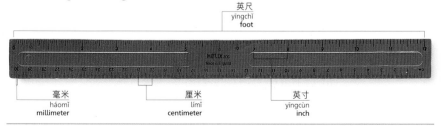

毫米
háomǐ
millimeter

厘米
límǐ
centimeter

英寸
yīngcùn
inch

中文 zhōngwén • **english**

容量 róngliàng · capacity

半升
bànshēng
half-liter

品脱
pǐntuō
pint

容积
róngjī
volume

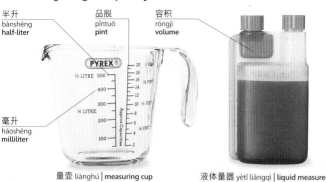

毫升
háoshēng
milliliter

量壶 liànghú | measuring cup

液体量器 yètǐ liángqì | liquid measure

词汇 cíhuì · vocabulary

加仑
jiālún
gallon

夸脱
kuātuō
quart

升
shēng
liter

容器 róngqì · container

硬纸盒
yìngzhǐhé
carton

包
bāo
packet

瓶
píng
bottle

袋
dài
bag

塑料盒 sùliàohé | tub

广口瓶 guǎngkǒupíng | jar

罐
guàn
can

罐头盒 guàntóuhé | tin

喷水器 pēnshuǐqì | spray bottle

块
kuài
bar

软管
ruǎnguǎn
tube

卷
juǎn
roll

纸盒
zhǐhé
pack

喷雾罐
pēnwùguàn
spray can

世界地图 shìjiè dìtú • **world map**

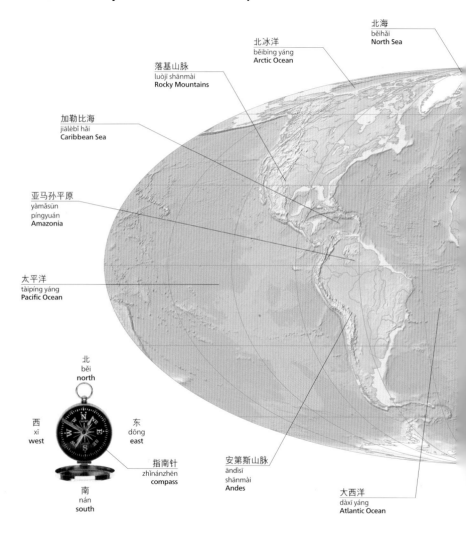

北海
běihǎi
North Sea

北冰洋
běibīng yáng
Arctic Ocean

落基山脉
luòjī shānmài
Rocky Mountains

加勒比海
jiālèbǐ hǎi
Caribbean Sea

亚马孙平原
yàmǎsūn
píngyuán
Amazonia

太平洋
tàipíng yáng
Pacific Ocean

北
běi
north

西
xī
west

东
dōng
east

指南针
zhǐnánzhēn
compass

安第斯山脉
āndìsī
shānmài
Andes

大西洋
dàxī yáng
Atlantic Ocean

南
nán
south

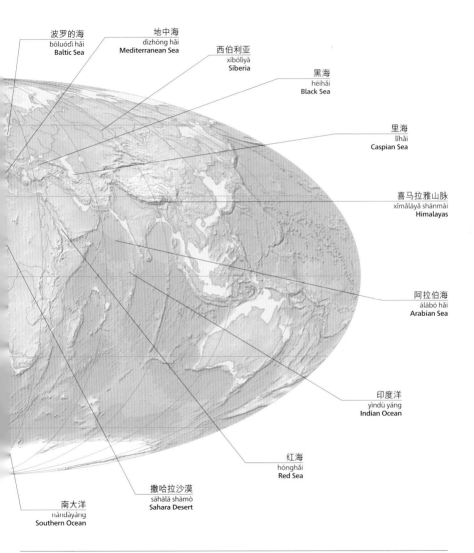

波罗的海
bōluódì hǎi
Baltic Sea

地中海
dìzhōng hǎi
Mediterranean Sea

西伯利亚
xībólìyà
Siberia

黑海
hēihǎi
Black Sea

里海
lǐhǎi
Caspian Sea

喜马拉雅山脉
xǐmǎlǎyǎ shānmài
Himalayas

阿拉伯海
ālābó hǎi
Arabian Sea

印度洋
yìndù yáng
Indian Ocean

红海
hónghǎi
Red Sea

撒哈拉沙漠
sāhālā shāmò
Sahara Desert

南大洋
nándàyáng
Southern Ocean

北美洲 běiměizhōu • **North and Central America**

巴巴多斯 bābāduōsī •
Barbados

加拿大 jiānádà • **Canada**

哥斯达黎加 gēsīdálíjiā •
Costa Rica

古巴 gǔbā • **Cuba**

牙买加 yámǎijiā • **Jamaica**

墨西哥 mòxīgē • **Mexico**

巴拿马 bānámǎ • **Panama**

特立尼达和多巴哥 tèlìnídá hé
duōbāgē • **Trinidad and Tobago**

美利坚合众国
měilìjiānhézhòngguó •
United States of America

阿拉斯加 ālāsījiā • **Alaska**

安提瓜和巴布达 āntíguā hé
bābùdá • **Antigua and Barbuda**

巴哈马 bāhāmǎ • **Bahamas**

巴巴多斯 bābāduōsī • **Barbados**

伯利兹 bólìzī • **Belize**

加拿大 jiānádà • **Canada**

哥斯达黎加 gēsīdálíjiā • **Costa Rica**

古巴 gǔbā • **Cuba**

多米尼克 duōmǐníkè • **Dominica**

多米尼加 duōmǐníjiā •
Dominican Republic

萨尔瓦多 sà'ěrwǎduō • **El Salvador**

格陵兰 gélínglán • **Greenland**

格林纳达 gélínnàdá • **Grenada**

危地马拉 wēidìmǎlā • **Guatemala**

海地 hǎidì • **Haiti**

夏威夷 xiàwēiyí • **Hawaii**

洪都拉斯 hóngdūlāsī • **Honduras**

牙买加 yámǎijiā • **Jamaica**

墨西哥 mòxīgē • **Mexico**

尼加拉瓜 níjiālāguā • **Nicaragua**

巴拿马 bānámǎ • **Panama**

波多黎各 bōduōlígè • **Puerto Rico**

圣基茨和尼维斯 shèngjīcí hé
níwéisī • **St. Kitts and Nevis**

圣卢西亚 shènglúxīyà • **St. Lucia**

圣文森特和格林纳丁斯
shèngwénsēntè hé gélínnàdīngsī •
St. Vincent and The Grenadines

特立尼达和多巴哥 tèlìnídá hé
duōbāgē • **Trinidad and Tobago**

美利坚合众国
měilìjiānhézhòngguó •
United States of America

南美洲 nánměizhōu ● **South America**

阿根廷 āgēntíng ● **Argentina**

玻利维亚 bōlìwéiyà ● **Bolivia**

巴西 bāxī ● **Brazil**

智利 zhìlì ● **Chile**

哥伦比亚 gēlúnbǐyà ●
Colombia

厄瓜多尔 èguāduōěr ●
Ecuador

秘鲁 bìlǔ ● **Peru**

乌拉圭 wūlāguī ●
Uruguay

委内瑞拉 wěinèiruìlā ●
Venezuela

阿根廷 āgēntíng ● **Argentina**

玻利维亚 bōlìwéiyà ● **Bolivia**

巴西 bāxī ● **Brazil**

智利 zhìlì ● **Chile**

哥伦比亚 gēlúnbǐyà ● **Colombia**

厄瓜多尔 èguāduōěr ● **Ecuador**

福克兰群岛（马尔维纳斯群岛）
fúkèlán qúndǎo (mǎ'ěrwéinàsī
qúndǎo) ● **Falkland Islands**

法属圭亚那 fǎshǔ guīyànà ●
French Guiana

加拉帕戈斯群岛 jiālāpàgēsī
qúndǎo ● **Galápagos Islands**

圭亚那 guīyànà ● **Guyana**

巴拉圭 bālāguī ● **Paraguay**

秘鲁 bìlǔ ● **Peru**

苏里南 sūlǐnán ● **Suriname**

乌拉圭 wūlāguī ● **Uruguay**

委内瑞拉 wěinèiruìlā ● **Venezuela**

词汇 cíhuì ● vocabulary

国家 guójiā country	省 shěng province	地域 dìyù zone
民族 mínzú nation	领土 lǐngtǔ territory	行政区 xíngzhèngqū district
大陆 dàlù continent	殖民地 zhímíndì colony	地区 dìqū region
主权国家 zhǔquán guójiā state	公国 gōngguó principality	首都 shǒudū capital

欧洲 ōuzhōu · Europe

法国 fǎguó · France

德国 déguó · Germany

意大利 yìdàlì · Italy

波兰 bōlán · Poland

葡萄牙 pútáoyá · Portugal

西班牙 xībānyá · Spain

阿尔巴尼亚 ā'ěrbāníyà · Albania

安道尔 āndào'ěr · Andorra

奥地利 àodìlì · Austria

巴利阿里群岛 bālìālǐ qúndǎo · Balearic Islands

白俄罗斯 bái'éluósī · Belarus

比利时 bǐlìshí · Belgium

波斯尼亚和黑塞哥维那(波黑) bōsīníyà hé hēisàigēwéinà(bōhēi) · Bosnia and Herzogovina

保加利亚 bǎojiālìyà · Bulgaria

科西嘉岛 kēxījiādǎo · Corsica

克罗地亚 kèluódìyà · Croatia

捷克 jiékè · Czech Republic

丹麦 dānmài · Denmark

爱沙尼亚 àishā'níyà · Estonia

芬兰 fēnlán · Finland

法国 fǎguó · France

德国 déguó · Germany

希腊 xīlà · Greece

匈牙利 xiōngyálì · Hungary

冰岛 bīngdǎo · Iceland

爱尔兰 ài'ěrlán · Ireland

意大利 yìdàlì · Italy

加里宁格勒 jiālǐnínggélè · Kaliningrad

科索沃 kēsuǒwò · Kosovo

拉脱维亚 lātuōwéiyà · Latvia

列支敦士登 lièzhīdūnshìdēng · Liechtenstein

立陶宛 lìtáowǎn · Lithuania

卢森堡 lúsēnbǎo · Luxembourg

马其顿 mǎqídùn · Macedonia

马耳他 mǎ'ěrtā · Malta

摩尔多瓦 mó'ěrduōwǎ · Moldova

摩纳哥 mónàgē · Monaco

黑山 hēishān · Montenegro

荷兰 hélán · Netherlands

挪威 nuówēi · Norway

波兰 bōlán · Poland

葡萄牙 pútáoyá · Portugal

罗马尼亚 luómǎníyà · Romania

俄罗斯联邦 éluósīliánbāng · Russian Federation

圣马力诺 shèngmǎlìnuò · San Marino

撒丁岛 sādīngdǎo · Sardinia

塞尔维亚 sài'ěrwéiyà · Serbia

西西里岛 xīxīlǐdǎo · Sicily

斯洛伐克 sīluòfákè · Slovakia

斯洛文尼亚 sīluòwénníyà · Slovenia

西班牙 xībānyá · Spain

瑞典 ruìdiǎn · Sweden

瑞士 ruìshì · Switzerland

乌克兰 wūkèlán · Ukraine

英国 yīngguó · United Kingdom

梵蒂冈 fàndìgāng · Vatican City

非洲 fēizhōu · **Africa**

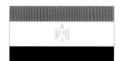

埃及 āijí · **Egypt**

埃塞俄比亚 āisài'ébǐyà · **Ethiopia**

肯尼亚 kěnníyà · **Kenya**

尼日利亚 nírìlìyà · **Nigeria**

南非 nánfēi · **South Africa**

乌干达 wūgāndá · **Uganda**

阿尔及利亚 ā'ěrjílìyà · **Algeria**

安哥拉 āngēlā · **Angola**

贝宁 bèiníng · **Benin**

博茨瓦纳 bócíwǎnà · **Botswana**

布基纳法索 bùjīnà fǎsuǒ · **Burkina Faso**

布隆迪 bùlóngdí · **Burundi**

卡奔达(安哥拉) kǎbēndá (āngēlā) · **Cabinda**

喀麦隆 kāmàilóng · **Cameroon**

中非共和国 zhōngfēi gònghéguó · **Central African Republic**

乍得 zhàdé · **Chad**

科摩罗群岛 kēmóluóqúndǎo · **Comoros**

刚果 gāngguǒ · **Congo**

刚果民主共和国 gāngguǒ mínzhǔ gònghéguó · **Democratic Republic of the Congo**

吉布提 jíbùtí · **Djibouti**

埃及 āijí · **Egypt**

赤道几内亚 chìdàojǐnèiyà · **Equatorial Guinea**

厄立特里亚 èlìtèlǐyà · **Eritrea**

埃塞俄比亚 āisài'ébǐyà · **Ethiopia**

加蓬 jiāpéng · **Gabon**

冈比亚 gāngbǐyà · **Gambia**

加纳 jiānà · **Ghana**

几内亚 jǐ'nèiyà · **Guinea**

几内亚比绍 jǐ'nèiyà bǐshào · **Guinea-Bissau**

科特迪瓦 kētèdíwǎ · **Ivory Coast**

肯尼亚 kěnníyà · **Kenya**

莱索托 láisuǒtuō · **Lesotho**

利比里亚 lìbǐlǐyà · **Liberia**

利比亚 lìbǐyà · **Libya**

马达加斯加 mǎdájiāsījiā · **Madagascar**

马拉维 mǎlāwéi · **Malawi**

马里 mǎlǐ · **Mali**

毛里塔尼亚 máolǐtǎníyà · **Mauritania**

毛里求斯 máolǐqiúsī · **Mauritius**

摩洛哥 móluògē · **Morocco**

莫桑比克 mòsāngbǐkè · **Mozambique**

纳米比亚 nàmǐbǐyà · **Namibia**

尼日尔 nírìěr · **Niger**

尼日利亚 nírìlìyà · **Nigeria**

卢旺达 lúwàngdá · **Rwanda**

圣多美和普林西比 shèngduōměi hé pǔlínxībǐ · **São Tomé and Principe**

塞内加尔 sàinèijiā'ěr · **Senegal**

塞拉利昂 sàilālì'áng · **Sierra Leone**

索马里 suǒmǎlǐ · **Somalia**

南非 nánfēi · **South Africa**

南苏丹 nán sūdān · **South Sudan**

苏丹 sūdān · **Sudan**

斯威士兰 sīwēishìlán · **Swaziland**

坦桑尼亚 tǎnsāngníyà · **Tanzania**

多哥 duōgē · **Togo**

突尼斯 tūnísī · **Tunisia**

乌干达 wūgāndá · **Uganda**

西撒哈拉 xīsāhālā · **Western Sahara**

赞比亚 zànbǐyà · **Zambia**

津巴布韦 jīnbābùwéi · **Zimbabwe**

亚洲 yàzhōu · **Asia**

孟加拉国 mèngjiālāguó ·
Bangladesh

中国 zhōngguó · **China**

印度 yìndù · **India**

日本 rìběn · **Japan**

约旦 yuēdàn · **Jordan**

菲律宾 fēilǜbīn · **Philippines**

韩国 hánguó · **South Korea**

泰国 tàiguó · **Thailand**

土耳其 tǔ'ěrqí · **Turkey**

阿富汗 āfùhàn · **Afghanistan**
亚美尼亚 yàměiníyà · **Armenia**
阿塞拜疆 ā'sàibàijiāng ·
Azerbaijan
巴林 bālín · **Bahrain**
孟加拉国 mèngjiālāguó ·
Bangladesh
不丹 bùdān · **Bhutan**
文莱 wénlái · **Brunei**
柬埔寨 jiǎnpǔzhài · **Cambodia**
中国 zhōngguó · **China**
塞浦路斯 sàipǔlùsī · **Cyprus**
东帝汶 dōngdìwèn · **East Timor**
斐济 fěijì · **Fiji**
格鲁吉亚 gélǔjíyà · **Georgia**
印度 yìndù · **India**

印度尼西亚 yìndùníxīyà ·
Indonesia
伊朗 yīlǎng · **Iran**
伊拉克 yīlākè · **Iraq**
以色列 yǐsèliè · **Israel**
日本 rìběn · **Japan**
约旦 yuēdàn · **Jordan**
哈萨克斯坦 hāsàkèsītǎn ·
Kazakhstan
科威特 kēwēitè · **Kuwait**
吉尔吉斯坦 jí'ěrjísītǎn · **Kyrgyzstan**
老挝 lǎowō · **Laos**
黎巴嫩 líbānèn · **Lebanon**
马来西亚 mǎláixīyà · **Malaysia**
马尔代夫 mǎ'ěrdàifū · **Maldives**
蒙古 měnggǔ · **Mongolia**

缅甸 miǎndiàn · **Myanmar
(Burma)**
尼泊尔 níbó'ěr · **Nepal**
朝鲜 cháoxiǎn · **North Korea**
阿曼 āmàn · **Oman**
巴基斯坦 bājīsītǎn · **Pakistan**
巴布亚新几内亚 bābùyà xīnjǐnèiyà
· **Papua New Guinea**
菲律宾 fēilǜbīn · **Philippines**
卡塔尔 kǎtǎ'ěr · **Qatar**
沙特阿拉伯 shātè'ālābó ·
Saudi Arabia
新加坡 xīnjiāpō · **Singapore**
所罗门群岛 suǒluómén qúndǎo ·
Solomon Islands
韩国 hánguó · **South Korea**

印度尼西亚 yìndùníxīyà ·
Indonesia

沙特阿拉伯 shātè'ālābó · **Saudi
Arabia**

越南 yuènán · **Vietnam**

斯里兰卡 sīlǐlánkǎ · **Sri Lanka**

叙利亚 xùlìyà · **Syria**

塔吉克斯坦 tǎjíkèsītǎn · **Tajikistan**

泰国 tàiguó · **Thailand**

土耳其 tǔ'ěrqí · **Turkey**

土库曼斯坦 tǔkùmànsītǎn ·
Turkmenistan

阿拉伯联合酋长国 ālābó liánhé
qiúzhǎngguó · **United Arab
Emirates**

乌兹别克斯坦 wūzībiékèsītǎn ·
Uzbekistan

瓦努阿图 wǎnǔ'ātú · **Vanuatu**

越南 yuènán · **Vietnam**

也门 yěmén · **Yemen**

大洋洲 dàyángzhōu ·
Australasia

澳大利亚 àodàlìyà · **Australia**

新西兰 xīnxīlán · **New Zealand**

澳大利亚 àodàlìyà · **Australia**

新西兰 xīnxīlán · **New Zealand**

塔斯马尼亚(岛) tǎsīmǎníyà(dǎo) ·
Tasmania

小品词与反义词 xiǎopǐncí yǔ fǎnyìcí •
particles and antonyms

到…去
dào…qù
to

从…来
cóng…lái
from

为
wèi
for

向…方向
xiàng…fāngxiàng
toward

在…上方
zài…shàngfāng
over

在…下方
zài…xiàfāng
under

沿着…
yánzhe…
along

越过
yuèguò
across

在…前面
zài…qiánmian
in front of

在…后面
zài…hòumian
behind

连同
liántóng
with

没有…
méiyǒu…
without

在…上
zài…shàng
onto

到…里
dào…lǐ
into

在…之前
zài…zhīqián
before

在…之后
zài…zhīhòu
after

在…里
zài…lǐ
in

在…外
zài…wài
out

不迟于…
bùchíyú…
by

直到…
zhídào…
until

在…上面
zài…shàngmian
above

在…下面
zài…xiàmian
below

早
zǎo
early

迟
chí
late

在…里面
zài…lǐmiàn
inside

在…外面
zài…wàimiàn
outside

现在
xiànzài
now

以后
yǐhòu
later

向上
xiàngshàng
up

向下
xiàngxià
down

一直
yīzhí
always

从不
cóngbù
never

在
zài
at

超出
chāochū
beyond

经常
jīngcháng
often

很少
hěnshǎo
rarely

穿越
chuānyuè
through

在…周围
zài…zhōuwéi
around

昨天
zuótiān
yesterday

明天
míngtiān
tomorrow

在…之上
zài…zhīshàng
on top of

在…旁边
zài…pángbiān
beside

第一
dìyī
first

最后
zuìhòu
last

在…之间
zài…zhījiān
between

在…对面
zài…duìmiàn
opposite

每…
měi…
every

一些
yīxiē
some

在…附近
zài…fùjìn
near

离…远
lí…yuǎn
far

关于
guānyú
about

准确地
zhǔnquède
exactly

这里
zhèlǐ
here

那里
nàlǐ
there

一点儿
yìdiǎn'er
a little

很多
hěnduō
a lot

大
dà
large

小
xiǎo
small

热
rè
hot

冷
lěng
cold

宽
kuān
wide

窄
zhǎi
narrow

开
kāi
open

关
guān
closed

高大
gāodà
tall

矮小
ǎixiǎo
short

满
mǎn
full

空
kōng
empty

高
gāo
high

低
dī
low

新
xīn
new

旧
jiù
old

厚
hòu
thick

薄
báo
thin

明亮
míngliàng
light

黑暗
hēiàn
dark

轻
qīng
light

重
zhòng
heavy

容易
róngyì
easy

困难
kùnnán
difficult

硬
yìng
hard

软
ruǎn
soft

空闲
kòngxián
free

忙碌
mánglù
occupied

潮湿
cháoshī
wet

干燥
gānzào
dry

强壮
qiángzhuàng
strong

虚弱
xūruò
weak

好
hǎo
good

坏
huài
bad

胖
pàng
fat

瘦
shòu
thin

快
kuài
fast

慢
màn
slow

年轻
niánqīng
young

年老
niánlǎo
old

正确
zhèngquè
correct

错误
cuòwù
wrong

更好
gènghǎo
better

更差
gèngchà
worse

干净
gānjìng
clean

脏
zāng
dirty

黑色
hēisè
black

白色
báisè
white

好看
hǎokàn
beautiful

丑
chǒu
ugly

有趣
yǒuqù
interesting

无聊
wúliáo
boring

贵
guì
expensive

便宜
piányi
cheap

生病的
shēngbìngde
sick

健康的
jiànkāngde
well

安静
ānjìng
quiet

吵闹
chǎonào
noisy

开始
kāishǐ
beginning

结束
jiéshù
end

中文 zhōngwén · english

常用语 cháng yòngyǔ · useful phrases

基本用语 jīběn yòngyǔ · essential phrases

是
shì
Yes

不
bù
No

也许
yěxǔ
Maybe

请
qǐng
Please

谢谢
xièxie
Thank you

不用谢
búyòngxiè
You're welcome

抱歉；打扰一下
bàoqiàn, dǎrǎoyíxià
Excuse me

对不起
duìbuqǐ
I'm sorry

不要
búyào
Don't

好
hǎo
OK

很好
hěnhǎo
That's fine

正确
zhèngquè
That's correct

不对
búduì
That's wrong

问候 wènhòu · greetings

你好
nǐ hǎo
Hello

再见
zàijiàn
Goodbye

早上好
zǎoshang hǎo
Good morning

下午好
xiàwǔ hǎo
Good afternoon

晚上好
wǎnshang hǎo
Good evening

晚安
wǎn'ān
Good night

你好吗？
nǐ hǎo ma?
How are you?

我叫…
wǒ jiào…
My name is …

您怎么称呼？
nín zěnme chēnghu?
What is your name?

他/她叫什么名字？
tā/tā jiào shénme míngzi?
What is his/her name?

我介绍一下…
wǒ jièshào yíxià…
May I introduce …

这是…
zhèshì…
This is …

很高兴见到你
hěngāoxìng jiàndào nǐ
Pleased to meet you

待会儿见
dài huǐ'er jiàn
See you later

标志 biāozhì · signs

游客问询处
yóukè wènxúnchù
Tourist information

入口
rùkǒu
Entrance

出口
chūkǒu
Exit

紧急出口
jǐnjí chūkǒu
Emergency exit

推
tuī
Push

危险
wēixiǎn
Danger

禁止吸烟
jìnzhǐxīyān
No smoking

故障
gùzhàng
Out of order

开放时间
kāifàng shíjiān
Opening times

免费入场
miǎnfèi rùchǎng
Free admission

减价
jiǎnjià
Reduced

打折
dǎzhé
Sale

进前敲门
jìnqiánqiāomén
Knock before entering

禁止践踏草坪
jìnzhǐ jiàntàcǎopíng
Keep off the grass

求助 qiúzhù · help

你能帮帮我吗？
nǐ néng bāngbāng wǒ ma?
Can you help me?

我不懂
wǒ bù dǒng
I don't understand

我不知道
wǒ bù zhīdào
I don't know

你说英语吗？
nǐ shuō yīngyǔ ma?
Do you speak English?

我会说英语
wǒ huì shuō yīngyǔ
I speak English

请说得再慢些
qǐng shuōdé zài màn xiē
Please speak more slowly

请帮我写下来
qǐng bāng wǒ xiě xiàlái
Please write it down for me

我丢了…
wǒ diūle…
I have lost …

方向 fāngxiàng ·
directions

我迷路了
wǒ mílùle
I am lost

...在哪里?
zàinǎli
Where is the ...?

最近的...在哪里?
zuìjinde...zàinǎli?
Where is the nearest ...?

洗手间在哪儿?
xǐshǒujiān zàinǎer?
Where is the restroom?

我怎么去…?
wǒ zěnme qù…?
How do I get to …?

右转
yòuzhuǎn
To the right

左转
zuǒzhuǎn
To the left

向前直行
xiàngqián zhíxíng
Straight ahead

到...有多远?
dào ...yǒu duōyuǎn?
How far is ...?

交通标志 jiāotōng biāozhì · road signs

各方通行
gèfāng tōngxíng
All directions

谨慎驾驶
jǐnshèn jiàshǐ
Caution

禁入
jinru
Do not enter

减速
jiǎnsù
Slow down

绕行
ràoxíng
Detour

靠右侧行驶
kào yòucè xíngshǐ
Keep right

高速公路
gāosùgōnglù
Freeway

禁止停车
jinzhǐ tíngchē
No parking

禁止通行
jinzhǐ tōngxíng
Dead end

单行道
dānxíngdào
One-way street

让路
rànglù
Yield

只限本区居民(停车)
zhǐxiànběnqūjūmín (tíngchē)
Residents only

道路管制
dàolùguǎnzhì
Roadwork

危险弯道
wēixiǎnwāndào
Dangerous curve

住宿 zhùsù ·
accommodation

我订了房间
wǒ ding le fángjiān
I have a reservation

餐厅在哪儿?
cāntīng zàinǎ'er
Where is the dining room?

几点吃早餐?
jǐdiǎn chī zǎocān?
What time is breakfast?

我将在...点回来
wǒ jiāng zài...diǎn huílái
I'll be back at ... o'clock

我明天离开
wǒ míngtiān líkāi
I'm leaving tomorrow

饮食 yǐnshí ·
eating and drinking

干杯!
gānbēi
Cheers!

很好吃/很难吃
hěn hǎochī/hěn nánchī
It's delicious/awful

我不喝酒/抽烟
wǒ bù hējiǔ/chōuyān
I don't drink/smoke

我不吃肉
wǒ bù chīròu
I don't eat meat

够了，谢谢
gòule, xièxiè
No more for me, thank you

请再来点儿
qǐng zàilái diǎn'ér
May I have some more?

我们要结账
wǒmen yào jiézhàng
May we have the check?

请开张收据
qǐng kāi zhāng shōujù
Can I have a receipt?

吸烟区
xīyānqū
Smoking area

健康 jiànkāng ·
health

我不舒服
wǒ bù shūfu
I don't feel well

我难受
wǒ nánshòu
I feel sick

我这儿疼
wǒ zhè'er téng
It hurts here

我发烧了
wǒ fāshāole
I have a fever

我怀孕...个月了
wǒ huáiyùn...gè yuèle
I'm ... months pregnant

我需要...处方
wǒ xūyào...chǔfāng
I need a prescription for ...

我通常服用...
wǒ tōngcháng fúyòng...
I normally take ...

我对...过敏
wǒ duì...guòmǐn
I'm allergic to ...

他/她没事吧?
tā/tā méishi ba?
Will he/she be all right?

中文索引 zhōngwén suŏyǐn • Chinese index

zhōngwén

zhōngwén

guónèi hángxiàn 212
guŏrén 122, 129
guŏrén qiāokělì cuìbĭng 141
guŏròu 124, 127, 129
guŏshànchē 262
guŏwèisuānnǎi 157
guŏwèixiàngpítáng 113
guŏyuán 183
guŏzhī 149, 156
guŏzhī bīnggāo 141
gǔpén 17
gǔpiào jiàgé 97
gǔpiào jīngjìrén 97
gǔquán 97
gùshìpiàn 269
gǔshŏu 258
gùtǐfēngmì 134
gùtou 119, 121
gùwèn 55
gǔwù 130
gǔxì 97
gùyuán 24
gùzhàng 203
gǔzhānghèchǎi 255
gǔzhé 46
gùzhìhuán 89
gùzhǔ 24

H

hǎi 264, 282
hǎi'àn 285
hǎi'àn jīngwèidùi 217
hǎi'òu 292
hǎibào 255, 290
hǎibīn bùdào 265
hǎibīn yóuyŏngdài 264
hǎidǐ 314
hǎiguān 212, 216
hǎiguī 293
hǎilánbǎoshí 288
hǎiláng 264
hǎilú 120
hǎimǎ 294
hǎimián 73, 74, 83
hǎimiáncéng 126
hǎishī 290
hǎitān 264
hǎitān xiǎowū 264
hǎitān yújìn 265
hǎitún 290
hǎiwángxīng 280
hǎixiàn 121
hǎixiàng 290
hǎixīng 295
hǎiyáng bǔlāo 245
hǎizi 23
hàn jiǔjiāng yǐnliào 145
hànbǎobāo 154, 155
hànbǎotàoàcān 154
hángbānhào 212
hángféng 277
hángkōng mǔjiàn 215
hángkōng yóujiàn 98
hángtiān fēijī 281
hánguó 318

hángxíng 240
hànjié 79
hánqián 199
hànxì 79, 81
hánzhàn 44
hǎo 321
hǎogōu 300
hǎokàn 321
hǎokè 310
hǎomǐ 310
hǎoqiú 228
hǎoshèng 311
hásàkèsītǎn 318
hé 127
hè 292
hé'àn 284
hé'èrméng 20
héchéngdé 31
hégǔ 17
hégǔxiàn 89
hèiàn 321
hēibǎn 162
hēicùlì 127
hēidài 237
hēidòng 280
hēifúshuāng 41
hēigǎnlǎn 143
hēigé 272
hēihǎi 313
hēikāfēi 148
hēimáimiànfěn 138
hēiméi 127
hēimiànbāo 138, 139, 149
hēiqiǎokělì 113
hēisàigéwèinà 316
hēisè 39, 274, 321
hēishān 316
hēitáo 273
hēixiànxuě 120
hēiyǎndòu 131
hēiyàoyán 288
hēiyú 288
hèkǎ 27
hékŏu 285
hélán 316
héliú 284
hémǎ 291
hénduŏ 320
hénggàn 235
hénggǎng 250
hénggémó 19
héngliáng 207
héngzuò'àn 242
hěnshǎo 320
héqìdào 236
hèsè 274
hèsèxiǎobiǎndòu 131
héshì cídàilùyīnjī 269
héshì lùyīndài 269
hétáo 129
hétaoyóu 134
hóng (pútáojiǔ) 145
hóngbǎoshí 288
hóngchá 149

hóngcùlì 127
hóngdòu 131
hóngdúlāsī 314
hónghǎi 313
hónghèsè 39
hónghuācàidòu 122
hóngkǎo càiyáopán 69
hóngkǎo shípǐn 107
hóngkǎode 129
hóngmó 51
hóngpái 223
hóngqiújújù 123
hóngròu 118
hóngsè 274
hóngshǔ 125
hóngshuǐ 287
hóngxīn 273
hóngyǎn 271
hóngyú 294
hóngyúndòu 131
hóngzhàjī 211
hóngzī 67, 138, 159
hóngzōngsè 39
hóngzūnyú 120
hòu 272, 321
hòudǐxiē 37
hòujiǎbǎn 214
hòujìdàtíng 213
hòujié 19
hòujìlóu 212
hòujǐng 13
hòulún 197
hòutiān 307
hòutóu 19
hòutuǐròu 119
hòuzhěnshì 45
hòuzi 291
hòuzuò 200, 204
hú 164, 285
hǔ 291
huà 62, 162, 274
huà 110, 297
huà'è 297
huàbǎn 249, 263
huàbān 297
huàbǎn yùndòng 249
huàbāo 111
huàbǐ 274
huàbiàn 35
huàbù 274
huàchuán 241
huàchuánjī 250
huàdiàn 110
huàfěn 276
huàfúbīng 157
huàgāngyán 288
huàgěpíng 84
huàguǎn 111
huàhànbīng 249
huàhuán 111
huài 321
huàiyùn 20, 52
huàiyùnde 52
huàiyùnsāngèyuè 52
huàjì 99

huàjià 274
huàjià 191, 274
huàjiàn 249
huàjiǎngchuán 214
huàkuàng 62
huàlěi 229
huàlěi 297
huàn píndào 269
huànchéng 209
huàndēngjī 163, 174
huàngféng 295
huánggǎidiē 120
huángguā 125
huánghún 305
huángpái 223
huángsè 274
huángshuǐxiàn 111
huángyóu 137, 156
huángyú 288
huánjìng 280
huànrén 223
huànshùriqì 168
huànxióng 290
huànyìdiàn 74
huànzhě 45
huàpén 89
huàpíng 63, 111
huàshàng 188
huàshēng 129, 151
huàshēngjiàng 135
huàshēngyóu 135
huàshìqíshù 243
huàshù 296
huàshù 35, 111
huàshuǐqiáo 241
huàshuǐzhě 241
huàtán 85, 90
huàtí 263
huàtōng 179
huáxiàng 248
huáxiángjī 211, 248
huáxiàngsàn 248
huáxíng 224
huáxuě 246
huáxuě 162
huáxuě pōdào 246
huáxuěbǎn 246
huáxuěfú 246
huáxuějìng 247
huáxuěshàn 31, 33
huáxuěxuē 246
huáxuězhàng 246
huáxuězhě 246
huàyàng 83
huàyàng huábīng 247
huàyàng yóuyŏng 239
huàyècài 124
huàyuán 84
huàyuán zhuāngshì 84
huàyuánfēnggé 84
huàyuánzhìwù 86
huàzhuāng 40
huàzhuāngjìng 40
huàzhuāngpǐn 107

huàzhuāngshuā 40
húchǐ 237
húdié 295
húfàsù 38
huì 293
huídá 163
huígān 232
huíhé 230, 237
huíhuà 261, 274
huíjiàng 187
huílù 97
huìpiào 98
huíqiú 231
huìsè 39, 274
huíshŏuzhàn 177
huìsuŏ 232
huíwěi 280
huìxiàng 122, 133
huìxiàngzǐ 133
huìxīng 280
huìyàn 19
huìyì 174
huìyìjìlù 174
huìyìshì 174
huìzhāng 189
hùjiàn 224
hùjiào ànniǔ 48
hùjiàofēn 64, 152
hùjiāolì 132
húkuì 236
húli 290
húlǐ 91
húliànwàng 177
húlubā 132
húluóbo 124
húmíng 81, 167
húnjué 44
húnlí 26, 35
húnlǐ dàngāo 141
hùnníngtǔkuài 187
hūnyàn 26
hūnyīntái 179
huòbì 97
huòbì miànè 97
huòcāng 215
huòchái 112
huòchē 208
huòchéngyùn 288
huòchētóu 208
huòchēzhàn 208
huòchuán 215
huódòng 245, 263
huódòng wánjù 74
huódòngguàtú 174
huŏhuāsāi 203
huŏjī 119, 185, 293
huòjià 106
huŏliènǎo 292
huŏlú 67
huŏmiàn 138
huòpàngjiàn 16
huòqícúnkuǎn zhànghù 96
huŏqíng 95
huŏshān 283
huŏshāndǎo 283

M

zhōngwén

zhōngwén

zhōngwén

zhōngwén

英文索引 yīngwén suǒyǐn • English index

A

à la carte 152
abdomen 12
abdominals 16
above 320
acacia 110
accelerator 200
access road 216
accessories 36, 38
accident 46
account number 96
accountant 97, 190
accounting department 175
accused 180
ace 230, 273
Achilles tendon 16
acorn squash 125
acquaintance 24
acquitted 181
across 320
acrylic paints 274
actions 237, 229, 227, 233, 183
activities 263, 245, 162, 77
actor 254, 191
actors 179
actress 254
acupressure 55
acupuncture 55
Adam's apple 19
add v 165
addition 58
address 98
adhesive bandage 47
adhesive tape 47
adjustable wrench 80
admissions office 168
admitted 48
adult 23
advantage 230
adventure movie 255
advertisement 269
adzuki beans 131
aerate v 91
Afghanistan 318
Africa 317
after 320
afternoon 305
aftershave 73
aftersun lotion 108
agate 289
agenda 174
aikido 236
aileron 210
air bag 201
air-conditioning 200
air cylinder 239

air filter 202, 204
air letter 98
air mattress 267
air vent 210
aircraft 210
aircraft carrier 215
airliner 210, 212
airport 212
aisle 106, 168, 210, 254
alarm clock 70
Alaska 314
Albania 316
alcoholic drinks 145
alfalfa 184
Algeria 317
all meals included 101
all-purpose flour 139
Allen wrench 80
allergy 44
alley 298
alligator 293
alligator clip 167
allspice 132
almond 129
almond oil 134
almonds 151
along 320
alpine 87
alpine skiing 247
alternating current 60
alternative therapy 54
alternator 203
altitude 211
aluminium 289
Amazonia 312
ambulance 94
amethyst 288
amniocentesis 52
amniotic fluid 52
amount 96
amp 60
amphibians 294
amplifier 268
analog 179
anchor 179, 191, 214, 240
Andes 312
Andorra 316
anesthetist 48
angle 164
angler 244
Angola 317
angry 25
animals 292, 294
animated movie 255
ankle 13, 15
ankle length 34
anniversary 26
annual 86, 307

answer 163
answer v 99, 163
answering machine 99
ant 295
antenna 295
antifreeze 199, 203
anti-inflammatory 109
antique store 114
antiseptic 47
antiseptic wipe 47
antiwrinkle 41
antler 291
apartment 59
apartment building 59, 298
apéritif 153
aperture dial 270
apex 165
app 99
appeal 181
appearance 30
appendix 18
appetizer 153
applaud v 255
apple 126
apple corer 68
apple juice 149
appliances 66
application 176
appointment 45, 175
apricot 126
April 306
apron 30, 50, 69, 212
aquamarine 288
Arabian Sea 313
arbor 84
arborio rice 130
arc 164
arch 15, 85, 301
archery 249
architect 190
architecture 300
architrave 301
Arctic Circle 283
Arctic Ocean 312
area 165, 310
areas 299
arena 243
Argentina 315
arithmetic 165
arm 13
armchair 63
Armenia 318
armpit 13
armrest 200, 210
aromatherapy 55
around 320

arrangements 111
arrest 94
arrivals 213
arrow 249
art 162
art college 169
Art Deco 301
art gallery 261
art history 169
Art Nouveau 301
art supply store 115
artery 19
artichoke 124
artist 274
arts and crafts 274, 276
arugula 123
ash 283
ashtray 150
Asia 318
asparagus 124
asphalt 187
assault 94
assistant 24
assisted delivery 53
asteroid 280
asthma 44
astigmatism 51
astronaut 281
astronomy 281
asymmetric bars 235
at 320
athlete 234
athletic shoes 31
Atlantic Ocean 312
ATM 97
atmosphere 282, 286
atrium 104
attachment 177
attack 220
attack zone 224
attend v 174
attic 58
attractions 261
auburn 39
audience 254
August 306
aunt 22
aurora 286
Australasia 319
Australia 319
Austria 316
auto racing 249
automatic 200
automatic door 196
automatic payment 96
avalanche 247
avenue 299
avocado 128

awning 148
ax 95
axle 205
ayurveda 55
Azerbaijan 318

B

baby 23, 30
baby bath 74
baby care 74
baby carriage 75
baby changing room 104
baby monitor 75
baby products 107
baby sling 75
back 13
back brush 73
backboard 226
backdrop 254
backgammon 272
backhand 231
backpack 31, 37, 267
backseat 200
backsplash 66
backstroke 239
backswing 233
bacon 118, 157
bacon strip 119
bad 321
badge 94, 189
badminton 231
bag 311
bag cart 233
bagel 139
baggage carousel 212
baggage claim 213
baggage trailer 212
bags 37
baguette 138
Bahamas 314
bail 181
bailiff 180
bait 244
bait v 245
bake v 67, 138
baked 159
baker 139
bakery 107, 114, 138
baking 69
balance wheel 276
balcony 59
balcony seats 254
bald 39
bale 184
Balearic Islands 316
ball 15, 75, 221, 224, 226, 228, 230
ball boy 231

english

english

choke v 47
chop 119, 237
chorizo 143
choux pastry 140
christening 26
Christmas 27
chrysanthemum 110
chuck 78
church 298, 300
chutney 134
cider vinegar 135
cigar 112
cigarettes 112
cilantro 133
cinder block 187
cinnamon 133
circle 165
circuit training 251
circular saw 78
circulation desk 168
circumference 164
citrus fruit 126
city 298, 299
clam 121
clamp 78, 166
clapper board 179
clarinet 257
clasp 36
classical music 255, 259
classroom 162
claw 291
clay 85, 275
clean v 77
clean clothes 76
cleaned 121
cleaner 188
cleaning equipment 77
cleaning fluid 51
cleanser 41
clear honey 134
cleat 220, 223, 240
cleaver 68
clementine 126
client 38, 175, 180
cliff 285
climber 87
climbing frame 263
clinic 48
clipboard 173
clitoris 20
clock radio 70
closed 260, 321
closet 71
cloth diaper 30
clothesline 76
clothespin 76
clothing 205
cloud 287
cloudy 286
clove 125
clover 297
cloves 133
club 273

club sandwich 155
clubhouse 232
clutch 200, 204
coal 288
coast 285
coast guard 217
coaster 150
coat 32
coat hanger 70
cockatoo 293
cockle 121
cockpit 210
cockroach 295
cocktail 151
cocktail shaker 150
cocoa powder 148
coconut 129
cocoon 295
cod 120
coffee 144, 148, 153, 156, 184
coffee cup 65
coffee machine 148, 150
coffee milkshake 149
coffee table 62
coffee with milk 148
cog 206
coin 97
coin return 99
cola 144
colander 68
cold 44, 286, 321
cold faucet 72
cold-pressed oil 135
collage 275
collar 32
collarbone 17
colleague 24
collect call 99
college 168
Colombia 315
colony 315
coloring pencil 163
colors 39, 274
comb 38
comb v 38
combat sports 236
combine 182
comedy 255
comet 280
comforter 71
comic book 112
commission 97
communications 98
commuter 208
Comoros 317
compact 40
company 175
compartment 209
compass 165, 312, 240
complaint 94

complexion 41
compliments slip 173
composite sketch 181
compost 88
compost pile 85
computer 176
concealer 40
conceive v 20
conception 52
concert 255, 258
concourse 209
concussion 46
condensed milk 136
conditioner 38
condom 21
conductor 256
cone 164, 187
confectioner 113
candy 107, 113
confident 25
confused 25
conglomerate 288
Congo 317
conifer 86
connect v 177
connection 212
conning tower 215
console 269
constellation 281
construction 186
construction site 186
construction worker 186, 188
consultation 45
contact lenses 51
container 216, 311
container port 216
container ship 215
continent 282, 315
contraception 21, 52
contraction 52
control tower 212
controller 269
controls 201, 204
convector heater 60
convertible 199
conveyer belt 106
cooked meat 118, 143
cookie sheet 69
cookies 113, 141
cooking 67
coolant reservoir 202
cooling rack 69
copilot 211
copper 289
copy v 172
coral reef 285
cordless drill 78
cordless phone 99
core 127
cork 134
corkscrew 150
corn 122, 130, 184

corn bread 139
corn oil 135
cornea 51
corner 223
corner flag 223
cornice 300
corset 35
Corsica 316
cosmetics 105
Costa Rica 314
costume 255
cottage cheese 136
cottage garden 84
cotton 184, 277
cotton balls 41
cough 44
cough medicine 108
counselor 55
count v 165
counter 96, 98, 100, 142, 272
countertop 66
country 259, 315
couple 24
courier 99
courses 153
court 226
court case 180
court clerk 180
court date 180
courtroom 180
courtyard 58, 84
couscous 130
cousin 22
coveralls 82
cow 185
cow's milk 136
crab 121, 295
cracked wheat 130
craft knife 81
crafts 275
cramp 239
cramps 44
cranberry 127
crane 187, 216, 292
crater 283
crayfish 121
cream 109, 137, 140
cream cheese 136
cream pie 141
crease 225
credit card 96
creel 245
creeper 87
crème caramel 141
crème pâtissière 140
crepes 155, 157
crescent moon 280
crew 241
crew hatch 201
crew neck 33
crib 74
cricket 225, 295

cricket ball 225
cricket player 225
crime 94
criminal 181
criminal record 181
crisp 127
crispbread 139, 156
crisper 67
Croatia 316
crochet 277
crochet hook 277
crockery 64
crockery 65
crocodile 293
croissant 156
crop 39, 183
crop farm 183
crops 184
crossbar 207, 222, 235
cross-country skiing 247
crosswalk 195
crow 292
crown 50
crucible 166
crushed 132
crust 139, 282
cry v 25
crystal healing 55
Cuba 314
cube 164
cucumber 125
cuff 32, 45
cuff links 36
cultivate v 91
cultivator 182
cumin 132
curb 298
cured 118, 159, 143
curling 247
curling iron 38
curly 39
currant 129
currency exchange 97
curry 158
curry powder 132
curtain 63, 254
curved 165
cushion 62
custard 140
customer 96, 104, 106, 152
customer service department 175
customer services 104
customs 212
customs house 216
cut 46
cut v 38, 79, 277
cuticle 15
cutlery 65
cuts 119

english

english

groom 243
ground 60, 132
ground coffee 144
ground cover 87
ground floor 104
ground meat 119
ground sheet 267
group therapy 55
grout 83
guard 236
guardrail 195
Guatemala 314
guava 128
guest 64, 100
guidebook 260
guided tour 260
guilty 181
Guinea 317
Guinea-Bissau 317
guitarist 258
gull 292
gum 50
gumdrop 113
gun 94
gurney 48
gutter 58, 299
guy rope 266
Guyana 315
gym 101, 250
gym machine 250
gymnast 235
gymnastics 235
gynecologist 52
gynecology 49
gypsophila 110

H

hacksaw 81
haddock 120
hemorrhage 46
hail 286
hair 14, 38
hair dye 40
hair straightener 38
hairdresser 38, 188
hairspray 38
Haiti 314
half an hour 304
half-and-half 137
half-liter 311
halftime 223
halibut fillets 120
Halloween 27
halter 243
halter neck 35
ham 119, 143, 156
hammer 80
hammer v 79
hammock 266
hamper 263
hamster 290
hamstring 16
hand 13, 15
hand drill 81

hand fork 89
hand rail 59, 196
hand towel 73
handbag 37
handcuffs 94
handicap 233
handkerchief 36
handle 36, 88, 106, 187, 200, 230
handlebar 207
handles 37
handsaw 81, 89
handset 99
hang v 82
hang-glider 248
hang-gliding 248
hanging basket 84
hanging file 173
happy 25
harbor 217
harbor master 217
hard 129, 321
hard candy 113
hard cheese 136
hard cider 145
hard hat 186
hardboard 79
hardware 176
hardware store 114
hardwood 79
haricot beans 131
harness race 243
harp 256
harvest v 91, 183
hat 36
hatchback 199, 200
have a baby v 26
Hawaii 314
hay 184
hay fever 44
hazard 195
hazard lights 201
hazelnut 129
hazelnut oil 134
head 12, 19, 81, 230
head v 222
head injury 46
head office 175
headache 44
headband 39
headboard 70
headlight 198, 205, 207
headphones 268
headrest 200
headsail 240
health 44
health center 168
health food store 115
heart 18, 119, 122, 273
heart attack 44
heater controls 201
heather 297
heating element 61

heavy 321
heavy cream 137
heavy metal 259
hedge 85, 90, 182
hedgehog 290
heel 13, 15, 37
height 165
helicopter 211
hello 322
helmet 95, 204, 206, 220, 224, 228
help desk 168
hem 34
hematite 289
hen's egg 137
herb 55, 86
herb garden 84
herbaceous border 85
herbal remedies 108
herbal tea 149
herbalism 55
herbicide 183
herbs 133, 134
herbs and spices 132
herd 183
hexagon 164
high 321
high chair 75
high definition 269
high dive 239
high-heeled shoe 37
high jump 235
high speed train 208
highlights 39
hiking 263
hiking boot 37, 267
hill 284
Himalayas 313
hip 12
hippopotamus 291
historic building 261
history 162
hit v 224
hob 67
hockey 224
hockey stick 224
hoe 88
hold 215, 237
hole 232
hole in one 233
hole punch 173
holly 296
home 58
home delivery 154
home entertainment 268
home furnishings 105
home plate 228
homeopathy 55
homework 163
homogenized 137
Honduras 314
honeycomb 135
honeymoon 26

honeysuckle 297
hood 31, 75, 198
hoof 242, 291
hook 187, 276
hoop 226, 277
horizontal bar 235
hormone 20
horn 201, 204, 291
horror movie 255
horse 185, 235, 242
horse race 243
horseback riding 242, 263
horseradish 125
horseshoe 242
hose 89, 95
hose reel 89
hosepipe 89
hospital 48
host 64, 178
hostess 64
hot 124, 286, 321
hot-air balloon 211
hot chocolate 144, 156
hot dog 155
hot drinks 144
hot faucet 72
hot-water bottle 70
hotel 100, 264
hour 304
hour hand 304
house 58
household current 60
household products 107
hovercraft 215
hub 206
hubcap 202
hull 214, 240
human resources department 175
humerus 17
humid 286
hummingbird 292
hump 291
hundred 308
hundred and ten 308
hundred thousand 308
hundredth 309
Hungary 316
hungry 64
hurdles 235
hurricane 287
husband 22
husk 130
hydrant 95
hydrofoil 215
hydrotherapy 55
hypnotherapy 55
hypoallergenic 41
hypotenuse 164

I

ice 120, 287
ice and lemon 151
ice bucket 150
ice climbing 247
ice cream 137, 149
ice-cream scoop 68
ice cube 151
ice hockey 224
ice hockey player 224
ice hockey rink 224
ice maker 67
ice skate 224
ice-skating 247
iced coffee 148
iced tea 149
Iceland 316
icicle 287
icon 177
identity tag 53
igneous 288
ignition 200
iguana 293
illness 44
immigration 212
impotent 20
in 320
in brine 143
in front of 320
in oil 143
in sauce 159
in syrup 159
inbox 177
inch 310
incisor 50
incubator 53
index finger 15
India 318
Indian Ocean 312
indigo 274
Indonesia 319
induce labour v 53
industrial park 299
infection 44
infertile 20
infield 228
inflatable dinghy 215
inflatable ring 265
information 261
information screen 213
in-goal area 221
inhaler 44, 109
injection 48
injury 46
ink 275
ink pad 173
inlet 61
inline skating 249
inner core 282
inner tube 207
inning 228
innocent 181

english

english

english

english

english

english

problems 271
processed grains 130
procession 27
processor 176
produce seller 188
produce stand 114
producer 254
professor 169
program 176, 254, 269
programming 178
propagate v 91
propeller 211, 214
proposal 174
prosciutto 143
prosecution 180
prostate 21
protractor 165
proud 25
prove v 139
province 315
prow 215
prune 129
prune v 91
pruners 89
psychiatry 49
psychotherapy 55
public address system 209
puck 224
Puerto Rico 314
puff pastry 140
pull up v 251
pulp 127
pulse 47
pumice 288
pumice stone 73
pump 37, 207
pumpkin 125
pumpkin seed 131
punch 237
punching bag 237
pup 290
pupil 51
puppy 290
purple 274
push-up 251
putt v 233
putter 233
pyramid 164

Q

Qatar 318
quadriceps 16
quail 119
quail egg 137
quart 311
quarter of an hour 304
quarterdeck 214
quartz 289
quay 216
queen 272, 273

question 163
question v 163
quiche 142
quiche pan 69
quick cooking 130
quilt 71
quilting 277
quince 128
quinoa 130
quiver 249

R

rabbit 118, 290
raccoon 290
race 234
race-car driver 249
racecourse 243
racehorse 243
racing bike 205, 206
racing dive 239
rack 166
racket 230
racket games 231
racquetball 231
radar 214, 281
radiator 60, 202
radicchio 123
radio 179, 268
radio antenna 214
radio station 179
radiology 49
radish 124
radius 17, 164
rafter 186
rafting 241
rail 208
railcar 208
railroad network 209
rain 287
rain boots 31
rain forest 285
rain gear 245, 267
rainbow 287
rainbow trout 120
raincoat 31, 32
raisin 129
rake 88
rake v 90
rally 230
rally driving 249
RAM 176
Ramadan 26
ramekin 69
rap 259
rapeseed 184
rapids 240, 284
rappelling 248
rash 44
raspberry 127
raspberry jam 134
rat 290
rattle 74
raw 124, 129

ray 294
razor blade 73
razorshell clam 121
read v 162
reading light 210
reading list 168
reading room 168
real estate office 115
realtor 189
reamer 80
rear light 207
rear wheel 197
rearview mirror 198
receipt 152
receive v 177
receiver 99
reception 100
receptionist 100, 190
record 234, 269
record player 268
record store 115
recording studio 179
rectangle 164
rectum 21
recycling bin 61
red 274
red (wine) 145
red card 223
red currant 127
red eye 271
red kidney beans 131
red lentils 131
red meat 118
red mullet 120
Red Sea 313
reduce v 172
reduced-fat milk 136
reel 244
reel in v 245
referee 220, 222, 226
referral 49
reflector 50, 204, 207
reflector strap 205
reflexology 54
reggae 259
region 315
regional office 175
register 100
registered mail 98
regulator 239
reheat v 154
reiki 55
reins 242
relationships 24
relatives 23
relaxation 55
relay race 235
release v 245
remote control 269
Renaissance 301
renew v 168
rent 58
rent v 58

repair kit 207
report 174
reporter 179
reproduction 20
reproductive 19
reproductive organs 20
reptiles 293
research 169
reserve v 168
residence hall 168
respiratory 19
rest 256
restaurant 101, 152
restrooms 104, 266
result 49
resurfacing 187
resuscitation 47
retina 51
retire v 26
return 231
return address 98
reverse v 195
rewind 269
rhinoceros 291
rhombus 164
rhubarb 127
rhythmic gymnastics 235
rib 17, 119, 155
rib cage 17
ribbon 27, 39, 111, 141, 235
rice 130, 158, 184
rice pudding 140
rider 242
riding boot 242
riding crop 242
riding hat 242
rigging 215, 240
right 260
right field 229
right-hand drive 201
right lane 194
rim 206
rind 119, 127, 136, 142
ring 36
ring finger 15
ring ties 89
rings 235
rinse v 38, 76
ripe 129
rise v 139
river 284
road bike 206
road markings 194
road roller 83, 187
road signs 195
roads 194
roadwork 187, 195
roast 158
roast v 67
roasted 129

robe 31, 32, 35, 38
rock climbing 248
rock concert 258
rock garden 84
rocks 284, 288
Rocky Mountains 312
Rococo 301
rodeo 243
roll 139, 311
roll v 67
roller coaster 262
roller shade 63
rollerblading 263
rolling pin 69
romance 255
Romania 316
romper 30
roof 58, 203
roof garden 84
roof rack 198
roof tile 187
rook 272
room 58
room key 100
room number 100
room service 101
rooms 100
rooster 185
root 50, 124, 296
roots 39
rope 248
rose 89, 110
rosé 145
rosemary 133
rotor blade 211
rotten 127
rough 232
round 237
roundabout 195
route number 196
router 78
row 210, 254
row v 241
row boat 214
row house 58
rower 241
rowing machine 250
rubber band 173
rubber boots 89
rubber stamp 173
ruby 288
ruck 221
rudder 210, 241
rug 63
rugby 221
rugby field 221
ruler 163, 165
rum 145
rum and cola 151
rump steak 119
run 228
run v 228

english

english

english

鸣谢 míngxiè • acknowledgments

DORLING KINDERSLEY would like to thank Christine Lacey for design assistance, Georgina Garner for editorial and administrative help, Kopal Agarwal, Polly Boyd, Sonia Gavira, Cathy Meeus, Antara Raghavan, and Priyanka Sharma for editorial help, Claire Bowers for compiling the DK picture credits, Nishwan Rasool for picture research, and Suruchi Bhatia, Miguel Cunha, Mohit Sharma, and Alex Valizadeh for app development and creation.

The publisher would like to thank the following for their kind permission to reproduce their photographs.

Abbreviations key: a-above; b-below/bottom; c-center; f-far; l-left; r-right; t-top)

123RF.com: Andriy Popov 34tl; Brad Wynnyk 172bc; Daniel Ernst 179tc; Hongqi Zhang 24cla, 175cr; Ingvar Bjork 60c; Kidsada Manchinda 270br; Kobby Dagan 259c; leonardo255 269c; Liubov Vadimovna (Luba) Nel 39cla; Ljupco Smokovski 75crb; Oleksandr Marynchenko 60bl; Olga Popova 33c; oneblink 49bc; Robert Churchill 94c; Roman Gorielov 33bc; Ruslan Kudrin 35bc, 35br; Subbotina 39cra; Sutichak Yachaingkham 39tc; Tarzhanova 37tc; Vitaly Valua 39tl; Wavebreak Media Ltd 188bl; Wilawan Khasawong 75cb; **Action Plus:** 224bc; **Alamy Images:** 154t; A.T. Willett 287bcl; Alex Segre 105ca, 195cl; Ambrophoto 24cra; Blend Images 168cr; Cultura RM 33r; Doug Houghton 107fbr; Hugh Threlfall 35tl; 176tr; Ian Allenden 48br; Ian Dagnall 270tc; Levgen Chepil 250bc; Imagebroker 199tl, 249c; Keith Morris 178c; Martyn Evans 210b; MBI 175tl; Michael Burrell 213cra; Michael Foyle 184bl; Oleksiy Maksymenko 105tc; Paul Weston 168br; Prisma Bildagentur AG 246b; Radharc Images 197tr; RBtravel 112tl; Ruslan Kudrin 176tl; Sasa Huzjak 258t; Sergey Kravchenko 37ca; Sergio Azenha 270bc; Stanca Sanda (iPad is a trademark of Apple Inc., registered in the U.S. and other countries) 176bc; Stock Connection 287bcr; tarczas 35c; Vitaly Suprun 176cl; Wavebreak Media ltd 39cl, 174b, 175tr; **Allsport/Getty Images:** 238cl; **Alvey and Towers:** 209 acr, 215bcl, 215bcr, 241cr; **Peter Anderson:** 188cbr, 271br. **Anthony Blake Photo Library:** Charlie Stebbings 114cl; John Sims 114tcl; **Andyalte:** 98tl; **Arcaid:** John Edward Linden 301bl; Martine Hamilton Knight, Architects: Chapman Taylor Partners, 213cl; Richard Bryant 301br; **Argos:** 41tcl, 66cbl, 66cl, 66br, 66bcl, 69cl, 70bcl, 71t, 77tl, 269tc, 270tl; **Axiom:** Eitan Simanor 105bcr; Ian Cumming 104t; Vicki Couchman 148cr; **Beken Of Cowes Ltd:** 215cbc; **Bosch:** 76tcr, 76tc, 76tcl; **Camera Press:** 38tr, 256t, 257cr; Barry J. Holmes 148tr; Jane Hanger 159cr; Mary Germanou 259bc; **Corbis:** 78b; Anna Clopet 247tr; Ariel Skelley / Blend Images 52l; Bettmann 181tl, 181tr; Blue Jean Images 48bl; Bo Zauders 156t; Bob Rowan 152bl; Bob Winsett 247cbl; Brian Bailey 247br; Chris Rainer 247ctl; Craig Aurness 215bl; David H.Wells 249cdr; Dennis Marsico 274bl;

Dimitri Lundt 236bc; Duomo 211tl; Gail Mooney 277ctcr; George Lepp 248c; Gerald Nowak 239b; Gunter Marx 248cr; Jack Hollingsworth 231bl; Jacqui Hurst 277cbr; James L. Amos 247bl, 191ctr, 220bcr; Jan Butchofsky 277cbc; Johnathan Blair 243cr; Jose F. Poblete 191br; Jose Luis Pelaez.Inc 153tc; Karl Weatherly 220bl, 247tcr; Kelly Mooney Photography 259tl; Kevin Fleming 249bc; Kevin R. Morris 105tr, 243tl, 243tc; Kim Sayer 249tcr; Lynn Goldsmith 258t; Macduff Everton 231bcl; Mark Gibson 249bl; Mark L. Stephenson 249tcl; Michael Pole 115tr; Michael S. Yamashita 247ctcl; Mike King 247cbl; Neil Rabinowitz 214br; Pablo Corral 115bc; Paul A. Sounders 169br, 249ctcl; Paul J. Sutton 224c, 224br; Phil Schermeister 227b, 248tr; R. W Jones 309; Richard Morrell 189bc; Rick Doyle 241ctr; Robert Holmes 97br, 277ctc; Roger Ressmeyer 169tr; Russ Schleipman 229; The Purcell Team 211ctr; Vince Streano 194t; Wally McNamee 220br, 220bcl, 224bl; Wavebreak Media LTD 191bc; Yann Arhus-Bertrand 249tl; **Demetrio Carrasco / Dorling Kindersley (c) Herge / Les Editions Casterman:** 112ccl; **Dorling Kindersley:** Banbury Museum 35c; Five Napkin Burger 152t; **Dixons:** 270cl, 270cr, 270bl, 270bcl, 270bcr, 270ccr; **Dreamstime.com:** Alexander Podshivalov 179tr, 191cr; Alexxl66 268tl; Andersastphoto 176tc; Andrey Popov 191bl; Arne9001 190tl; Chaoss 26c; Designsstock 269cl; Monkey Business Images 26clb; Paul Michael Hughes 162tr; Serghei Starus 190bc; Isselee 292fcrb; Zerbor 296tr; **Education Photos:** John Walmsley 26tl; **Empics Ltd:** Adam Day 236br; Andy Heading 243c; Steve White 249cbc; **Getty Images:** 48bcl, 94tr; 100t, 114bcr, 154bl, 287tr; David Leahy 162tl; Don Farrall / Digital Vision 176c; Ethan Miller 270bl; Inti St Clair 179bl; Liam Norris 188br; Sean Justice / Digital Vision 24br; **Dennis Gilbert:** 106tc. **Hulsta:** 70t; **Ideal Standard Ltd:** 72r; **The Image Bank/Getty Images:** 58; **Impact Photos:** Eliza Armstrong 115cr; Philip Achache 246t; **The Interior Archive:** Henry Wilson, Alfie's Market 114bl; Luke White, Architect: David Mikhail, 59tl; Simon Upton, Architect: Phillippe Starck, St Martins Lane Hotel 100bcr, 100br; **iStockphoto.com:** asterix0597 163tl; EdStock 190br; RichLegg 26bc; SorinVidis 27cr; **Jason Hawkes Aerial Photography:** 216t; **Dan Johnson:** 35r; **Kos Pictures Source:** 215cbl, 240tc, 240tr; David Williams 216b; **Lebrecht Collection:** Kate Mount 169bc; **MP Visual.com:** Mark Swallow 202t; **NASA:** 280cr, 280ccl, 281tl; **P&O Princess Cruises:** 214bl; **P A Photos:** 181br; **The Photographers' Library:** 186bl, 186bc, 186t; **Plain and Simple Kitchens:** 66t; **Powerstock Photolibrary:** 169tl, 256t, 287tc; **PunchStock:** Image Source 195tr; **Rail Images:** 208c, 208 cbl, 209br; **Red Consultancy:** Odeon cinemas 257br; **Redferns:** 259br; Nigel Crane 259c;

Rex Features: 106br, 259tc, 259tr, 259bl, 280b; Charles Ommaney 114tcr; J.F.F Whitehead 243cl; Patrick Barth 101tl; Patrick Frilet 189cbl; Scott Wiseman 287bl; **Royalty Free Images:** Getty Images/Eyewire 154bl; **Science & Society Picture Library:** Science Museum 202b; **Science Photo Library:** IBM Research 190cla; NASA 281cr; **SuperStock:** Ingram Publishing 62; Juanma Aparicio / age fotostock 172t; Nordic Photos 269tl; **Skyscan:** 168t, 182c, 298; Quick UK Ltd 212; **Sony:** 268bc; **Robert Streeter:** 154br; **Neil Sutherland:** 82tr, 83tl, 90t, 118, 188ctr, 196tl, 196tr, 299cl, 299bl; **The Travel Library:** Stuart Black 264t; **Travelex:** 97cl; **Vauxhall:** Technik 198t, 199tl, 199tr, 199cl, 199cr, 199ctcl, 199tcr, 199tl, 199tcr, 200; **View Pictures:** Dennis Gilbert, Architects: ACDP Consulting, 106t; Dennis Gilbert, Chris Wilkinson Architects, 209tr; Peter Cook, Architects: Nicholas Crimshaw and partners, 208t; **Betty Walton:** 185br; **Colin Walton:** 2, 4, 7, 9, 10, 28, 40l, 42, 56, 92, 95c, 99tl, 99tcl, 102, 116, 120t, 138t, 146, 150t, 160, 170, 191ctcl, 192, 218, 252, 260br, 260l, 261tr, 261c, 261cr, 271cbl, 271cbr, 271ctl, 278, 287br, 302.

DK PICTURE LIBRARY:

Akhil Bahkshi; Patrick Baldwin; Geoff Brightling; British Museum; John Bulmer; Andrew Butler; Joe Cornish; Brian Cosgrove; Andy Crawford and Kit Hougton; Philip Dowell; Alistair Duncan; Gables; Bob Gathany; Norman Hollands; Kew Gardens; Peter James Kindersley; Vladimir Kozlik; Sam Lloyd; London Northern Bus Company Ltd; Tracy Morgan; David Murray and Jules Selmes; Musée Vivant du Cheval, France; Museum of Broadcast Communications; Museum of Natural History; NASA; National History Museum; Norfolk Rural Life Museum; Stephen Oliver; RNLI; Royal Ballet School; Guy Ryecart; Science Museum; Neil Setchfield; Ross Simms and the Winchcombe Folk Police Museum; Singapore Symphony Orchestra; Smart Museum of Art; Tony Souter; Erik Svensson and Jeppe Wikstrom; Sam Tree of Keygrove Marketing Ltd; Barrie Watts; Alan Williams; Jerry Young.

Additional photography by Colin Walton.

Colin Walton would like to thank:
A&A News, Uckfield; Abbey Music, Tunbridge Wells; Arena Mens Clothing, Tunbridge Wells; Burrells of Tunbridge Wells; Gary at Di Marco's; Jeremy's Home Store, Tunbridge Wells; Noakes of Tunbridge Wells; Ottakar's, Tunbridge Wells; Selby's of Uckfield; Sevenoaks Sound and Vision; Westfield, Royal Victoria Place, Tunbridge Wells.

All other images © Dorling Kindersley
For further information see: www.dkimages.com